MILES' DIARY

THE LIFE OF MILES DAVIS 1947-1961

Published by Sanctuary Publishing Ltd,
The Colonnades, 82 Bishops Bridge Road,
London W2 6BB.

ISBN 1 86074 159 2

Printed and bound in the UK by Staples Printers Rochester Limited

Acknowledgements

My grateful thanks to:
My wife, Marian, and my children, Sam and Emily, for taking care of
business so that I could write this book;
Rolf Dahlgren for his generosity in sharing his photographs;
Down Beat and *Metronome* magazines;
Ron Fritts for sharing material and information from his Washington
D.C. and Baltimore M.D. collection;
Bob Frost for sharing his collection of programmes and magazines;
Ira Gitler for his memories of recording sessions;
Jimmy Heath for sharing his photographs and his recollections;
Franz Hoffmann for his amazing series of books, *Jazz Advertised*;
Ken Jones of the National Jazz Foundation Archive at Loughton;
Melody Maker for permission to use extracts;
Mosaic Records for permission to use photographs by Francis Wolff;
Brian Peerless for sharing his collection of *Metronomes* and *Down Beats*
and much more besides;
Tony Shoppee for sharing his *Down Beat* collection;
and David Stonard for his diligent proof-reading and pertinent
observations.

I would also like to acknowledge the kind assistance of
George Avakian, Bill Crow, Mona Heath, Charlie Lourie, Teo Macero,
Hank O'Neal, Boris Rose, Duncan Schiedt and Peter Vacher.

I have also been grateful for the writings of W. Bruynincx, Ian Carr,
Jack Chambers, Marc Crawford, Michael Cuscuna, Leonard Feather,
Yasuhiro Fujioka, Barbara Gardner, Mark Gardner, Gary Giddins, Ira
Gitler, Ralph Gleason, Burt Goldblatt, Nat Hentoff, Jorgen Grunnet
Jepsen, Gene Lees, Mike Levin, Barry McRae, Alun Morgan, Eric
Nisenson, Bob Porter, Lewis Porter, Brian Priestley, Robert Reisner,
Ross Russell, Phil Schaap, Quincy Troup, Barry Ulanov and Richard
Williams.

Photographs from the collections of Bill Crow, Rolf Dahlgren, Frank
Driggs, Brian Foskett, Jean-Pierre Leloir, Jimmy Heath, Herman
Leonard/The Special Photographers Library, London Features, Bengt
Malmquist, Mosaic Records, Redferns, Duncan Schiedt, Dennis
Stock/Magnum, and the author.

Preface

Miles' Diary sets out to provide a fascinating insight into the life and times of the most intense and innovative trumpeter in jazz... Miles Davis. Using contemporary photographs, newspaper reports, advertisements and reviews, I have attempted to chronicle his life month-by-month from joining the famous Charlie Parker Quintet in April 1947 to the legendary Carnegie Hall concert in May 1961, preceded by a brief resumé of his life up to April 1947. I have tried to include all known club, concert, television, film and jam session appearances as well as his recordings, although this is not intended to be a discography.

I hope that you, the reader, will find this book an informative accompaniment when listening to Miles' records or reading any of his biographies. I am grateful to Penny Braybrooke of Sanctuary Books for the faith she has shown in the project, and to Michelle Knight for her dedication and energy in the exacting task of sourcing the photographs.

Ken Vail, Cambridge, September 1996

WEDNESDAY 26 MAY 1926

Miles Dewey Davis III is born in Alton, Illinois to Miles II and Cleota Davis.

1927

The family move to East St. Louis, Illinois, where Miles' father sets up a dental practice.

1929

Miles' brother Vernon is born. Miles already has a sister, Dorothy, who is two years older.

1936

Miles begins taking private music lessons.

FRIDAY 26 MAY 1939

On his 13th birthday, Miles gets a trumpet from his father. He soon joins the Lincoln High School Band and receives special tuition from his teacher, Elwood Buchanan.

1942

Miles starts playing weekend gigs while still at High School. He meets, and is attracted to, Irene Birth.

1943

Miles joins Eddie Randle's Blue Devils Band at the Rhumboogie Club in St. Louis. He becomes friendly with trumpeter Clark Terry.

Below: Seventeen year old Miles (far right, back row) in Eddie Randle's Orchestra at the Rhumboogie Club.

Left: Dizzy Gillespie, Charlie Parker and Billy Eckstine in front of the 1944 Billy Eckstine Band.

ANUARY 1944

...iles decides to leave High School. Irene is pregnant, and ...ter in the year, gives birth to Cheryl.

RIDAY 26 MAY 1944

...iles' 18th birthday.

JNE 1944

...iles leaves Eddie Randle to join Adam Lambert's Six ...rown Cats. Singer Joe Williams is with the band and they ...egin a short residency in Springfield, Illinois. After three ...eeks, Miles leaves and returns to St. Louis.

JLY 1944

...lly Eckstine's Big Band arrive in St. Louis to play a two-...eek engagement at the Riviera Club. Trumpeter Buddy ...nderson has just contracted tuberculosis and is forced to ...ave the band. Miles is asked to substitute and spends two ...eeks playing next to Charlie Parker, Dizzy Gillespie and ...rt Blakey. He is mortified when the band leaves town ...ithout him, but Charlie Parker tells Miles to look him up if ...e is in New York. He realises that this is what he has to do ...d persuades his father to let him attend Juilliard in New ...ork. Mr Davis agrees to pay for tuition fees, and even ...ovides Miles with a monthly allowance.

SEPTEMBER 1944

Miles arrives in New York City and enrols at Juilliard. He spends the first week looking for Charlie Parker, eventually finding him at the Heat Wave Club in Harlem. Soon Parker has moved into Miles' room at 147th and Broadway.

DECEMBER 1944

Irene arrives in New York with Cheryl and moves in with Miles. Charlie Parker finds a room in another part of the building.

SPRING 1945

Miles spends his days at Juilliard and nights on 52nd Street, sitting in whenever possible.

TUESDAY 24 APRIL 1945

Miles makes his recording debut with Herbie Fields' Band for Savoy in New York City. The producer is Teddy Reig. HERBIE FIELDS (clarinet/tenor sax), MILES DAVIS (trumpet), RUBBERLEGS WILLIAMS (vocal), TEDDY BRANNON (piano), AL CASEY (guitar), LEONARD GASKIN (bass), ED NICHOLSON (drums) *That's The Stuff You Gotta Watch / Pointless Mama Blues / Deep Sea Blues / Bring It On Home*

THURSDAY 26 MAY 1945

Miles' 19th birthday.

Highlight on 52nd Street is Charlie Parker and his combo, which opened last month at the Spotlite club. Parker's great alto, complemented by drummer Stan Levy, Sir Charles on piano, bassist Leonard Gaskin, tenorman Dexter Gordon and Miles Davis on trumpet, cannot be outranked by the many other outstanding attractions on the street. The Buster Bailey Trio (William Smith, bass; Hank Jones, piano; Buster Bailey, clarinet) and singer Billy Daniels accompanied by pianist Kenny Wyatt alternate with Parker at the Spotlite.

JUNE 1945

Miles frequently sits in with Coleman Hawkins' Band at the Downbeat Club. The regular trumpeter in the band is Joe Guy, recently married to Billie Holiday who is also on the bill at the Downbeat. Joe is often absent from the gig, and Miles takes full advantage.

OCTOBER 1945

Sometime during October Miles quits Juilliard and joins the Charlie Parker Combo (Charlie Parker, alto sax; Miles Davis, trumpet; Al Haig, piano; Curley Russell, bass; Max Roach and Stan Levey, drums) at the Three Deuces on 52nd Street. After two weeks, the group moves down the street to the Spotlite Club. Dexter Gordon comes in on tenor sax, and Sir Charles Thompson and Leonard Gaskin replace Haig and Russell.

NOVEMBER 1945

When the Spotlite Club is temporarily closed by a police crackdown on 52nd Street, Charlie Parker moves his combo up to Minton's Playhouse in Harlem.

MONDAY 26 NOVEMBER 1945

Recording session by Charlie Parker's Reboppers for Savoy in New York City.

CHARLIE PARKER (alto sax), MILES DAVIS (trumpet), DIZZY GILLESPIE (piano), CURLEY RUSSELL (bass), MAX ROACH (drums)

Billie's Bounce (5 takes) / *Now's The Time* (4 takes)

CHARLIE PARKER (alto sax), MILES DAVIS (trumpet), SADIK HAKIM (piano), CURLEY RUSSELL (bass), MAX ROACH (drums)

Thriving On A Riff (3 takes)

Dizzy takes over on trumpet from Miles to record *Ko Ko*, *Warming Up A Riff* and *Meanderin'*.

DECEMBER 1945

When Bird leaves for California, Sir Charles Thompson takes over the Minton job with a trio. He hires Miles on trumpet and Connie Kay on drums. Miles takes Irene and Cheryl home to St. Louis for Christmas with his family.

JANUARY 1946

The Benny Carter Big Band plays at the Riviera Club in St. Louis. Miles goes to hear them and Benny asks him to join the band. The band is working its way west to Los Angeles, and the prospect of meeting up with Diz and Bird again is enough to persuade Miles.

FEBRUARY 1946

The Benny Carter Big Band reaches Los Angeles and plays an engagement at the Orpheum Theatre. At the end of the engagement, Benny breaks up the big band and forms a small band including Miles, trombonist Al Grey and tenor saxophonist Bumps Myers to play gigs around Los Angeles.

MARCH 1946

Miles locates Charlie Parker and begins sitting in with him at an after-hours club called the Finale where Bird has the band. A number of local musicians feature in the Finale sessions, including Howard McGhee, Art Farmer and his twin brother Addison, Sonny Criss, Red Callender and Charlie Mingus. Miles is in the band that broadcast from the Finale in early March:
CHARLIE PARKER (alto sax), MILES DAVIS (trumpet), JOE ALBANY (piano), ADDISON FARMER (bass), CHUCK THOMPSON (drums)
Anthropology / Billie's Bounce / Blue'n'Boogie / All The Things You Are / Ornithology

THURSDAY 28 MARCH 1946

Recording session as Charlie Parker Septet for Dial at Radio Recorders Studios in Glendale.
CHARLIE PARKER (alto sax), MILES DAVIS (trumpet), LUCKY THOMPSON (tenor sax), DODO MARMAROSA (piano), ARVIN GARRISON (guitar on Moose The Mooche only), VIC McMILLAN (bass), ROY PORTER (drums)
Moose The Mooche (3 takes) / Yardbird Suite (2 takes) / Ornithology (3 takes) / Famous Alto Break / Night In Tunisia (2 takes)
The recording session lasts from 1pm until 9pm because the sidemen are having difficulty playing some of Parker's music. Ross Russell later blames it on Miles, saying 'Miles Davis, wooden and deadpanned, not playing much on his solos but warming the ensemble parts with his broad tone… was slow to learn new material.'

SUNDAY 31 MARCH 1946

Benny Carter's small band broadcast from Los Angeles.
BENNY CARTER (alto sax), MILES DAVIS (trumpet), BUMPS MYERS (tenor sax), AL GREY (trombone), SONNY WHITE (piano), JIMMY CANNADY (guitar), TOMMY MOULTRIE (bass), PERCY BRICE (drums)
Just You, Just Me / Don't Blame Me / Sweet Georgia Brown
Shortly after this, Miles becomes tired of the music Benny's band is playing, and quits. Money is scarce and Irene, back in St. Louis, is pregnant again. Miles moves in with Lucky Thompson and they become good friends.

FRIDAY 12 APRIL 1946

Miles takes part in a concert at the Carver Club on the UCLA campus. The concert stars Herb Jeffries, Kay Starr and the Nat Cole Trio. Also appearing are Benny Carter and Lester Young. Charlie Parker opens the concert with an 8-piece group comprising: Charlie Parker (alto sax), Miles Davis (trumpet), Lucky Thompson (tenor sax), Britt Woodman (trombone), Dodo Marmarosa (piano), Arv Garrison (guitar), Red Callender (bass) and Perc White (drums). After intermission, Charlie plays a set with Lester Young. The *Metronome* reviewer says: *This was by far the best number of the program.*

APRIL 1946

The Finale Club closes and Miles gigs around town with Lucky Thompson and Charlie Mingus. When Howard McGhee reopens the Finale and re-installs Charlie Parker, Miles is not included in the band.

SUNDAY 26 MAY 1946

Miles' 20th birthday.

MONDAY 29 JULY 1946

Miles is not around to see the fateful *Lover Man* recording session and Charlie Parker's breakdown. Miles is shocked by the whole episode that ends with Bird being committed to Camarillo State Hospital. He feels that Bird is going to die.

AUGUST 1946

Miles is featured in Lucky Thompson's Band at the Elk's Ballroom on Central Avenue. During this engagement, Miles and Lucky are involved in a recording session organised by Charlie Mingus:
Baron Mingus and his Symphonic Airs
MILES DAVIS, VERN CARLSON (trumpet), HENRY COKER (trombone), BOOTS MUSSULLI (alto sax), LUCKY THOMPSON (tenor sax), BUDDY COLLETTE (tenor sax/flute), HERB CARROLL (baritone sax), BUZZ WHEELER (piano), CHARLIE MINGUS (bass), WARREN THOMPSON (drums), HERB GAYLE (vocal)
He's Gone (vHG) / *The Story Of Love* / *Portrait*

SEPTEMBER 1946

Billy Eckstine's Band arrives in Los Angeles, and Eckstine asks Miles to join the band to replace Fats Navarro who has stayed in New York. It gives Miles the chance to work his way back to New York.

LOS ANGELES, Calif.—Pandemonium reigned on Central Avenue here as Billy Eckstine, young America's new singing idol, opened with his orchestra on the stage of the Lincoln Theatre amidst surging mobs of squealing, shrieking, screaming youngsters who refused to let anything—not even a detail of special police—stand in the way of their seeing the ecstatic bronze balladeer.

Eckstine had previously not been impressed by Miles' playing, but now he says:

> BY THE TIME WE GOT TO CALIFORNIA HE HAD BLOSSOMED OUT. HE'D BEEN GOING TO JUILLIARD, AND PLAYING WITH BIRD, SO HE CAME IN AND TOOK OVER THE SAME BOOK, THE SOLO BOOK WHICH WAS ORIGINALLY DIZZY'S. MILES STAYED WITH ME UNTIL I BROKE UP, WHICH WAS IN 1947.

SATURDAY 5 OCTOBER 1946
Recording session by Billy Eckstine and his Orchestra for National in Los Angeles.

Miles Davis, Hobart Dotson, Leonard Hawkins, King Kolax (trumpet), Walter Knox, Chippy Outcalt, Gerry Valentine (trombone), Sonny Stitt, John Cobbs (alto sax), Gene Ammons, Arthur Samson (tenor sax), Cecil Payne (baritone sax), Linton Garner (piano), Connie Wainwright (guitar), Tommy Potter (bass), Art Blakey (drums), Billy Eckstine (vocal/trombone)

Oo Bop Sh'Bam (2 takes) / *I Love The Loveliness* / *In The Still Of The Night* / *Jelly Jelly*

SUNDAY 6 OCTOBER 1946
Recording session by Billy Eckstine and his Orchestra for National in Los Angeles.

Miles Davis, Hobart Dotson, Leonard Hawkins, King Kolax (trumpet), Walter Knox, Chippy Outcalt, Gerry Valentine (trombone), Sonny Stitt, John Cobbs (alto sax), Gene Ammons, Arthur Samson (tenor sax), Cecil Payne (baritone sax), Linton Garner (piano), Connie Wainwright (guitar), Tommy Potter (bass), Art Blakey (drums), Billy Eckstine (vocal/trombone) plus string section

My Silent Love / *Time On My Hands* / *All The Things You Are* / *In A Sentimental Mood*

Billy Eckstine and his Orchestra make their way back toward New York City. They hold over in Chicago for a few days, giving Miles the chance to visit his family in East St. Louis and see his new son, Gregory. While in Chicago Miles, Sonny Stitt and Gene Ammons play an engagement at the Jumptown Club.

SUNDAY 1 DECEMBER 1946
Billy Eckstine and his Orchestra open at the Rio Casino in Boston for a four-week engagement.

WEDNESDAY 25 DECEMBER 1946
Billy Eckstine and his Orchestra play a Christmas night dance at the Grand Ballroom at Hunts Point Palace in the Bronx.

FRIDAY 10 JANUARY 1947
Billy Eckstine and his Orchestra open at the Apollo Theatre in Harlem for a one-week engagement. Also on the bill are Kitty Murray, Norma Miller, Tampa Boys, Sybil Lewis, John Bunn and Pigmeat Markham.

JANUARY/FEBRUARY 1947
Billy Eckstine and his Orchestra complete their commitments in the New York area before Billy breaks up the band for good. It is during this period with Billy Eckstine's Band that Miles uses cocaine and heroin for the first time.

MARCH 1947
One of Miles' first jobs after the Eckstine break-up is a recording session by Illinois Jacquet and his Orchestra organised by Leonard Feather for Aladdin in New York City.

Miles Davis, Joe Newman or Russell Jacquet, Marion Hazel, Fats Navarro (trumpet), Gus Chappel, Fred Robinson, Ted Kelly, Dicky Wells (trombone), Ray Perry, Jimmy Powell (alto sax), George Nicholas, Illinois Jacquet (tenor sax), Bill Doggett or Leonard Feather (piano), Al Lucas (bass), Shadow Wilson (drums)

For Europeans Only / *Big Dog* / *You Left Me Alone* / *Jivin' With Jack The Bellboy*

TUESDAY 1 APRIL 1947
Trumpeter Freddie Webster, a major influence and a close friend of Miles, dies in Chicago from an overdose of heroin.

SATURDAY 5 APRIL 1947
Miles joins Dizzy Gillespie's Big Band for a one-week engagement at the Savoy Ballroom in Harlem.

TUESDAY 8 APRIL 1947
Charlie Parker, newly arrived in New York, joins Dizzy's band at the Savoy. During the first show, Dizzy realises that Parker is high and, not wanting to be known as a band full of junkies, immediately fires him.

FRIDAY 11 APRIL 1947
The Dizzy Gillespie band close at the Savoy. Parker takes Miles and Max as the nucleus of a new band. With the addition of Duke Jordan (piano) and Tommy Potter (bass) the Charlie Parker Quintet is ready to open at the Three Deuces on 52nd Street opposite Lennie Tristano.

MONDAY 14 APRIL 1947
Miles appears at a Blue Monday Jazz Concert at Smalls Paradise in Harlem. The special feature is a 'Battle of the Baritone Sax' between Leo Parker and Serge Chaloff. Miles and Art Blakey are in the accompanying group.

TUESDAY 15 APRIL 1947
The Charlie Parker Quintet with Miles opens at the Three Deuces opposite Lennie Tristano.

JES	1
VED	2
HUR	3
RI	4
AT	5
JN	6
MON	7
JES	8
VED	9
HUR	10
RI	11
AT	12
JN	13
MON	14
JES	15
VED	16
HUR	17
RI	18
AT	19
JN	20
MON	21
JES	22
VED	23
HUR	24
RI	25
AT	26
JN	27
MON	28
JES	29
VED	30

THUR	1	SUN	1
FRI	2	MON	2
SAT	3	TUES	3
SUN	4	WED	4
MON	5	THUR	5
TUES	6	FRI	6
WED	7	SAT	7
THUR	8	SUN	8
FRI	9	MON	9
SAT	10	TUES	10
SUN	11	WED	11
MON	12	THUR	12
TUES	13	FRI	13
WED	14	SAT	14
THUR	15	SUN	15
FRI	16	MON	16
SAT	17	TUES	17
SUN	18	WED	18
MON	19	THUR	19
TUES	20	FRI	20
WED	21	SAT	21
THUR	22	SUN	22
FRI	23	MON	23
SAT	24	TUES	24
SUN	25	WED	25
MON	26	THUR	26
TUES	27	FRI	27
WED	28	SAT	28
THUR	29	SUN	29
FRI	30	MON	30
SAT	31		

THURSDAY 8 MAY 1947

Recording session as Charlie Parker All Stars for Savoy at the Harris Smith Studios, New York City.
CHARLIE PARKER (alto sax), MILES DAVIS (trumpet), BUD POWELL (piano), TOMMY POTTER (bass), MAX ROACH (drums)
Donna Lee (5 takes) / *Chasing the Bird* (4 takes) / *Cheryl* (2 takes) / *Buzzy* (5 takes)

Miles writes *Donna Lee* for the session, named after Tommy Potter's daughter. It is the first tune by Miles to be recorded, but when the record is released Charlie Parker is listed as the composer.

MONDAY 26 MAY 1947

Miles' 21st birthday.

JUNE 1947

Miles sits in with Coleman Hawkins at the Three Deuces and also gets to record with Hawk for a small independent label, Aladdin, in New York City.
MILES DAVIS (trumpet), COLEMAN HAWKINS (tenor sax), possibly HOWARD JOHNSON (alto sax), KAI WINDING (trombone), HANK JONES (piano), UNKNOWN (bass), MAX ROACH (drums)
Bean-A-Re-Bop / Phantomesque / The Way You Look Tonight / Isn't It Romantic

MONDAY 30 JUNE 1947

Miles plays at a Blue Monday Swing Session at Smalls Paradise in Harlem.

UES	**1**	FRI	**1**
VED	**2**	SAT	**2**
HUR	**3**	SUN	**3**
RI	**4**	MON	**4**
AT	**5**	TUES	**5**
UN	**6**	WED	**6**
MON	**7**	THUR	**7**
UES	**8**	FRI	**8**
VED	**9**	SAT	**9**
HUR	**10**	SUN	**10**
RI	**11**	MON	**11**
AT	**12**	TUES	**12**
UN	**13**	WED	**13**
MON	**14**	THUR	**14**
UES	**15**	FRI	**15**
VED	**16**	SAT	**16**
HUR	**17**	SUN	**17**
RI	**18**	MON	**18**
AT	**19**	TUES	**19**
UN	**20**	WED	**20**
MON	**21**	THUR	**21**
UES	**22**	FRI	**22**
VED	**23**	SAT	**23**
HUR	**24**	SUN	**24**
RI	**25**	MON	**25**
AT	**26**	TUES	**26**
UN	**27**	WED	**27**
MON	**28**	THUR	**28**
UES	**29**	FRI	**29**
VED	**30**	SAT	**30**
HUR	**31**	SUN	**31**

FRIDAY 18 JULY 1947
The Charlie Parker Quintet with Miles, Duke Jordan, Tommy Potter and Max Roach open at the New Bali in Washington, D.C. for a two-week engagement.

THURSDAY 31 JULY 1947
The Charlie Parker Quintet closes at the New Bali in Washington, D.C.

THURSDAY 7 AUGUST 1947
The Charlie Parker Quintet with Miles, Duke Jordan, Tommy Potter and Max Roach open at the Three Deuces on 52nd Street in New York City for a two-week engagement opposite Coleman Hawkins.

TUESDAY 12 AUGUST 1947
Rehearsals for the Miles Davis recording session on 14th. It is to be Miles' first date as leader and he writes and arranges all four tunes for the session. Charlie Parker is persuaded to play tenor sax.

WEDNESDAY 13 AUGUST 1947
Rehearsals for recording session.

THURSDAY 14 AUGUST 1947
Recording session as Miles Davis All Stars for Savoy at the Harris Smith Studios, New York City. The producer is Teddy Reig.
MILES DAVIS (trumpet), CHARLIE PARKER (tenor sax), JOHN LEWIS (piano), NELSON BOYD (bass), MAX ROACH (drums)
Milestones (3 takes) / *Little Willie Leaps* (3 takes) / *Half Nelson* (2 takes) / *Sippin' At Bells* (4 takes)

WEDNESDAY 20 AUGUST 1947
The Charlie Parker Quintet close at the Three Deuces.

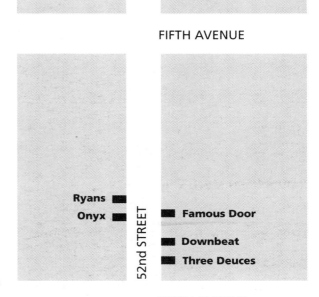

FIFTH AVENUE

Ryans ■
Onyx ■

52nd STREET

■ Famous Door
■ Downbeat
■ Three Deuces

SIXTH AVENUE

MON	1	WED	1	SAT	1
TUES	2	THUR	2	SUN	2
WED	3	FRI	3	MON	3
THUR	4	SAT	4	TUES	4
FRI	5	SUN	5	WED	5
SAT	6	MON	6	THUR	6
SUN	7	TUES	7	FRI	7
MON	8	WED	8	SAT	8
TUES	9	THUR	9	SUN	9
WED	10	FRI	10	MON	10
THUR	11	SAT	11	TUES	11
FRI	12	SUN	12	WED	12
SAT	13	MON	13	THUR	13
SUN	14	TUES	14	FRI	14
MON	15	WED	15	SAT	15
TUES	16	THUR	16	SUN	16
WED	17	FRI	17	MON	17
THUR	18	SAT	18	TUES	18
FRI	19	SUN	19	WED	19
SAT	20	MON	20	THUR	20
SUN	21	TUES	21	FRI	21
MON	22	WED	22	SAT	22
TUES	23	THUR	23	SUN	23
WED	24	FRI	24	MON	24
THUR	25	SAT	25	TUES	25
FRI	26	SUN	26	WED	26
SAT	27	MON	27	THUR	27
SUN	28	TUES	28	FRI	28
MON	29	WED	29	SAT	29
TUES	30	THUR	30	SUN	30
		FRI	31		

TUESDAY 28 OCTOBER 1947

Recording session by the Charlie Parker Quintet for Dial at WOR Studios, 1440 Broadway, New York under the supervision of Ross Russell. This is the first recording by the working Quintet.
CHARLIE PARKER (alto sax), MILES DAVIS (trumpet), DUKE JORDAN (piano), TOMMY POTTER (bass), MAX ROACH (drums)
Dexterity (2 takes) / *Bongo Bop* (2 takes) / *Dewey Square* (3 takes) / *The Hymn* / *Superman (The Hymn)* / *Bird Of Paradise* (3 takes) / *Embraceable You* (2 takes)

TUESDAY 4 NOVEMBER 1947

Second recording session by the Charlie Parker Quintet for Dial at WOR Studios, 1440 Broadway, New York under the supervision of Ross Russell.
CHARLIE PARKER (alto sax), MILES DAVIS (trumpet), DUKE JORDAN (piano), TOMMY POTTER (bass), MAX ROACH (drums)
Bird Feathers / Klact-oveeseds-tene (2 takes) / *Scrapple From The Apple* (2 takes) / *My Old Flame / Out Of Nowhere* (3 takes) / *Don't Blame Me*

TUESDAY 11 NOVEMBER 1947

The Charlie Parker Quintet with Miles open at the Argyle Lounge in Chicago for a two-week engagement.

During the engagement some private recordings are made:
My Old Flame / How High The Moon /Big Foot / Slow Boat To China / All Of Me / Cheryl / Home Sweet Home / Wee / Ko Ko / Little Willie Leaps / The Way You Look Tonight / A Night In Tunisia / The Way You Look Tonight

SUNDAY 23 NOVEMBER 1947

The Charlie Parker Quintet with Miles close at the Argyle Lounge in Chicago.

TUESDAY 25 NOVEMBER 1947

The Charlie Parker Quintet with Miles are scheduled to open at the El Sino Club in Detroit. Charlie Parker has trouble making a connection in Detroit, gets drunk, argues with the manager of the club and walks out. The engagement is cancelled. Miles reports that Bird was so angry he threw his saxophone out of the hotel window and smashed it up on the street.

SATURDAY 29 NOVEMBER 1947

The Charlie Parker Quintet with Miles appear in a One-Nite Stand Concert at Town Hall in New York City. Pearl Bailey and Babs Gonzales are also featured.

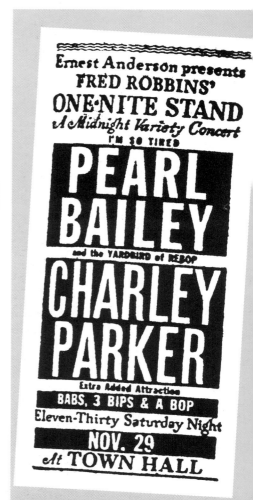

MON	1	THUR	1
TUES	2	FRI	2
WED	3	SAT	3
THUR	4	SUN	4
FRI	5	MON	5
SAT	6	TUES	6
SUN	7	WED	7
MON	8	THUR	8
TUES	9	FRI	9
WED	10	SAT	10
THUR	11	SUN	11
FRI	12	MON	12
SAT	13	TUES	13
SUN	14	WED	14
MON	15	THUR	15
TUES	16	FRI	16
WED	17	SAT	17
THUR	18	SUN	18
FRI	19	MON	19
SAT	20	TUES	20
SUN	21	WED	21
MON	22	THUR	22
TUES	23	FRI	23
WED	24	SAT	24
THUR	25	SUN	25
FRI	26	MON	26
SAT	27	TUES	27
SUN	28	WED	28
MON	29	THUR	29
TUES	30	FRI	30
WED	31	SAT	31

TUESDAY 2 DECEMBER 1947
The Charlie Parker Quintet with Miles open at the Downbeat Club in Philadelphia for a one-week engagement. Charlie doesn't have a horn and borrows Jimmy Heath's.

SATURDAY 6 DECEMBER 1947
The Charlie Parker Quintet with Miles close at the Downbeat in Philadelphia.

MONDAY 15 DECEMBER 1947
Rehearsal by the Charlie Parker Quintet plus trombonist J. J. Johnson for the forthcoming recording session.

WEDNESDAY 17 DECEMBER 1947
Final recording session for Dial as the Charlie Parker Sextet at the WOR Studios in New York City. Ross Russell has flu and cannot attend. CHARLIE PARKER (alto sax), MILES DAVIS (trumpet), J. J. JOHNSON (trombone), DUKE JORDAN (piano), TOMMY POTTER (bass), MAX ROACH (drums)
Drifting On A Reed (3 takes) / *Quasimodo* (2 takes) / *Charlie's Wig* (3 takes) / *Bongo Beep* (2 takes) / *Crazeology* (4 takes) / *How Deep Is The Ocean* (2 takes)

For this date Charlie has a brand new Selmer saxophone.

FRIDAY 19 DECEMBER 1947
The Charlie Parker Quintet open at El Sino in Detroit opposite Sarah Vaughan for a two-week engagement. The engagement is a great success and they sell-out.

SUNDAY 21 DECEMBER 1947
Recording session as Charlie Parker All Stars for Savoy at the United Sound Studios, Detroit. CHARLIE PARKER (alto sax), MILES DAVIS (trumpet), DUKE JORDAN (piano), TOMMY POTTER (bass), MAX ROACH (drums)
Another Hairdo (4 takes) / *Bluebird* (3 takes) / *Klaunstance* / *Bird Gets The Worm* (3 takes)

THURSDAY 1 JANUARY 1948
The Charlie Parker Quintet close at the El Sino in Detroit.

SATURDAY 3 JANUARY 1948
The Charlie Parker Quintet open at the Pershing Ballroom in Chicago for a four-night engagement. They double at a Saturday night dance at the New Savoy opposite Claude McLin and his Combo. During the engagement some private recordings are made:
CHARLIE PARKER (alto sax), MILES DAVIS (trumpet), DUKE JORDAN (piano), TOMMY POTTER (bass), MAX ROACH (drums)
The Chase / *Drifting On A Reed*

TUESDAY 6 JANUARY 1948
The Charlie Parker Quintet close at the Pershing Ballroom.

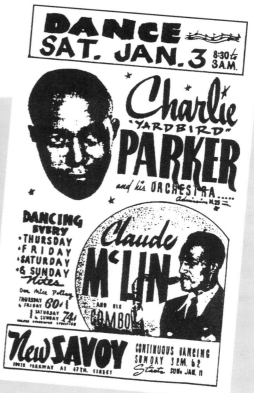

SUN	**1**	MON	**1**
MON	**2**	TUES	**2**
TUES	**3**	WED	**3**
WED	**4**	THUR	**4**
THUR	**5**	FRI	**5**
FRI	**6**	SAT	**6**
SAT	**7**	SUN	**7**
SUN	**8**	MON	**8**
MON	**9**	TUES	**9**
TUES	**10**	WED	**10**
WED	**11**	THUR	**11**
THUR	**12**	FRI	**12**
FRI	**13**	SAT	**13**
SAT	**14**	SUN	**14**
SUN	**15**	MON	**15**
MON	**16**	TUES	**16**
TUES	**17**	WED	**17**
WED	**18**	THUR	**18**
THUR	**19**	FRI	**19**
FRI	**20**	SAT	**20**
SAT	**21**	SUN	**21**
SUN	**22**	MON	**22**
MON	**23**	TUES	**23**
TUES	**24**	WED	**24**
WED	**25**	THUR	**25**
THUR	**26**	FRI	**26**
FRI	**27**	SAT	**27**
SAT	**28**	SUN	**28**
SUN	**29**	MON	**29**
		TUES	**30**
		WED	**31**

SUNDAY 29 FEBRUARY 1948

The Charlie Parker Quintet battle with Gene Ammons and his Band at the New Savoy in Chicago.

TUESDAY 30 MARCH 1948

Charlie Parker Quintet opens at the Three Deuces on 52nd Street for a two-week engagement opposite Margie Hyams' group.

WEDNESDAY 31 MARCH 1948

Dean Benedetti is at the Three Deuces with hi new recording equipment, a Brush Sound Mirror tape recorder. The Deuces managemen allow him to tape two sets but when they realise he is not going to spend any money, he is thrown out.

CHARLIE PARKER (alto sax), MILES DAVIS (trumpet), DUKE JORDAN (piano), TOMMY POTTE (bass), MAX ROACH (drums), plus KENNY 'PANCHO' HAGOOD (vocal)

52nd Street Theme / Big Foot / Dizzy Atmosphere / My Old Flame / 52nd Street Theme / Half Nelson / All The Things You Are (vocal) */ 52nd Street Them*

HUR	**1**	SAT	**1**
RI	**2**	SUN	**2**
AT	**3**	MON	**3**
UN	**4**	TUES	**4**
MON	**5**	WED	**5**
UES	**6**	THUR	**6**
VED	**7**	FRI	**7**
HUR	**8**	SAT	**8**
RI	**9**	SUN	**9**
AT	**10**	MON	**10**
UN	**11**	TUES	**11**
MON	**12**	WED	**12**
UES	**13**	THUR	**13**
VED	**14**	FRI	**14**
HUR	**15**	SAT	**15**
RI	**16**	SUN	**16**
AT	**17**	MON	**17**
UN	**18**	TUES	**18**
MON	**19**	WED	**19**
UES	**20**	THUR	**20**
VED	**21**	FRI	**21**
HUR	**22**	SAT	**22**
RI	**23**	SUN	**23**
AT	**24**	MON	**24**
UN	**25**	TUES	**25**
MON	**26**	WED	**26**
UES	**27**	THUR	**27**
VED	**28**	FRI	**28**
HUR	**29**	SAT	**29**
RI	**30**	SUN	**30**
		MON	**31**

SUNDAY 11 APRIL 1948
The Charlie Parker Quintet close at the Three Deuces.

SUNDAY 18 APRIL 1948
Charlie Parker Quintet plus Sarah Vaughan join a 26-day JATP tour in Cincinnati.
CHARLIE PARKER (alto sax), MILES DAVIS (trumpet), DUKE JORDAN (piano), TOMMY POTTER (bass), MAX ROACH (drums), plus Sarah's trumpet playing husband/manager George Treadwell, and tenor saxists Dexter Gordon and Flip Phillips.

TUESDAY 20 APRIL 1948
JATP appears at Kleinhans Music Hall in Buffalo, NY.

THURSDAY 22 APRIL 1948
JATP appears in Pittsburgh.

FRIDAY 23 APRIL 1948
JATP appears at the Public Music Hall in Cleveland.

SATURDAY 24 APRIL 1948
JATP appears at the Masonic Auditorium in Detroit.

SUNDAY 25 APRIL 1948
JATP appears in Indianapolis.

MONDAY 26 APRIL 1948
JATP appears in Milwaukee.

TUESDAY 27 APRIL 1948
JATP appears in Kansas City.

WEDNESDAY 28 APRIL 1948
JATP appears in Des Moines.

FRIDAY 30 APRIL 1948
JATP appears in St Louis.

SATURDAY 1 MAY 1948
JATP appears at the Civic Opera House in Chicago.

SUNDAY 2 MAY 1948
JATP appears in Minneapolis.

FRIDAY 7 MAY 1948
JATP begin a one-week engagement at the Paradise Theatre, Detroit.

THURSDAY 13 MAY 1948
JATP closes at the Paradise Theatre, Detroit.

FRIDAY 14 MAY 1948
JATP appears in Philadelphia.

SATURDAY 15 MAY 1948
JATP appears in Newark, NJ at 8.30 followed by a midnight concert at Carnegie Hall, NYC.

SUNDAY 16 MAY 1948
JATP appears in Boston.

WEDNESDAY 26 MAY 1948
Miles' 22nd birthday.

TUES	1	THUR	1	SUN	1
WED	2	FRI	2	MON	2
THUR	3	SAT	3	TUES	3
FRI	4	SUN	4	WED	4
SAT	5	MON	5	THUR	5
SUN	6	TUES	6	FRI	6
MON	7	WED	7	SAT	7
TUES	8	THUR	8	SUN	8
WED	9	FRI	9	MON	9
THUR	10	SAT	10	TUES	10
FRI	11	SUN	11	WED	11
SAT	12	MON	12	THUR	12
SUN	13	TUES	13	FRI	13
MON	14	WED	14	SAT	14
TUES	15	THUR	15	SUN	15
WED	16	FRI	16	MON	16
THUR	17	SAT	17	TUES	17
FRI	18	SUN	18	WED	18
SAT	19	MON	19	THUR	19
SUN	20	TUES	20	FRI	20
MON	21	WED	21	SAT	21
TUES	22	THUR	22	SUN	22
WED	23	FRI	23	MON	23
THUR	24	SAT	24	TUES	24
FRI	25	SUN	25	WED	25
SAT	26	MON	26	THUR	26
SUN	27	TUES	27	FRI	27
MON	28	WED	28	SAT	28
TUES	29	THUR	29	SUN	29
WED	30	FRI	30	MON	30
		SAT	31	TUES	31

TUESDAY 6 JULY 1948

The Charlie Parker Quintet opens at the Onyx Club in New York for one week. Dean Benedetti is on hand with his tape recorder and records on at least four nights. The sequence for opening night is guesswork by Phil Schaap.
CHARLIE PARKER (alto sax), MILES DAVIS (trumpet), DUKE JORDAN (piano), TOMMY POTTER (bass), MAX ROACH (drums)
52nd Street Theme / Out Of Nowhere / My Old Flame / Chasin' The Bird / The Way You Look Tonight / This Time The Dream's On Me / Shaw Nuff / 52nd Street Theme / 52nd Street Theme / Cheryl / Bird Lore / These Foolish Things / Groovin' High / Little Willie Leaps / Night And Day / This Time The Dream's On Me / 52nd Street Theme / The Way You Look Tonight / Out Of Nowhere / My Old Flame / Blues

WEDNESDAY 7 JULY 1948

CHARLIE PARKER (alto sax), MILES DAVIS (trumpet), DUKE JORDAN (piano), TOMMY POTTER (bass), MAX ROACH (drums)
Out Of Nowhere / How High The Moon / 52nd Street Theme

SATURDAY 10 JULY 1948

Benedetti is present at an afternoon rehearsal in the Onyx.
CHARLIE PARKER (alto sax), MILES DAVIS (trumpet), DUKE JORDAN (piano), TOMMY POTTER (bass), MAX ROACH (drums)
Chasin' The Bird / Don't Blame Me / Tico Tico / Out Of Nowhere / Medley: Indiana, Donna Lee

Benedetti returns to the club for the evening performance.
CHARLIE PARKER (alto sax), MILES DAVIS (trumpet), DUKE JORDAN (piano), TOMMY POTTER (bass), MAX ROACH (drums) plus CARMEN McRAE (vocal) and an unidentified tenor saxist sits in on Groovin' High
52nd Street Theme / How High The Moon / I'm In The Mood For Love / This Time The Dream's On Me / Yesterdays / 52nd Street Theme / 52nd Street Theme / How High The Moon / Groovin' High / What Price Love (Yardbird Suite) (Carmen McRae vocal, followed by an encore as Bird scolds the audience for not listening) */ 52nd Street Theme / Cheryl*

SUNDAY 11 JULY 1948

Closing night at the Onyx. Benedetti is again present with his tape recorder.
CHARLIE PARKER (alto sax), MILES DAVIS (trumpet), DUKE JORDAN (piano), TOMMY POTTER (bass), MAX ROACH (drums) plus THELONIOUS MONK (piano) on *Well, You Needn't* and PANCHO HAGOOD (vocal) on *All The Things You Are, Spotlite* and *September Song* and either Pancho or EARL COLEMAN (vocal) on *My Old Flame.*
All The Things You Are / Well You Needn't / Big Foot / I Can't Get Started / Dizzy Atmosphere / Spotlite / 52nd Street Theme / How High The Moon / September Song / Hot House / 52nd Street Theme / Night In Tunisia / My Old Flame / The Hymn
Bird is not present on the final two numbers on Benedetti's tape and it is possible that he left early.
Half Nelson / Little Willie Leaps

FRIDAY 23 JULY 1948

The Charlie Parker Quintet begin a week at the Apollo Theatre, Harlem. Also on the bill is the Buddy Johnson Band.

WEDNESDAY 28 JULY 1948

Amateur Nite at the Apollo.

THURSDAY 29 JULY 1948

Bird and the quintet close at the Apollo.

AUGUST 1948

Duke Ellington, newly returned from a variety tour of Great Britain, calls Miles up to his office in the Brill Building and offers him a job in the orchestra he is reassembling. Miles, despite his great admiration for Duke and his music, turns him down and goes back to rehearsing a nine-piece orchestra with Gil Evans and Gerry Mulligan.

FRIDAY 3 SEPTEMBER 1948

Charlie Parker and the quintet appear for the first time at the Royal Roost. They are an added star attraction over the Labor Day weekend.

SATURDAY 4 SEPTEMBER 1948

Charlie Parker broadcasts from the Royal Roost on Broadway between 47th and 48th Street.
CHARLIE PARKER (alto sax), MILES DAVIS (trumpet), TADD DAMERON (piano), CURLEY RUSSELL (bass), MAX ROACH (drums), SYMPHONY SID TORIN (mc)
52nd Street Theme / Koko / 52nd Street Theme

AND AS OUR SURPRISE FOR THIS MORNING HERE ON THE ALL NIGHT ALL FRANTIC ONE WITH OUR MICROPHONES DOWN HERE AT THE **ROYAL ROOST**, WE BRING YOU ONCE AGAIN THE WONDERFUL AND OUTSTANDING **CHARLIE PARKER** AND HIS WONDERFUL ORGANISATION. THAT'S RIGHT... FOR THE WEEKEND, LADIES AND GENTLEMEN, WE'RE BRINGING YOU THE GREAT CHARLIE PARKER AND HIS WONDERFUL ORGANISATION FEATURING **MILES DAVIS** ON TRUMPET, **MAX ROACH** ON DRUMS, **TADD DAMERON** ON PIANO AND **CURLEY RUSSELL** ON BASS. I KNOW YOU'LL HAVE A LOT OF FUN OVER THE WEEKEND ... C'MON ON DOWN AND DIG THE GREAT CHARLIE PARKER, THE ONE AND ONLY ... THE MAN OF JAZZ!

THURSDAY 9 SEPTEMBER 1948

The Miles Davis Nonet open at the Royal Roost in New York City for a two-week engagement opposite the Count Basie Orchestra and Dinah Washington. Miles persuades the owners, Monte Kay and Ralph Watkins, to display a sign outside that says:

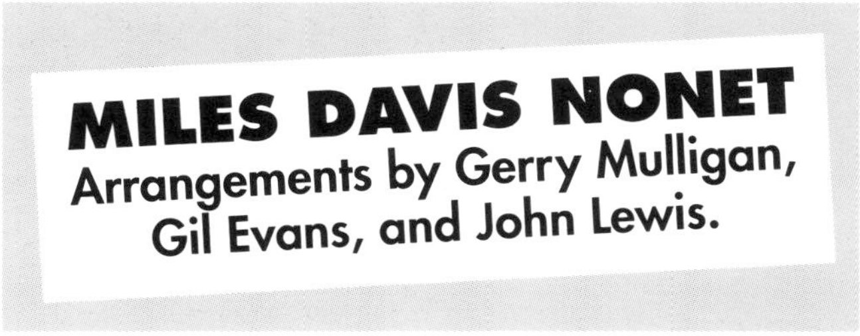

MILES DAVIS NONET
Arrangements by Gerry Mulligan, Gil Evans, and John Lewis.

SATURDAY 11 SEPTEMBER 1948

Broadcast by the Miles Davis Nonet from the Royal Roost in New York City.
MILES DAVIS (trumpet), MIKE ZWERIN (trombone), JUNIOR COLLINS (french horn), BILL BARBER (tuba), LEE KONITZ (alto sax), GERRY MULLIGAN (baritone sax), JOHN LEWIS (piano), AL MCKIBBON (bass), MAX ROACH (drums), KENNY HAGOOD (vocal)
Move / Why Do I Love You? (vKH) / *Godchild / S'il Vous Plait / Moondreams / Hallucinations (Budo)*

SATURDAY 18 SEPTEMBER 1948

Recording session as the Charlie Parker All Stars for Savoy at the Harris Smith Studios.
CHARLIE PARKER (alto sax), MILES DAVIS (trumpet), JOHN LEWIS (piano), CURLEY RUSSELL (bass), MAX ROACH (drums)
Barbados (4 takes) / *Ah Leu Cha* (2 takes) / *Constellation* (5 takes) / *Parker's Mood* (5 takes, MD out)

That evening the Miles Davis Nonet broadcast from the Royal Roost, New York City.
MILES DAVIS (trumpet), MIKE ZWERIN (trombone), JUNIOR COLLINS (french horn), BILL BARBER (tuba), LEE KONITZ (alto sax), GERRY MULLIGAN (baritone sax), JOHN LEWIS (piano), CURLEY RUSSELL (bass), MAX ROACH (drums), KENNY HAGOOD (vocal)
Jumpin' With Symphony Sid / Move / Darn That Dream (vKH) / *Chasin' The Bird / Moondreams / Hallucinations (Budo)*

WEDNESDAY 22 SEPTEMBER 1948

The Miles Davis Nonet close at the Royal Roost in New York City.

THURSDAY 23 SEPTEMBER 1948

The Miles Davis All Star Quintet, a contraction of the Nonet open at the Royal Roost in New York City for a one-week engagement opposite the Count Basie Orchestra.

FRIDAY 24 SEPTEMBER 1948

Recording session as the Charlie Parker All Stars for Savoy at the Harris Smith Studios.
CHARLIE PARKER (alto sax), MILES DAVIS (trumpet), JOHN LEWIS (piano), CURLEY RUSSELL (bass), MAX ROACH (drums)
Perhaps (7 takes) / *Marmaduke* (12 takes) / *Steeplechase* (2 takes) / *Merry-Go-Round* (2 takes)

SATURDAY 25 SEPTEMBER 1948

Broadcast by the Miles Davis All Star Quintet from the Royal Roost, New York City.
MILES DAVIS (trumpet), LEE KONITZ (alto sax), JOHN LEWIS (piano), CURLEY RUSSELL (bass), MAX ROACH (drums), KENNY HAGOOD (vocal)
Jumpin' With Symphony Sid / 52nd Street Theme / Half Nelson / You Go To My Head (vKH) / *Chasin' The Bird*

WEDNESDAY 29 SEPTEMBER 1948

The Miles Davis All Star Quintet close at the Royal Roost in New York City.

VED	1
HUR	2
RI	3
AT	4
JN	5
ION	6
JES	7
VED	8
HUR	9
RI	10
AT	11
JN	12
ION	13
JES	14
VED	15
HUR	16
RI	17
AT	18
JN	19
ION	20
JES	21
VED	22
HUR	23
RI	24
AT	25
JN	26
ON	27
JES	28
VED	29
HUR	30

FRI **1**	MON **1**	WED **1**
SAT **2**	TUES **2**	THUR **2**
SUN **3**	WED **3**	FRI **3**
MON **4**	THUR **4**	SAT **4**
TUES **5**	FRI **5**	SUN **5**
WED **6**	SAT **6**	MON **6**
THUR **7**	SUN **7**	TUES **7**
FRI **8**	MON **8**	WED **8**
SAT **9**	TUES **9**	THUR **9**
SUN **10**	WED **10**	FRI **10**
MON **11**	THUR **11**	SAT **11**
TUES **12**	FRI **12**	SUN **12**
WED **13**	SAT **13**	MON **13**
THUR **14**	SUN **14**	TUES **14**
FRI **15**	MON **15**	WED **15**
SAT **16**	TUES **16**	THUR **16**
SUN **17**	WED **17**	FRI **17**
MON **18**	THUR **18**	SAT **18**
TUES **19**	FRI **19**	SUN **19**
WED **20**	SAT **20**	MON **20**
THUR **21**	SUN **21**	TUES **21**
FRI **22**	MON **22**	WED **22**
SAT **23**	TUES **23**	THUR **23**
SUN **24**	WED **24**	FRI **24**
MON **25**	THUR **25**	SAT **25**
TUES **26**	FRI **26**	SUN **26**
WED **27**	SAT **27**	MON **27**
THUR **28**	SUN **28**	TUES **28**
FRI **29**	MON **29**	WED **29**
SAT **30**	TUES **30**	THUR **30**
SUN **31**		FRI **31**

THURSDAY 28 OCTOBER 1948

With the Charlie Parker Quintet temporarily disbanded as Charlie goes out on tour with JATP, the Miles Davis Quartet, probably John Lewis, Curley Russell and Max Roach, open at the Three Deuces in New York City for a four-week engagement opposite singer Herb Jeffries.

WEDNESDAY 3 NOVEMBER 1948

Down Beat reports:

> Miles Davis Quartet replaced Stan Hassel-gard unit at 3 Deuces and set to stay on through the current engagement of Herb Jeffries to 24 November.

WEDNESDAY 24 NOVEMBER 1948

Miles and the Quartet close at the Three Deuces.

THURSDAY 9 DECEMBER 1948

Charlie Parker Quintet with Al Haig on piano in place of Duke Jordan open at the Royal Roost for an extended engagement which lasts four months. Also on the bill is Billy Eckstine and the Charlie Ventura Group.

SATURDAY 11 DECEMBER 1948

In the early hours of Saturday, Charlie Parker and the Quintet broadcast from the Royal Roost.

CHARLIE PARKER (alto sax), MILES DAVIS (trumpet), AL HAIG (piano), TOMMY POTTER (bass), MAX ROACH (drums), SYMPHONY SID TORIN (announcer)
Groovin' High / Big Foot / Ornithology / Slow Boat To China

AND SO, LADIES AND GENTLEMEN, ONCE AGAIN HERE AT THE METROPOLITAN BOPERA HOUSE, THE ORIGINAL HOUSE THAT BOP BUILT, ON BROADWAY BETWEEN 47TH AND 48TH, WE'RE PRESENTING TO YOU, OVER THE CHRISTMAS HOLIDAY, RIGHT UP INTO THE NEW YEAR... THE GREAT CHARLIE PARKER AND THE ALL STARS, MISTER B – BILLY ECKSTINE, AND THE WONDERFUL CHARLIE VENTURA AND THE BOP GROUP. WE INVITE YOU TO COME DOWN, SIT BACK AND RELAX AND HAVE A WONDERFUL TIME.

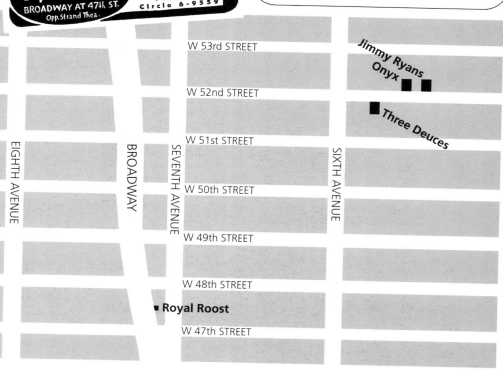

WED **1**

HUR **2**

RI **3**

AT **4**

UN **5**

MON **6**

UES **7**

WED **8**

HUR **9**

RI **10**

AT **11**

UN **12**

MON **13**

UES **14**

WED **15**

HUR **16**

RI **17**

AT **18**

UN **19**

MON **20**

UES **21**

WED **22**

HUR **23**

RI **24**

AT **25**

UN **26**

MON **27**

UES **28**

WED **29**

HUR **30**

RI **31**

After the show at the Roost, the whole company move up to the Apollo Theatre on 125th Street.

AND DON'T BE SURPRISED IF WE GO OFF THE AIR AND GO BACK TO THE APOLLO THEATRE. I'D LIKE TO REMIND YOU THAT IT'S DONE FOR A WONDERFUL CAUSE, AND I ALSO WOULD LIKE TO REMIND YOU THAT WE'RE GONNA TAKE THE SAME GROUP AROUND 4.15 ... AND WE'RE GONNA TAKE CHARLIE PARKER AND THE ALL STARS, THE GREAT MISTER B – BILLY ECKSTINE, AND THE WONDERFUL CHARLIE VENTURA AND THE BOP GROUP, AND TAKE THEM RIGHT UP TO THE APOLLO THEATRE WHERE WE'LL DO EXACTLY THE SAME THING AS WE'RE HAVING DOWN HERE AT THE ROOST. SO STAND BY, AND HAVE A LOT OF FUN. I KNOW THAT YOU WILL ... DIGGIN' THE GREAT BIRD AND THE ALL STARS.

SUNDAY 12 DECEMBER 1948

In the early hours of Sunday, Charlie Parker and the Quintet broadcast from the Royal Roost.
CHARLIE PARKER (alto sax), MILES DAVIS (trumpet), AL HAIG (piano), TOMMY POTTER (bass), MAX ROACH (drums), ART FORD (announcer)
Hot House / Salt Peanuts

Below: The building that housed the Royal Roost, pictured in 1990 shortly before being demolished to make way for a hotel. Pictured from the corner of Broadway and 48th Street.

SATURDAY 18 DECEMBER 1948

In the early hours of Saturday, Charlie Parker and the Quintet broadcast from the Royal Roost.
CHARLIE PARKER (alto sax), MILES DAVIS (trumpet), AL HAIG (piano), TOMMY POTTER (bass), MAX ROACH (drums), SYMPHONY SID TORIN (announcer)
Chasin' The Bird / Out Of Nowhere / How High The Moon

THURSDAY 23 DECEMBER 1948

Miles Davis storms off the stand at the Royal Roost complaining: 'Bird makes you feel about one foot high'. Max Roach also quits but agrees to stay two more nights until Joe Harris can take over on drums.

What is Be-Bop!

The House that Bop Built...

NIGHTLY CONCERTS OF PROGRESSIVE JAZZ

Produced by MONTE KAY
Staged by ALBERT CARLO
Publicity by MIKE HALL

Bill and Ralph's

Royal Roost

"Metropolitan Bopera House"

Broadway, at 47th Street, N.Y.

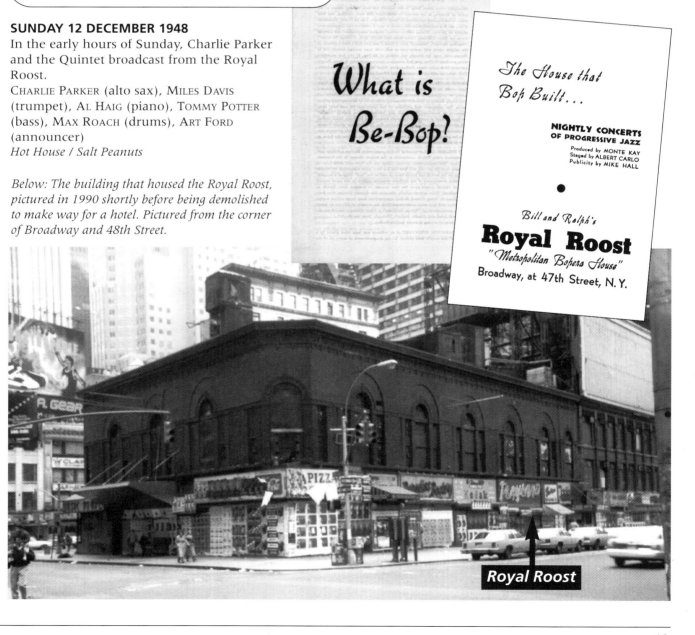

Royal Roost

SAT	1
SUN	2
MON	3
TUES	4
WED	5
THUR	6
FRI	7
SAT	8
SUN	9
MON	10
TUES	11
WED	12
THUR	13
FRI	14
SAT	15
SUN	16
MON	17
TUES	18
WED	19
THUR	20
FRI	21
SAT	22
SUN	23
MON	24
TUES	25
WED	26
THUR	27
FRI	28
SAT	29
SUN	30
MON	31

MONDAY 3 JANUARY 1949

Miles takes part in the Metronome All Stars recording session in New York City.

MILES DAVIS, DIZZY GILLESPIE, FATS NAVARRO (trumpet), J. J. JOHNSON, KAI WINDING (trombone), BUDDY DEFRANCO (clarinet), CHARLIE PARKER (alto sax), CHARLIE VENTURA (tenor sax), ERNIE CACERES (baritone sax), LENNIE TRISTANO (piano), BILLY BAUER (guitar), EDDIE SAFRANSKI (bass), SHELLY MANNE (drums), PETE RUGOLO (director)

Overtime (2 takes) / *Victory Ball* (3 takes)

WEDNESDAY 5 JANUARY 1949

Miles joins an all star combo led by Oscar Pettiford at the Clique Club (later to become famous as Birdland) on Broadway at 52nd Street. Also in the band are Fats Navarro, Kai Winding, Lucky Thompson, Milt Jackson, Bud Powell and Kenny Clarke.

Down Beat reports on the new band:

As a replacement for Buddy Rich & Orchestra, who moved to the Adams Theatre, Newark, the Clique Club built an all-star band around Oscar Pettiford. Miles Davis left JATP to join the new combo.

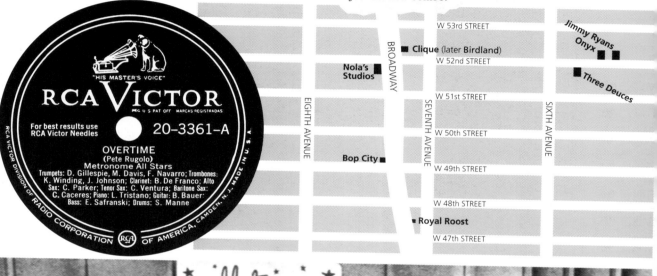

AT	**1**
UN	**2**
1ON	**3**
UES	**4**
VED	**5**
HUR	**6**
RI	**7**
AT	**8**
UN	**9**
1ON	**10**
UES	**11**
VED	**12**
THUR	**13**
FRI	**14**
SAT	**15**
SUN	**16**
MON	**17**
TUES	**18**
WED	**19**
THUR	**20**
FRI	**21**
SAT	**22**
SUN	**23**
MON	**24**
TUES	**25**
WED	**26**
THUR	**27**
FRI	**28**
SAT	**29**
SUN	**30**
MON	**31**

Crowd Gives Enthusiastic Welcome To Extreme Bop By Pettiford All-Stars

New York—With Sarah Vaughan held over as the box office attraction, the Clique turned on a strictly bop show for its big band policy, bringing in a stable of the best publicized boppists in the big city. Taking Kenny Clarke and Oscar Pettiford away from their background spot behind pianist George Shearing, and building a new combo there, managers Sammy Kaye and Irv Alexander let fly to capture whatever excitement bop may be creating hereabouts.

The all-star group, so billed, under the direction of Pettiford, goes to extremes in presenting the new fetish of jazzophiles.

It is doubtful if more than a small part of the audience can decipher even a little of the arrangements, but the capacity crowd there when reviewed was enthusiastic and did plenty of talking about what was happening on the stand.

The band does some good ensemble stuff that shows the results of a week's constant rehearsing. Miles Davis and Fats Navarro do some trumpet duet studies in bop—good listening, flashy presentation, and good salesmanship of their product.

Not more than three or four of the men get a real crack at the solo spotlight during a half-hour set, loaded as the outfit is with stars.

Kai Winding stood out on the individual stuff, choosing slower numbers for his solo stints.

Milt Jackson on vibes; Lucky Thompson, tenor; Bud Powell, piano, and Clarke, drums, all get the spotlight to themselves in good time. Pettiford, with his own individual pin spot, always gets a heavy reception.

All, individually and collectively, are experts in the dishes they're serving. For bop extremists, this is something of an ideal collection.

Somewhat tastier and more delicate are the performances of George Shearing and his three cohorts. These boys, too, deal in bop, but not exclusively, and the English pianist gets at least one good crack at the piano for some of the best solo keyboard work in these parts, at least once each set.

De Franco Gets Break

Buddy De Franco, the *Beat* poll winning clarinetist, also gets plenty of opportunity to give out with the only worthwhile music played on that instrument in any of the midtown metropolitan clubs or ballrooms.

Backing up the two solo stars are Denzil Best on drums and John Levy, bass.

SAT **1**

SUN **2**

MON **3**

TUES **4**

WED **5**

THUR **6**

FRI **7**

SAT **8**

SUN **9**

MON **10**

TUES **11**

WED **12**

THUR **13**

FRI **14**

SAT **15**

SUN **16**

MON **17**

TUES **18**

WED **19**

THUR **20**

FRI **21**

SAT **22**

SUN **23**

MON **24**

TUES **25**

WED **26**

THUR **27**

FRI **28**

SAT **29**

SUN **30**

MON **31**

AT **1**

UN **2**

ON **3**

JES **4**

ED **5**

HUR **6**

.I **7**

AT **8**

UN **9**

ON **10**

JES **11**

ED **12**

HUR **13**

.I **14**

AT **15**

UN **16**

ON **17**

JES **18**

ED **19**

HUR **20**

.I **21**

AT **22**

UN **23**

ON **24**

JES **25**

ED **26**

HUR **27**

.I **28**

AT **29**

UN **30**

ON **31**

Opposite page: Miles poses in a booth at the Clique Club on Broadway.

Below: With two other members of the Oscar Pettiford Band at the Clique – trumpeter Fats Navarro and trombonist Kai Winding.

SAT	1
SUN	2
MON	3
TUES	4
WED	5
THUR	6
FRI	7
SAT	8
SUN	9
MON	10
TUES	11
WED	12
THUR	13
FRI	14
SAT	15
SUN	16
MON	17
TUES	18
WED	19
THUR	20
FRI	21
SAT	22
SUN	23
MON	24
TUES	25
WED	26
THUR	27
FRI	28
SAT	29
SUN	30
MON	31

Above l to r: Junior Collins (french horn), Bill Barber (tuba), Kai Winding (trombone), Max Roach (drums), Gerry Mulligan (baritone sax), Miles Davis (trumpet), Lee Konitz (alto sax), Al Haig (piano) and Joe Shulman (bass) at the 21 January recording session.

FRIDAY 21 JANUARY 1949

Recording session by the Miles Davis Nonet for Capitol in New York City.
MILES DAVIS (trumpet), KAI WINDING (trombone), JUNIOR COLLINS (french horn), BILL BARBER (tuba), LEE KONITZ (alto sax), GERRY MULLIGAN (baritone sax), AL HAIG (piano), JOE SHULMAN (bass), MAX ROACH (drums)
Jeru / Move / Godchild / Budo

MONDAY 24 JANUARY 1949

Miles and the Oscar Pettiford All-Stars close at the Clique Club.

JES 1
ED 2
HUR 3
RI 4
AT 5
JN 6
ON 7
JES 8
ED 9
HUR 10
RI 11
AT 12
JN 13
ON 14
JES 15
ED 16
HUR 17
RI 18
AT 19
JN 20
ON 21
JES 22
ED 23
HUR 24
RI 25
AT 26
JN 27
ON 28

THURSDAY 17 FEBRUARY 1949

Tadd Dameron Ten featuring Miles Davis open at the Royal Roost in New York City opposite the Charlie Parker Quintet. Miles is deputising for Fats Navarro.

SATURDAY 19 FEBRUARY 1949

Tadd Dameron Ten broadcast from the Royal Roost in New York City.

MILES DAVIS (trumpet), KAI WINDING (trombone), SAHIB SHIHAB (alto sax), BENJAMIN LUNDY (tenor sax), CECIL PAYNE (baritone sax), TADD DAMERON (piano), JOHN COLLINS (guitar), CURLEY RUSSELL (bass), KENNY CLARKE (drums), CARLOS VIDAL (conga)
Focus / April In Paris / Good Bait / Webb's Delight

SUNDAY 20 FEBRUARY 1949

Miles is among a host of other bop stars who play an afternoon benefit for Leo Parker at the Royal Roost.

SATURDAY 26 FEBRUARY 1949

Tadd Dameron Ten broadcast from the Royal Roost in New York City.

MILES DAVIS (trumpet), KAI WINDING (trombone), SAHIB SHIHAB (alto sax), BENJAMIN LUNDY (tenor sax), CECIL PAYNE (baritone sax), TADD DAMERON (piano), JOHN COLLINS (guitar), CURLEY RUSSELL (bass), KENNY CLARKE (drums), CARLOS VIDAL (conga)
Miles / Casbah

TUES	**1**	FRI	**1**
WED	**2**	SAT	**2**
THUR	**3**	SUN	**3**
FRI	**4**	MON	**4**
SAT	**5**	TUES	**5**
SUN	**6**	WED	**6**
MON	**7**	THUR	**7**
TUES	**8**	FRI	**8**
WED	**9**	SAT	**9**
THUR	**10**	SUN	**10**
FRI	**11**	MON	**11**
SAT	**12**	TUES	**12**
SUN	**13**	WED	**13**
MON	**14**	THUR	**14**
TUES	**15**	FRI	**15**
WED	**16**	SAT	**16**
THUR	**17**	SUN	**17**
FRI	**18**	MON	**18**
SAT	**19**	TUES	**19**
SUN	**20**	WED	**20**
MON	**21**	THUR	**21**
TUES	**22**	FRI	**22**
WED	**23**	SAT	**23**
THUR	**24**	SUN	**24**
FRI	**25**	MON	**25**
SAT	**26**	TUES	**26**
SUN	**27**	WED	**27**
MON	**28**	THUR	**28**
TUES	**29**	FRI	**29**
WED	**30**	SAT	**30**
THUR	**31**		

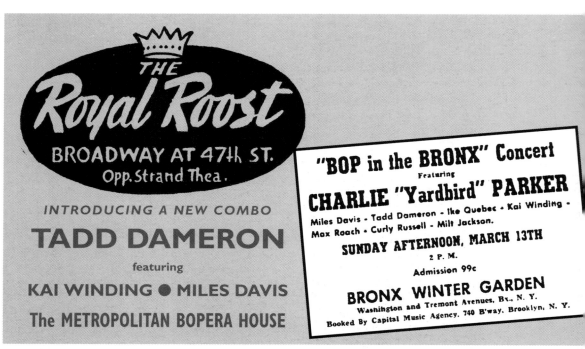

FRIDAY 4 MARCH 1949
Miles appears on a CBS television show 'Adventures in Jazz'.
CHARLIE PARKER (alto sax), MILES DAVIS (trumpet), MAX KAMINSKY (trumpet), KAI WINDING (trombone), JOE MARSALA (clarinet), MIKE CALUCCIO (piano), SPECS POWELL, MAX ROACH (drums), WILLIAM B. WILLIAMS (MC)
Anthropology (JOE SULLIVAN plays piano) / *Bop City* (trombone: BILL BRADLEY) / *I Get A Kick Out Of You* (vocal: ANN HATHAWAY) / *Big Foot* (Finale jam session)

SATURDAY 5 MARCH 1949
Tadd Dameron Ten broadcast from the Royal Roost in New York City.
MILES DAVIS (trumpet), KAI WINDING (trombone), SAHIB SHIHAB (alto sax), BENJAMIN LUNDY (tenor sax), CECIL PAYNE (baritone sax), TADD DAMERON (piano), JOHN COLLINS (guitar), CURLEY RUSSELL (bass), KENNY CLARKE (drums), CARLOS VIDAL (conga)
Good Bait / The Squirrel

SUNDAY 13 MARCH 1949
Miles appears in a Sunday afternoon 'Bop in the Bronx' Concert at the Bronx Winter Garden. Also taking part are Charlie Parker, Tadd Dameron, Ike Quebec, Kai Winding, Milt Jackson, Curley Russell and Max Roach.

WEDNESDAY 16 MARCH 1949
Miles and the Tadd Dameron Ten close at the Royal Roost in New York City.

THURSDAY 21 APRIL 1949
Recording session by the Tadd Dameron Ten fo Capitol in New York City.
MILES DAVIS (trumpet), J. J. JOHNSON (trombone), SAHIB SHIHAB (alto sax), BENJAMIN LUNDY (tenor sax), CECIL PAYNE (baritone sax), TADD DAMERON (piano), JOHN COLLINS (guitar), CURLEY RUSSELL (bass), KENNY CLARKE (drums), KAY PENTON (vocal)
John's Delight / What's New (vKP) / *Heaven's Doors Are Wide Open* (vKP) / *Focus*

FRIDAY 22 APRIL 1949
Recording session by the Miles Davis Nonet for Capitol in New York City.
MILES DAVIS (trumpet), J. J. JOHNSON (trombone), SANDY SIEGELSTEIN (french horn), BILL BARBER (tuba), LEE KONITZ (alto sax), GERRY MULLIGAN (baritone sax), JOHN LEWIS (piano), NELSON BOYD (bass), KENNY CLARKE (drums)
Venus de Milo / Rouge / Boplicity / Israel

JUN 1
MON 2
TUES 3
WED 4
THUR 5
FRI 6
SAT 7
SUN 8
MON 9
TUES 10
WED 11
THUR 12
FRI 13
SAT 14
SUN 15
MON 16
TUES 17
WED 18
THUR 19
FRI 20
SAT 21
SUN 22
MON 23
TUES 24
WED 25
THUR 26
FRI 27
SAT 28
SUN 29
MON 30
TUES 31

Above: Some of the visiting American musicians arrive in Paris for the International Jazz Festival. L to r: Hot Lips Page, Tommy Potter, unknown lady, Big Chief Russell Moore, Sidney Bechet, Al Haig, Charlie Parker, Max Roach, Miles Davis and Kenny Dorham.

SATURDAY 7 MAY 1949
Miles flies to Paris to appear at the International Jazz Festival.

SUNDAY 8 MAY 1949
The Tadd Dameron/Miles Davis Quintet appear at the opening concert at the Salle Pleyel in Paris.
MILES DAVIS (trumpet), JAMES MOODY (tenor sax), TADD DAMERON (piano), BARNEY SPIELER (bass), KENNY CLARKE (drums)
Don't Blame Me / Rifftide / The Squirrel / Embraceable You / Ornithology / Good Bait / Lady Bird / Perdido / All The Things You Are / Crazy Rhythm

FESTIVAL INTERNATIONAL 1949
JAZZ

OUVERTURE DU FESTIVAL
*
SYDNEY BECHET
*
PETE JOHNSON
*
« HOT LIPS » PAGE - « Big » RUSSEL MOORE DON BYAS, GEORGE JOHNSON, etc...
*
MILES DAVIS, TAD DAMERON Quintet,
featuring : James MOODY,
Kenny CLARKE - « bass » SPIELER
*
CHARLIE PARKER'S Quintet
featuring : Kenny DORHAM, AL. HAIG, Tommy POTTER et Max ROACH

SUN	**1**
MON	**2**
TUES	**3**
WED	**4**
THUR	**5**
FRI	**6**
SAT	**7**
SUN	**8**
MON	**9**
TUES	**10**
WED	**11**
THUR	**12**
FRI	**13**
SAT	**14**
SUN	**15**
MON	**16**
TUES	**17**
WED	**18**
THUR	**19**
FRI	**20**
SAT	**21**
SUN	**22**
MON	**23**
TUES	**24**
WED	**25**
THUR	**26**
FRI	**27**
SAT	**28**
SUN	**29**
MON	**30**
TUES	**31**

Miles meets Juliette Greco at a rehearsal and falls in love. He later recalls the time in his autobiography:

Juliette and I used to walk down by the Seine River together, holding hands and kissing, looking into each other's eyes, and kissing some more, and squeezing each other's hands. It was like magic, almost like I had been hypnotized, was in some kind of trance. I had never done this before. I was always so into the music I never had time for any kind of romance. Music had been my total life until I met Juliette Greco and she taught me what it was to love someone other than music.

MONDAY 9 MAY 1949
The Tadd Dameron/Miles Davis Quintet appear at the Salle Pleyel in Paris.
MILES DAVIS (trumpet), JAMES MOODY (tenor sax), TADD DAMERON (piano), BARNEY SPIELER (bass), KENNY CLARKE (drums)
Wahoo / Allen's Alley / Embraceable You / Ornithology / All The Things You Are

WEDNESDAY 11 MAY 1949
The Tadd Dameron/Miles Davis Quintet appear at the Salle Pleyel in Paris.

THURSDAY 12 MAY 1949
The Tadd Dameron/Miles Davis Quintet appear at matinée and evening performances at the Salle Pleyel in Paris.

SATURDAY 14 MAY 1949
The Tadd Dameron/Miles Davis Quintet appear at the Salle Pleyel in Paris.
MILES DAVIS (trumpet), JAMES MOODY (tenor sax), TADD DAMERON (piano), BARNEY SPIELER (bass), KENNY CLARKE (drums)
Lady Be Good / Don't Blame Me / Allen's Alley / Crazy Rhythm / All The Things You Are

SUNDAY 15 MAY 1949
The Tadd Dameron/Miles Davis Quintet appear at matinée and evening performances at the Salle Pleyel in Paris. In the final concert (8.45pm) Miles jams with Charlie Parker, Sidney Bechet and Don Byas in the finale session.
KENNY DORHAM, AIME BARELLI, BILL COLEMAN, MILES DAVIS, HOT LIPS PAGE (trumpets), 'BIG CHIEF' RUSSELL MOORE (trombone), HUBERT ROSTAING (clarinet), PIERRE BRASLAVSKY, SIDNEY BECHET (soprano sax), CHARLIE PARKER (alto sax), DON BYAS, JAMES MOODY (tenor sax), AL HAIG, BERNARD PEIFFER (piano), HAZY OSTERWALD (vibes), TOOTS THIELEMANS (guitar), TOMMY POTTER (bass), MAX ROACH (drums)
Farewell Blues

THURSDAY 26 MAY 1949
Miles' 23rd birthday.

Crowds Jam Paris Jazz Festival

By MARIAN McPARTLAND

Paris—Backstage at the Salle Pleyel, an excited crowd shuffled back and forth. Musicians were warming up, stage technicians barked last minute directions, critics and kibitzers chattered excitedly and craned their necks as, 15 minutes late, a French emcee sidled in front of the curtain and announced "Le Festival Internationale de Jazz est ouvert."

And for a whole week the 25,000-capacity auditorium was jammed. Devotees of New Orleans music rubbed shoulders with bop disciples. When, on opening night, the first notes of Vic Lewis' bop-styled, 15-piece British band were heard, purists in the audience booed and hissed.

And, when Carlo Krahmer's Dixie band held the stage, the progressive element loudly registered disapproval.

Listen to Tadd

But when Tadd Dameron's quintet, with Miles Davis, trumpet; James Moody, tenor; Bass Speiler, bass, and Kenny Clarke, drums, was announced, the entire audience settled to hear, if not always to understand, some of the most controversial music of the day.

Bespectacled, goateed Parisians nodded bereted heads sagely at each exciting harmonic change, screaming and whistling their approval of every soloist.

Left: Miles and Kenny Dorham enjoy a final drink in a Paris bar before the return flight to New York.

WED	**1**	FRI	**1**	MON	**1**	THUR	**1**
THUR	**2**	SAT	**2**	TUES	**2**	FRI	**2**
FRI	**3**	SUN	**3**	WED	**3**	SAT	**3**
SAT	**4**	MON	**4**	THUR	**4**	SUN	**4**
SUN	**5**	TUES	**5**	FRI	**5**	MON	**5**
MON	**6**	WED	**6**	SAT	**6**	TUES	**6**
TUES	**7**	THUR	**7**	SUN	**7**	WED	**7**
WED	**8**	FRI	**8**	MON	**8**	THUR	**8**
THUR	**9**	SAT	**9**	TUES	**9**	FRI	**9**
FRI	**10**	SUN	**10**	WED	**10**	SAT	**10**
SAT	**11**	MON	**11**	THUR	**11**	SUN	**11**
SUN	**12**	TUES	**12**	FRI	**12**	MON	**12**
MON	**13**	WED	**13**	SAT	**13**	TUES	**13**
TUES	**14**	THUR	**14**	SUN	**14**	WED	**14**
WED	**15**	FRI	**15**	MON	**15**	THUR	**15**
THUR	**16**	SAT	**16**	TUES	**16**	FRI	**16**
FRI	**17**	SUN	**17**	WED	**17**	SAT	**17**
SAT	**18**	MON	**18**	THUR	**18**	SUN	**18**
SUN	**19**	TUES	**19**	FRI	**19**	MON	**19**
MON	**20**	WED	**20**	SAT	**20**	TUES	**20**
TUES	**21**	THUR	**21**	SUN	**21**	WED	**21**
WED	**22**	FRI	**22**	MON	**22**	THUR	**22**
THUR	**23**	SAT	**23**	TUES	**23**	FRI	**23**
FRI	**24**	SUN	**24**	WED	**24**	SAT	**24**
SAT	**25**	MON	**25**	THUR	**25**	SUN	**25**
SUN	**26**	TUES	**26**	FRI	**26**	MON	**26**
MON	**27**	WED	**27**	SAT	**27**	TUES	**27**
TUES	**28**	THUR	**28**	SUN	**28**	WED	**28**
WED	**29**	FRI	**29**	MON	**29**	THUR	**29**
THUR	**30**	SAT	**30**	TUES	**30**	FRI	**30**
		SUN	**31**	WED	**31**		

On his return to the USA Miles finds jobs hard to come by and he spend
much of the rest of the year unemployed. The boredom and frustration
lead him into drugs and he soon has an expensive heroin habit.
He is living with Irene and the kids, Gregory and Cheryl, in an
apartment in St Albans, driving into Harlem in his 1948 Dodge
convertible to score drugs. The relentless search for drugs keeps him
away from home more and more until he eventually breaks with Irene,
leaving her stranded. Singer Betty Carter steps in to take care of Irene
and the kids.

AUGUST 1949
Miles and Tadd Dameron rehearse an 18-piece band but when they fail
to get work or a recording date the band breaks up.

TUESDAY 6 SEPTEMBER 1949
Miles Davis appears at a Town Hall Concert which also features Erroll
Garner, Lennie Tristano, Bud Powell, Charlie Parker & Harry Belafonte.

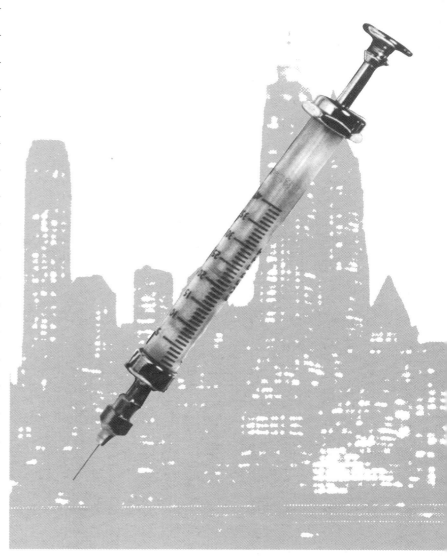

AT	**1**	TUES	**1**	THUR	**1**
JN	**2**	WED	**2**	FRI	**2**
ON	**3**	THUR	**3**	SAT	**3**
JES	**4**	FRI	**4**	SUN	**4**
'ED	**5**	SAT	**5**	MON	**5**
HUR	**6**	SUN	**6**	TUES	**6**
I	**7**	MON	**7**	WED	**7**
AT	**8**	TUES	**8**	THUR	**8**
JN	**9**	WED	**9**	FRI	**9**
ON	**10**	THUR	**10**	SAT	**10**
JES	**11**	FRI	**11**	SUN	**11**
'ED	**12**	SAT	**12**	MON	**12**
HUR	**13**	SUN	**13**	TUES	**13**
I	**14**	MON	**14**	WED	**14**
AT	**15**	TUES	**15**	THUR	**15**
JN	**16**	WED	**16**	FRI	**16**
ON	**17**	THUR	**17**	SAT	**17**
JES	**18**	FRI	**18**	SUN	**18**
'ED	**19**	SAT	**19**	MON	**19**
HUR	**20**	SUN	**20**	TUES	**20**
I	**21**	MON	**21**	WED	**21**
AT	**22**	TUES	**22**	THUR	**22**
JN	**23**	WED	**23**	FRI	**23**
ON	**24**	THUR	**24**	SAT	**24**
JES	**25**	FRI	**25**	SUN	**25**
'ED	**26**	SAT	**26**	MON	**26**
HUR	**27**	SUN	**27**	TUES	**27**
I	**28**	MON	**28**	WED	**28**
AT	**29**	TUES	**29**	THUR	**29**
JN	**30**	WED	**30**	FRI	**30**
ON	**31**			SAT	**31**

FRIDAY 7 OCTOBER 1949
Miles Davis opens with the Bud Powell Band at the Orchid Club (formerly the Onyx) on W52nd Street. The Bud Powell Band consists of Miles (trumpet), Bud Powell (piano), Nelson Boyd (bass), Roy Haynes (drums). Playing opposite them are the Wardell Gray Combo with Wardell (tenor sax), Sonny Stitt (alto sax), Tadd Dameron (piano), Gene Ramey (bass) and Charlie Perry (drums).

THURSDAY 13 OCTOBER 1949
Miles Davis and the Bud Powell Band close at the Orchid Club when it suddenly drops its modern music policy.

FRIDAY 21 OCTOBER 1949
Down Beat reviews Miles' latest Capitol release:

MILES DAVIS
**** Boplicity
*** Israel
The same wonderful sound as on Davis' previous side of *Jeru* and *Godchild*, this combines tuba, French horn, and other blowing gentry for very soft, melodious sounds as well as good solos. While the playing isn't quite as clean on these sides as the ones before, it is still delightful, relaxed bop, well conceived and integrated. Davis' playing, as well as Gerry Mulligan's baritone, is worth hearing. *Israel*, by brassman Johnny Carisi, utilizes some fine moving passages in single instrumentation, which, unfortunately, the boys don't render with quite the due justice necessary. **(Capitol 57-60011)**

NOVEMBER 1949
Miles Davis is at the Hi Note Club in Chicago opposite Anita O'Day. Miles is backed by local musicians Eddie Baker (piano), Bob Petersen (bass) and Hal Russell (vibes and drums).

SUNDAY 25 DECEMBER 1949
Miles Davis appears in a concert at Carnegie Hall promoted by Leonard Feather and called the *Stars of Modern Jazz Concert*. Sarah Vaughan and the Charlie Parker Quintet are top of the bill with Lennie Tristano and two pick-up groups featuring Stan Getz/Kai Winding and Miles as support. The concert is taped by Voice of America:
Miles Davis (trumpet), Benny Green (trombone), Sonny Stitt (alto sax), Serge Chaloff (baritone sax), Bud Powell (piano), Curley Russell (bass), Max Roach (drums)
Move / Hot House / Ornithology

SUN	1	WED	1	WED	1
MON	2	THUR	2	THUR	2
TUES	3	FRI	3	FRI	3
WED	4	SAT	4	SAT	4
THUR	5	SUN	5	SUN	5
FRI	6	MON	6	MON	6
SAT	7	TUES	7	TUES	7
SUN	8	WED	8	WED	8
MON	9	THUR	9	THUR	9
TUES	10	FRI	10	FRI	10
WED	11	SAT	11	SAT	11
THUR	12	SUN	12	SUN	12
FRI	13	MON	13	MON	13
SAT	14	TUES	14	TUES	14
SUN	15	WED	15	WED	15
MON	16	THUR	16	THUR	16
TUES	17	FRI	17	FRI	17
WED	18	SAT	18	SAT	18
THUR	19	SUN	19	SUN	19
FRI	20	MON	20	MON	20
SAT	21	TUES	21	TUES	21
SUN	22	WED	22	WED	22
MON	23	THUR	23	THUR	23
TUES	24	FRI	24	FRI	24
WED	25	SAT	25	SAT	25
THUR	26	SUN	26	SUN	26
FRI	27	MON	27	MON	27
SAT	28	TUES	28	TUES	28
SUN	29			WED	29
MON	30			THUR	30
TUES	31			FRI	31

FRIDAY 13 JANUARY 1950

Miles guests with the 18-piece Jay Burkhardt Orchestra which opens a one-week engagement at the Regal Theatre in Chicago opposite Billie Holiday. Wardell Gray and Leo Parker are also in the band.

THURSDAY 19 JANUARY 1950

Miles and the Jay Burkhardt Orchestra close at the Regal Theatre in Chicago.

Chicago—*Moose the Mooche*, *The Chase*, and other boppish ceiling-raisers had a brief fling at the Regal Theatre here recently, when Jay Burkhardt's 18-piece band worked a week at the spot, opposite Billie Holiday.

Hard to realize, until the Regal date, what Chicago's been missing during the last few months. Burkhardt and his big crew, however, are it.

The band played with enthusiasm and drive, sparked by Miles Davis' horn from the guest spot in the trumpet section. Wardell Gray, also advertised as appearing with the band, didn't make it until the last night. Evidently hated to leave that California sunshine. Tom Archia sat in Gray's spot, but the substitution ended there.

Chief interest, other than Miles' impeccable solos on *Mooche*, *Body and Soul*, and his tremendous little solo obligato behind a dance team, rested in the band's playing of *Sorrento*. A Bob Anderson arrangement that they've had in the books since Bob Dunne was singing with the band, it would be terrific in any band's library. Joe Williams sang it with fine feeling and a musical competency…

FRIDAY 20 JANUARY 1950

Miles Davis/Wardell Gray Quintet open at the Club Valley in Detroit for a one-week engagement.

THURSDAY 26 JANUARY 1950

Miles Davis/Wardell Gray Quintet close at the Club Valley in Detroit.

THURSDAY 9 FEBRUARY 1950

The Miles Davis/Stan Getz Sextet open at Birdland in New York City.
The sextet features Miles (trumpet), Stan Getz (tenor sax), J. J. Johnson (trombone), Tadd Dameron (piano), Gene Ramey (bass) and Art Blakey (drums). Also on the bill are Charlie Parker's Quintet (Red Rodney, Al Haig, Tommy Potter, Roy Haynes) and the Bud Powell Trio featuring Curley Russell (bass) and Max Roach (drums).

Miles is now living in Manhattan at the Hotel America on 48th Street. He hangs out up on Sugar Hill in Harlem with Sonny Rollins, Gil Coggins, Jackie McLean, Walter Bishop, Art Blakey, Art Taylor, Max Roach and Kenny Drew. Most of the group are using heroin.

FRIDAY 10 FEBRUARY 1950

The Miles Davis/Stan Getz Sextet broadcast from Birdland in New York City.
MILES DAVIS (trumpet), J. J. JOHNSON (trombone), STAN GETZ (tenor sax), TADD DAMERON (piano), GENE RAMEY (bass), MAX ROACH (drums)
Conception / Ray's Idea / That Old Black Magic (MD, JJJ out) / *Max Is Making Wax / Woody'n You*

FRIDAY 17 FEBRUARY 1950

Miles continues at Birdland with his own sextet, joined by Ella Fitzgerald and the Bud Powell Trio.

THURSDAY 2 MARCH 1950

Ella and Bud Powell close at Birdland. Miles stays on, joined by Lester Young, Jeri Southern and a new singing sensation Larry Darnell.

THURSDAY 9 MARCH 1950

Recording session by the Miles Davis Nonet for Capitol in New York City.
MILES DAVIS (trumpet), J. J. JOHNSON (trombone), GUNTHER SCHULLER (french horn), BILL BARBER (tuba), LEE KONITZ (alto sax), GERRY MULLIGAN (baritone sax), JOHN LEWIS (piano), AL McKIBBON (bass), MAX ROACH (drums), KENNY HAGOOD (vocal)
Deception / Rocker / Moondreams / Darn That Dream (vKH) / *The Coop*

T	**1**	MON	**1**
JN	**2**	TUES	**2**
ON	**3**	WED	**3**
JES	**4**	THUR	**4**
ED	**5**	FRI	**5**
IUR	**6**	SAT	**6**
I	**7**	SUN	**7**
T	**8**	MON	**8**
JN	**9**	TUES	**9**
ON	**10**	WED	**10**
IES	**11**	THUR	**11**
ED	**12**	FRI	**12**
IUR	**13**	SAT	**13**
I	**14**	SUN	**14**
T	**15**	MON	**15**
IN	**16**	TUES	**16**
ON	**17**	WED	**17**
IES	**18**	THUR	**18**
ED	**19**	FRI	**19**
IUR	**20**	SAT	**20**
I	**21**	SUN	**21**
T	**22**	MON	**22**
IN	**23**	TUES	**23**
ON	**24**	WED	**24**
IES	**25**	THUR	**25**
ED	**26**	FRI	**26**
IUR	**27**	SAT	**27**
	28	SUN	**28**
T	**29**	MON	**29**
IN	**30**	TUES	**30**
		WED	**31**

WEDNESDAY 17 MAY 1950

The Miles Davis Sextet broadcast from Birdland in New York City.
MILES DAVIS (trumpet), J. J. JOHNSON (trombone), BREW MOORE (tenor sax), TADD DAMERON (piano), CURLEY RUSSELL (bass), ART BLAKEY (drums), JIMMIE SCOTT (vocal)
Max Is Making Wax / Chubbie's Blues (vJS, MD, BM out) / *Poobah* (JJJ, BM out)
Miles also sits in with Charlie Parker's Band.
CHARLIE PARKER (alto sax), MILES DAVIS (trumpet), FATS NAVARRO (trumpet), WALTER BISHOP (piano), CURLEY RUSSELL (bass), ART BLAKEY (drums)
Conception

THURSDAY 18 MAY 1950

Miles enters Columbia's studios for the first time for a recording session by Sarah Vaughan with Jimmy Jones' Band in New York City.
SARAH VAUGHAN (vocal), MILES DAVIS (trumpet), BENNY GREEN (trombone), TONY SCOTT (clarinet), BUDD JOHNSON (tenor sax), JIMMY JONES (piano), FREDDIE GREEN (guitar), BILLY TAYLOR (bass), J. C. HEARD (drums)
Ain't Misbehavin' / Goodnight My Love / It Might As Well Be Spring

Miles later says of this session:

I LIKE THE THINGS WITH SARAH... I LIKE THE SOUND I GOT, ESPECIALLY ON 'IT MIGHT AS WELL BE SPRING'.

THURSDAY 18 MAY 1950

The Miles Davis Sextet broadcast from Birdland in New York City.
MILES DAVIS (trumpet), J. J. JOHNSON (trombone), BREW MOORE (tenor sax), TADD DAMERON (piano), CURLEY RUSSELL (bass), ART BLAKEY (drums)
Hot House / Theme

FRIDAY 19 MAY 1950

Miles is back at Columbia Studios for the completion of the recording session by Sarah Vaughan with Jimmy Jones' Band in New York City.
SARAH VAUGHAN (vocal), MILES DAVIS (trumpet), BENNY GREEN (trombone), TONY SCOTT (clarinet), BUDD JOHNSON (tenor sax), JIMMY JONES (piano), MUNDELL LOWE (guitar), BILLY TAYLOR (bass), J. C. HEARD (drums)
Mean To Me / Come Rain Or Come Shine / Nice Work If You Can Get It

SATURDAY 20 MAY 1950

The Miles Davis Sextet broadcast from Birdland in New York City.
MILES DAVIS (trumpet), J. J. JOHNSON (trombone), BREW MOORE (tenor sax), TADD DAMERON (piano), CURLEY RUSSELL (bass), ART BLAKEY (drums)
Round About Midnight / Embraceable You / Wee

SUNDAY 21 MAY 1950

The Miles Davis Sextet broadcast from Birdland in New York City.
MILES DAVIS (trumpet), J. J. JOHNSON (trombone), BREW MOORE (tenor sax), TADD DAMERON (piano), CURLEY RUSSELL (bass), ART BLAKEY (drums)
Ow! / For Now My Love / September In The Rain / Overturia / 52nd Street Theme

FRIDAY 26 MAY 1950

Miles' 24th birthday.

MONDAY 29 MAY 1950

The Miles Davis Sextet broadcast from Birdland in New York City.
MILES DAVIS (trumpet), J. J. JOHNSON (trombone), BREW MOORE (tenor sax), TADD DAMERON (piano), CURLEY RUSSELL (bass), ART BLAKEY (drums)
52nd Street Theme

TUESDAY 30 MAY 1950

The Miles Davis Sextet broadcast from Birdland in New York City.
MILES DAVIS (trumpet), J. J. JOHNSON (trombone), BREW MOORE (tenor sax), TADD DAMERON (piano), CURLEY RUSSELL (bass), ART BLAKEY (drums), JIMMIE SCOTT (vocal)
Wee / Chubbie's Blues (vJS, MD, BM out)

THUR 1	SAT 1	TUES 1
FRI 2	SUN 2	WED 2
SAT 3	MON 3	THUR 3
SUN 4	TUES 4	FRI 4
MON 5	WED 5	SAT 5
TUES 6	THUR 6	SUN 6
WED 7	FRI 7	MON 7
THUR 8	SAT 8	TUES 8
FRI 9	SUN 9	WED 9
SAT 10	MON 10	THUR 10
SUN 11	TUES 11	FRI 11
MON 12	WED 12	SAT 12
TUES 13	THUR 13	SUN 13
WED 14	FRI 14	MON 14
THUR 15	SAT 15	TUES 15
FRI 16	SUN 16	WED 16
SAT 17	MON 17	THUR 17
SUN 18	TUES 18	FRI 18
MON 19	WED 19	SAT 19
TUES 20	THUR 20	SUN 20
WED 21	FRI 21	MON 21
THUR 22	SAT 22	TUES 22
FRI 23	SUN 23	WED 23
SAT 24	MON 24	THUR 24
SUN 25	TUES 25	FRI 25
MON 26	WED 26	SAT 26
TUES 27	THUR 27	SUN 27
WED 28	FRI 28	MON 28
THUR 29	SAT 29	TUES 29
FRI 30	SUN 30	WED 30
	MON 31	THUR 31

FRIDAY 30 JUNE 1950

The Miles Davis Sextet broadcast from Birdland in New York City.
MILES DAVIS (trumpet), J. J. JOHNSON (trombone), BREW MOORE (tenor sax), TADD DAMERON (piano), CURLEY RUSSELL (bass), ART BLAKEY (drums)
Hot House / Embraceable You

Walter Bishop replaces Tadd Dameron on piano.
MILES DAVIS (trumpet), J. J. JOHNSON (trombone), BREW MOORE (tenor sax), WALTER BISHOP (piano), CURLEY RUSSELL (bass), ART BLAKEY (drums)
Eronel / 52nd Street Theme

FRIDAY 30 JUNE 1950

Down Beat carries a record review of the Charlie Parker Quintet: *Charlie's Wig* (tepid) and *Klactoveedsedstene* (tasty)

Quintet formation with Miles Davis, JJ Johnson, Max Roach, Duke Jordan, and Tommy Potter. JJ operates well on *Wig* as does Miles. *Klacto* is an esoteric title, graced with fair solos. Charlie himself is heard to better advantage here than on *Wig*. (**Dial 1040**)

THURSDAY 6 JULY 1950

The Miles Davis Sextet close at Birdland in New York City.

Miles and Irene are temporarily back together, but behind with their rent at the Hotel America. They pawn what the can, throw the rest into the 1948 Dodge and drive with the kids to East St. Louis. Irene is pregnant and they have the idea that once out of New York they will be able to patch up their marriage. Nothing changes, however, and the relationship ends. Miles returns to New York leaving Irene in East St. Louis where she gives birth to Miles IV.

SUNDAY 30 JULY 1950

Miles joins a small group that Billy Eckstine takes on tour and they open at the Frolics in Salisbury Beach, Massachusetts. Tenor saxophonist Budd Johnson is the musical director of the group which includes Tommy Potter on bass and Art Blakey on drums.

FRIDAY 11 AUGUST 1950

Miles and the Eckstine group open at the Chicago Theatre in Chicago for a two-week engagement.

THURSDAY 24 AUGUST 1950

Miles and the Eckstine group close at the Chicago Theatre in Chicago.

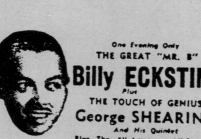

One Evening Only
THE GREAT "MR. B"
Billy ECKSTINE
Plus
THE TOUCH OF GENIUS
George SHEARING
And His Quintet
Plus The All-American All-Stars—
World's Most Exciting Jazz Group

One Evening Only
THE GREAT "MR. B"
Billy ECKSTINE
Plus
THE TOUCH OF GENIUS
George SHEARING
And His Quintet
Plus The All-American All-Stars—
World's Most Exciting Jazz Group

Shearing Five, Eckstine Plan Concert Tour

Hollywood — George Shearing unit will be teamed with Billy Eckstine for a concert tour this fall. The first date in the series is being set up for Sept. 15 at L.A.'s 6,000-seat Shrine auditorium, with Gene Norman as impresario.

William Morris agency, which handles Eckstine, is lining up other dates with aim of covering some 30 or more cities, with the final fling slated for New York. MGM records, which has both Eckstine and Shearing on that label, is playing an active part in the deal.

1	SUN **1**	WED **1**
T **2**	MON **2**	THUR **2**
N **3**	TUES **3**	FRI **3**
ON **4**	WED **4**	SAT **4**
ES **5**	THUR **5**	SUN **5**
ED **6**	FRI **6**	MON **6**
UR **7**	SAT **7**	TUES **7**
8	SUN **8**	WED **8**
T **9**	MON **9**	THUR **9**
N **10**	TUES **10**	FRI **10**
ON **11**	WED **11**	SAT **11**
ES **12**	THUR **12**	SUN **12**
ED **13**	FRI **13**	MON **13**
UR **14**	SAT **14**	TUES **14**
15	SUN **15**	WED **15**
T **16**	MON **16**	THUR **16**
N **17**	TUES **17**	FRI **17**
ON **18**	WED **18**	SAT **18**
ES **19**	THUR **19**	SUN **19**
ED **20**	FRI **20**	MON **20**
UR **21**	SAT **21**	TUES **21**
22	SUN **22**	WED **22**
T **23**	MON **23**	THUR **23**
N **24**	TUES **24**	FRI **24**
ON **25**	WED **25**	SAT **25**
ES **26**	THUR **26**	SUN **26**
ED **27**	FRI **27**	MON **27**
UR **28**	SAT **28**	TUES **28**
29	SUN **29**	WED **29**
30	MON **30**	THUR **30**
	TUES **31**	

FRIDAY 15 SEPTEMBER 1950
Miles and the Eckstine group appear in concert at the Shrine Auditorium in Los Angeles.

Leonard Feather, writing in the London *Melody Maker*, reports:

Miles is arrested in Los Angeles on suspicion of being a heroin addict. Along with Dexter Gordon and Art Blakey, fellow members of the Eckstine group, he is on his way to Burbank Airport at the end of the tour when the bust occurs. Miles goes to jail but a lawyer engaged by Miles' father gets him out on bail.

Miles Davis arrested on narcotics charge

MILES DAVIS, youngest and most widely respected of the current modern trumpet stars, has been arrested on narcotics charges. He and drummer Art Blakey were picked up by detectives at Los Angeles when boarding a plane to fulfil an engagement with Billy Eckstine in San Francisco.

Several capsules of heroin were found in their possession.

News of the arrest has shocked American music circles, for Miles has frequently expressed his disapproval of the habits of so many of his fellow-boppers (*writes Leonard Feather*).

The two musicians were both members of the original big band led by Billy Eckstine. Recently they were hired again as part of the small unit to accompany the singer on his current joint tour with the George Shearing Quintet.

Miles Davis is widely known to record-collectors in this country through his many waxings with Charlie Parker and by his own unique-sounding group on Capitol. He played at last year's Paris Jazz Festival with Parker's outfit.

Miles Davis Freed
Los Angeles—Miles Davis, arrested here in September on a narcotics count, was brought to trial in November and acquitted. Jury voted 10 to 2 in his favor.

Above: While awaiting trial Miles visits San Francisco's Bop City where he meets up with Dizzy Gillespie and his Sextet. Diz is at the piano with Miles at his shoulder. Also visible are vocalist Betty Bennett, drummers Roy Porter and Specs Wright, Kenny Dorham, Sonny Criss, Milt Jackson, Carl Perkins and the Heath brothers, Jimmy and Percy.

FRIDAY 17 NOVEMBER 1950
Down Beat magazine devotes its editorial to the narcotics problem in the music business, singling out Miles and Art Blakey in an unfortunate way.

This adverse publicity makes it virtually impossible for either man to find work.

FRI	**1**
SAT	**2**
SUN	**3**
MON	**4**
TUES	**5**
WED	**6**
THUR	**7**
FRI	**8**
SAT	**9**
SUN	**10**
MON	**11**
TUES	**12**
WED	**13**
THUR	**14**
FRI	**15**
SAT	**16**
SUN	**17**
MON	**18**
TUES	**19**
WED	**20**
THUR	**21**
FRI	**22**
SAT	**23**
SUN	**24**
MON	**25**
TUES	**26**
WED	**27**
THUR	**28**
FRI	**29**
SAT	**30**
SUN	**31**

FRIDAY 1 DECEMBER 1950

Down Beat carries a record review of Miles' latest record release:

MILES DAVIS
**** Venus De Milo
**** Darn That Dream

Two more sides with that softly-blended sound of French horn, tuba, trumpet, baritone sax, and trombone which Miles has used to great success before. I find this stuff extremely pretty, often movingly-stated music. Kenny Hagood sings *Dream*, takes it too impressively and misses the neatness of phrasing the song demands. The scoring behind him once again is well done. It would be a wonderful thing if every young arranger in the country were forced to write for units of this size so that he actually learned the individual instruments and their sound possibilities instead of the mere massed blotches of color the Kenton tradition demands. **(Capitol 7-1221)**

FRIDAY 22 DECEMBER 1950

Miles opens at the Hi-Note in Chicago, leading the band that plays opposite Billie Holiday. The engagement is a great success and they play to capacity audiences throughout the two-week run.

Miles is living in hotels in Chicago, probably paid for by his father, as pianist Gil Coggins recalls:

HE WAS IN A MARVELLOUS HOTEL THEN.
I THINK IT COST $28 A WEEK, AND <u>THEN</u>… $28!
…THAT WAS A PRETTY NICE HOTEL! AND THAT
TIME HE WAS MESSING AROUND WITH EVERYBODY.
HIS OLD MAN WAS SENDING HIM $75… HIS OLD
MAN WOULD PAY FOR HIS PHONE BILLS – $35…
THAT'S A LOT OF CALLING… SHIT WAS CHEAP, YOU
COULD GET A CAPSULE FOR A DOLLAR…
IT WAS PURE, YOU KNOW, POTENT.

DOWN BEAT

6

CHICAGO BAND BRIEFS

Hi-Note Inaugurates New Policy: Brings In Holiday

By JACK TRACY

Chicago—In an abrupt and surprising move, for these times at least, the Hi-Note sliced off half of their bar, tossed tables into the cavity, and brought in Billie Holiday backed by a Miles Davis-fronted group. All this after months of econ-omy-style bookings caused rival ops to say the club was foolish—it wouldn't work.

So Billie packed the joint night-ly. And although the management had nothing definite set to follow Lady after her Jan. 7 closing, a succession of similar talent was promised. Miles was scheduled to stay on, however.

Billie was looking and singin better than in her last appearan here about a year ago. And ga no trouble to op Marty Denenb who says, "She's a

sound) were Ollie Wilson brothers Swope (Earl ar making up the trombone and bassist Mert Oliver. Count Basie's option wa up again at the Brass

ON **1**

JES **2**

ED **3**

HUR **4**

I **5**

AT **6**

JN **7**

ON **8**

JES **9**

ED **10**

HUR **11**

I **12**

AT **13**

JN **14**

ON **15**

JES **16**

ED **17**

HUR **18**

I **19**

AT **20**

JN **21**

ON **22**

JES **23**

ED **24**

HUR **25**

I **26**

AT **27**

JN **28**

ON **29**

JES **30**

ED **31**

SUNDAY 7 JANUARY 1951

Miles and Billie close at the Hi-Note in Chicago.

Bob Weinstock, owner of Prestige Records, has been impressed by the Miles Davis Nonet recordings and wants to record Miles on Prestige. He has trouble locating Miles, but gets through to his family in East St. Louis:

THEY TOLD ME HE WAS IN CHICAGO. I SAID, 'PLEASE, IF YOU SHOULD HEAR FROM MILES, ASK HIM TO CALL ME IN NEW YORK. I WANT TO RECORD HIM.' FINALLY HE GOT IN TOUCH WITH ME, AND HE CAME BACK EAST. MILES, AT THAT TIME, ALTHOUGH HE STILL DUG THE COOL MUSIC OF MULLIGAN AND EVANS, SOME OF THE PRIMITIVENESS IN HIM STARTED TO COME OUT. I SAY PRIMITIVENESS, BECAUSE TO ME THE MUSIC OF THE BOP MASTERS IS PRIMITIVE MUSIC, LIKE THE ORIGINAL NEW ORLEANS MUSIC OF KING OLIVER AND LOUIS. HE SORT OF DRIFTED BACK INTO THAT ELEMENT, AND HE LIKED SONNY ROLLINS, AS CRUDE AS SONNY WAS AT THAT TIME, AND JOHN LEWIS. ON HIS FIRST DATE, YOU CAN HEAR A VERY DIFFERENT MILES DAVIS THAN ON THE CAPITOLS.

Miles returns to New York, his spirits lifted by the Prestige contract. He moves in with drummer Stan Levey until he can find a place of his own.

WEDNESDAY 17 JANUARY 1951

Recording session as Charlie Parker Quintet for Mercury/Verve in New York City.
CHARLIE PARKER (alto sax), MILES DAVIS (trumpet), WALTER BISHOP (piano), TEDDY KOTICK (bass), MAX ROACH (drums)
Au Privave (2 takes) / *She Rote* (2 takes) / *K.C. Blues* / *Star Eyes*

Recording session by the Miles Davis Sextet for Prestige in New York City.
MILES DAVIS (trumpet), BENNY GREEN (trombone), SONNY ROLLINS (tenor sax), JOHN LEWIS (piano), PERCY HEATH (bass), ROY HAYNES (drums)
Morpheus / Down / Blue Room (BG, SR out) / *Blue Room* (BG, JL out) / *Whispering*
This is Miles' first Prestige recording date and takes place in the evening, following the Charlie Parker session for Mercury. He plays piano on *Blue Room*. At the end of the session, Miles insists that Sonny Rollins is given a chance as a leader. As pianist John Lewis has already left, Miles plays piano:
SONNY ROLLINS (tenor sax), MILES DAVIS (piano), PERCY HEATH (bass), ROY HAYNES (drums)
I Know

Miles Back In NYC; Cuts Prestige Sides

New York—Shortly after arriving in New York following several months' absence, Miles Davis signed a three-year recording contract with Prestige and cut his first session Jan. 17.

Featured on the date were Sonny Rollins, tenor; Benny Green, trombone; John Lewis, piano; Percy Heath, bass; and Roy Haynes, drums. Miles also cut a side on piano accompanying a Sonny Rollins tenor solo.

MON	**1**
TUES	**2**
WED	**3**
THUR	**4**
FRI	**5**
SAT	**6**
SUN	**7**
MON	**8**
TUES	**9**
WED	**10**
THUR	**11**
FRI	**12**
SAT	**13**
SUN	**14**
MON	**15**
TUES	**16**
WED	**17**
THUR	**18**
FRI	**19**
SAT	**20**
SUN	**21**
MON	**22**
TUES	**23**
WED	**24**
THUR	**25**
FRI	**26**
SAT	**27**
SUN	**28**
MON	**29**
TUES	**30**
WED	**31**

TUESDAY 23 JANUARY 1951
Miles appears at a recording session by the Metronome All Stars for Capitol in New York City.
MILES DAVIS (trumpet), KAI WINDING (trombone), JOHN LA PORTA (clarinet), LEE KONITZ (alto sax), STAN GETZ (tenor sax), SERGE CHALOFF (baritone sax), TERRY GIBBS (vibes), GEORGE SHEARING (piano), BILLY BAUER (guitar), EDDIE SAFRANSKI (bass), MAX ROACH (drums)
Early Spring / Local 802 Blues

*Right: Stan Getz, arranger Ralph Burns and Miles at the Metronome All Stars session.
Below: Miles rehearses while Ralph Burns and Terry Gibbs listen.*

HUR	**1**
RI	**2**
AT	**3**
JN	**4**
ION	**5**
JES	**6**
VED	**7**
HUR	**8**
RI	**9**
AT	**10**
JN	**11**
ION	**12**
JES	**13**
VED	**14**
HUR	**15**
RI	**16**
AT	**17**
JN	**18**
ION	**19**
JES	**20**
VED	**21**
HUR	**22**
RI	**23**
AT	**24**
JN	**25**
ION	**26**
JES	**27**
VED	**28**

FRIDAY 9 FEBRUARY 1951

Down Beat runs a feature on trumpeter Bobby Hackett. This is what Miles has to say about Hackett:

> I LIKE THE WAY HE RUNS HIS CHORDS, STAYS AROUND LOW REGISTER, AND, ABOVE ALL, ALWAYS SAYS SOMETHING. THAT FRANK SINATRA RECORD HE MADE HAS ALWAYS BEEN ONE OF MY FAVOURITES. HACKETT'S ORIGINAL BECAUSE HE DOES KNOW MUSIC. HE SOUNDS GOOD TO ME.

THURSDAY 15 FEBRUARY 1951

The Miles Davis All Stars open at Birdland in New York City for a one-week engagement opposite Wynonie Harris. Miles includes 19-year-old Jackie McLean in the band. On opening night Jackie is so nervous that he leaves the stand in the middle of his solo to be sick.

SATURDAY 17 FEBRUARY 1951

The Miles Davis All Stars broadcast from Birdland. MILES DAVIS (trumpet), J. J. JOHNSON (trombone), SONNY ROLLINS (tenor sax), KENNY DREW (piano), TOMMY POTTER (bass), ART BLAKEY (drums)
Evance / Half Nelson / Tempus Fugit / Move

WEDNESDAY 21 FEBRUARY 1951

The Miles Davis All Stars close at Birdland in New York City.

Miles moves out of Stan Levey's place on Long Island and stays in various hotels in Manhattan, including the University Hotel on 20th Street and the Hotel America on 48th Street. He puts together a band including Sonny Rollins, Jackie McLean, Walter Bishop, Percy Heath and Art Blakey but jobs are scarce and Miles spends much of his time hanging out in Harlem with Jackie, Sonny, Kenny Drew, Walter Bishop and Art Taylor. His heroin habit is growing and the only club in New York that will hire him is Birdland.

W 55th STREET

W 54th STREET

W 53rd STREET

■ **Birdland**

W 52nd STREET

Nola's Studios ■

W 51st STREET

BROADWAY

W 50th STREET

EIGHTH AVENUE

SEVENTH AVENUE

W 49th STREET

SIXTH AVENUE

THUR 1	SUN 1	TUES 1
FRI 2	MON 2	WED 2
SAT 3	TUES 3	THUR 3
SUN 4	WED 4	FRI 4
MON 5	THUR 5	SAT 5
TUES 6	FRI 6	SUN 6
WED 7	SAT 7	MON 7
THUR 8	SUN 8	TUES 8
FRI 9	MON 9	WED 9
SAT 10	TUES 10	THUR 10
SUN 11	WED 11	FRI 11
MON 12	THUR 12	SAT 12
TUES 13	FRI 13	SUN 13
WED 14	SAT 14	MON 14
THUR 15	SUN 15	TUES 15
FRI 16	MON 16	WED 16
SAT 17	TUES 17	THUR 17
SUN 18	WED 18	FRI 18
MON 19	THUR 19	SAT 19
TUES 20	FRI 20	SUN 20
WED 21	SAT 21	MON 21
THUR 22	SUN 22	TUES 22
FRI 23	MON 23	WED 23
SAT 24	TUES 24	THUR 24
SUN 25	WED 25	FRI 25
MON 26	THUR 26	SAT 26
TUES 27	FRI 27	SUN 27
WED 28	SAT 28	MON 28
THUR 29	SUN 29	TUES 29
FRI 30	MON 30	WED 30
SAT 31		THUR 31

Jazz Festival at Civic Due March 25

Lovers of swing music and bop as well, may witness the greatest show of its kind when "Easter Jazz Festival" is presented at the Civic Opera House Sunday, Mar. 25. There will be two shows, one in afternoon at 3:30 and the other an evening performance at 8:00.

Stars galore will appear on the bill. To mention a few there will be the Orioles, vocal swing sensations, Benny Green and Helen Humes as headliners. Others will include Max Roach, Jay Jay Johnson, Bud Powell, Oscar Pettiford, Miles Davis, Joe Roland, Slam Stewart, Hot Lips Page, Grady Johnson, Dick Davis combo; Claude McLin, Harold Ousley and Rudy Richardson.

Top vocalists on the bill will include Helen Humes, Ethel Duncan and DeLores Bell. This trio of singers rate the best to be found in entertainment circles and will add much to the all-star group of horn tooters and drum beaters.

Following the Opera House concert the Orioles will combine with the bands of Binz Freeman and Eddie Williams to feature a dance at the Pershing ballroom. Yes, Easter will be quite a day and night for the bugs.

WEDNESDAY 7 MARCH 1951
Recording session with the Lee Konitz Sextet for Prestige in New York City. LEE KONITZ (alto sax), MILES DAVIS (trumpet), SAL MOSCA (piano), BILLY BAUER (guitar), ARNOLD FISHKIN (bass), MAX ROACH (drums)
Ezz-thetic / Odjenar / Hi, Beck / Yesterdays (MR out)

SUNDAY 11 MARCH 1951
Miles appears at a 3:00 Hi-Dance at the Audubon Ballroom in New York City.

SUNDAY 25 MARCH 1951
Miles appears at the 'Easter Jazz Festival' at the Civic Opera House in Chicago. There are two shows, at 3.30pm and 8.00pm (see newspaper cutting above). It seems likely that Miles is part of a quintet including Max Roach, J. J. Johnson, Bud Powell and Oscar Pettiford that either has a club engagement in Chicago or is on a short tour.

FRIDAY 6 APRIL 1951
Down Beat, using a new rating system of 1–10, reviews Miles' first Prestige release:

MILES DAVIS
6 Morpheus
4 Blue Room
Miles on *Morpheus* again attempts something different, this time using a sextet. Evidently he's trying for the same chamber music sound and feel he got on his Capitol sides, but here has only three horns to work with—trumpet, tenor (Sonny Rollins), and trombone (Benny Green). It isn't very cleanly played, however, and the arrangement allows for few solo opportunities, although Miles sounds fine in his short burst.

Blue Room is another recording director's attempt to get sales by playing the melody straight. Davis is rather unfamiliar with the tune. **(Prestige 734)**

FRIDAY 13 APRIL 1951
Miles is at Birdland to receive his *Down Beat* plaque on Symphony Sid's WJZ radio show. It is Roy Eldridge's opening night at Birdland after returning from a year in Europe. Roy tells Sid: 'I'm sure glad to be back. It's good to see the lights of Broadway again.' Miles interrupts: 'Why don't you tell 'em what you were just telling me?' Sid changes the subject.

SATURDAY 26 MAY 1951
Miles' 25th birthday.

THURSDAY 31 MAY 1951
The Miles Davis All Stars open at Birdland in New York City for a two-week engagement.

I	**1**	SUN	**1**	WED	**1**	SAT	**1**
AT	**2**	MON	**2**	THUR	**2**	SUN	**2**
UN	**3**	TUES	**3**	FRI	**3**	MON	**3**
ON	**4**	WED	**4**	SAT	**4**	TUES	**4**
JES	**5**	THUR	**5**	SUN	**5**	WED	**5**
ED	**6**	FRI	**6**	MON	**6**	THUR	**6**
IUR	**7**	SAT	**7**	TUES	**7**	FRI	**7**
I	**8**	SUN	**8**	WED	**8**	SAT	**8**
AT	**9**	MON	**9**	THUR	**9**	SUN	**9**
UN	**10**	TUES	**10**	FRI	**10**	MON	**10**
ON	**11**	WED	**11**	SAT	**11**	TUES	**11**
JES	**12**	THUR	**12**	SUN	**12**	WED	**12**
ED	**13**	FRI	**13**	MON	**13**	THUR	**13**
IUR	**14**	SAT	**14**	TUES	**14**	FRI	**14**
I	**15**	SUN	**15**	WED	**15**	SAT	**15**
AT	**16**	MON	**16**	THUR	**16**	SUN	**16**
UN	**17**	TUES	**17**	FRI	**17**	MON	**17**
ON	**18**	WED	**18**	SAT	**18**	TUES	**18**
JES	**19**	THUR	**19**	SUN	**19**	WED	**19**
ED	**20**	FRI	**20**	MON	**20**	THUR	**20**
IUR	**21**	SAT	**21**	TUES	**21**	FRI	**21**
I	**22**	SUN	**22**	WED	**22**	SAT	**22**
AT	**23**	MON	**23**	THUR	**23**	SUN	**23**
UN	**24**	TUES	**24**	FRI	**24**	MON	**24**
ON	**25**	WED	**25**	SAT	**25**	TUES	**25**
JES	**26**	THUR	**26**	SUN	**26**	WED	**26**
ED	**27**	FRI	**27**	MON	**27**	THUR	**27**
IUR	**28**	SAT	**28**	TUES	**28**	FRI	**28**
I	**29**	SUN	**29**	WED	**29**	SAT	**29**
AT	**30**	MON	**30**	THUR	**30**	SUN	**30**
		TUES	**31**	FRI	**31**		

SATURDAY 2 JUNE 1951
The Miles Davis All Stars broadcast from Birdland in New York City.
MILES DAVIS (trumpet), J. J. JOHNSON (trombone), SONNY ROLLINS (tenor sax), KENNY DREW (piano), TOMMY POTTER (bass), ART BLAKEY (drums)
Jumpin' With Symphony Sid / Move / Half Nelson / Down

WEDNESDAY 13 JUNE 1951
The Miles Davis All Stars close at Birdland in New York City.

FRIDAY 7 SEPTEMBER 1951
Down Beat reviews Miles' latest Prestige release:

> **MILES DAVIS**
> **3 Down**
> **4 Whispering**
> Two very bad sides from Miles, cut at the same session last January that produced *Blue Room*. Sonny Rollins, Benny Green, John Lewis, Percy Heath, and Roy Haynes give aid. But no one seems at all interested in playing, and a completely lifeless and uninspired performance results. Release of items like this can do neither the artist or the label much good. **(Prestige 742)**

THURSDAY 20 SEPTEMBER 1951
The Miles Davis All Stars open at Birdland in New York City for a two-week engagement.

SATURDAY 29 SEPTEMBER 1951
The Miles Davis All Stars broadcast from Birdland in New York City.
MILES DAVIS (trumpet), GEORGE 'BIG NICK' NICHOLAS (tenor sax), EDDIE 'LOCKJAW' DAVIS (tenor sax), BILLY TAYLOR (piano), CHARLIE MINGUS (bass), ART BLAKEY (drums)
Jumpin' With Symphony Sid / Move / The Squirrel / Lady Bird

MON	**1**	THUR	**1**	SAT	**1**
TUES	**2**	FRI	**2**	SUN	**2**
WED	**3**	SAT	**3**	MON	**3**
THUR	**4**	SUN	**4**	TUES	**4**
FRI	**5**	MON	**5**	WED	**5**
SAT	**6**	TUES	**6**	THUR	**6**
SUN	**7**	WED	**7**	FRI	**7**
MON	**8**	THUR	**8**	SAT	**8**
TUES	**9**	FRI	**9**	SUN	**9**
WED	**10**	SAT	**10**	MON	**10**
THUR	**11**	SUN	**11**	TUES	**11**
FRI	**12**	MON	**12**	WED	**12**
SAT	**13**	TUES	**13**	THUR	**13**
SUN	**14**	WED	**14**	FRI	**14**
MON	**15**	THUR	**15**	SAT	**15**
TUES	**16**	FRI	**16**	SUN	**16**
WED	**17**	SAT	**17**	MON	**17**
THUR	**18**	SUN	**18**	TUES	**18**
FRI	**19**	MON	**19**	WED	**19**
SAT	**20**	TUES	**20**	THUR	**20**
SUN	**21**	WED	**21**	FRI	**21**
MON	**22**	THUR	**22**	SAT	**22**
TUES	**23**	FRI	**23**	SUN	**23**
WED	**24**	SAT	**24**	MON	**24**
THUR	**25**	SUN	**25**	TUES	**25**
FRI	**26**	MON	**26**	WED	**26**
SAT	**27**	TUES	**27**	THUR	**27**
SUN	**28**	WED	**28**	FRI	**28**
MON	**29**	THUR	**29**	SAT	**29**
TUES	**30**	FRI	**30**	SUN	**30**
WED	**31**			MON	**31**

WEDNESDAY 3 OCTOBER 1951

The Miles Davis All Stars close at Birdland in New York City.

FRIDAY 5 OCTOBER 1951

Recording session by the Miles Davis Sextet for Prestige in New York. This is one of the first recording sessions to use the new microgroove technology and enough music is recorded to fill two 10-inch LP records. In the sleeve notes to the first of the LPs issued, the producer Ira Gitler writes: 'This album gives Miles more freedom than he has ever had on records for time limits were not strictly enforced. There is an opportunity to build ideas into a definite cumulative effect.'
MILES DAVIS (trumpet), JACKIE MCLEAN (alto sax), SONNY ROLLINS (tenor sax), WALTER BISHOP JR (piano), TOMMY POTTER (bass), ART BLAKEY (drums)
Conception (JML out) / *Out Of The Blue* / *Denial* / *Bluing* / *Dig* / *My Old Flame* (JML out) / *It's Only A Paper Moon* (JML out)

For the rest of 1951 into early 1952, Miles resorts to pimping off prostitutes to support himself and his habit. He has a stable of around seven girls working for him, but he realises that he is going to have to kick his habit. He wonders if working out at the gym will help and asks boxing coach Bobby McQuillen to train him. McQuillen tells him that he won't train anybody with a drug habit, and that Miles should go back to St. Louis and kick the habit. Miles is shocked by the candour of his friend and telephones his father to come and get him.

Miles is on the stand at Le Downbeat at 263 W54th Street when he sees his father in the audience. He finishes the set and takes the train to East St. Louis with his father. Miles tries to relax by riding horses on his father's farm, but boredom and withdrawal sickness lead him to seek out a supplier and he starts shooting heroin again. He also meets up with tenor saxophonist Jimmy Forrest in St. Louis and they start playing together at a club called the Barrelhouse.

One of the sessions at the Barrelhouse Club in St Louis is privately taped:
MILES DAVIS (trumpet), JIMMY FORREST (tenor sax), CHARLES FOX (piano), JOHN HIXON (bass), OSCAR OLDHAM (drums), UNKNOWN (bongos)
All The Things You Are / Wahoo / Our Delight / Ow! (vJF) / *Lady Bird / What's New*

Miles is taking money from his father to feed his habit and when Miles Senior finds out he stops the money and has his son thrown into jail in Belleville, Illinois for a week. When he gets out of jail, Miles promises his father that he will join a rehabilitation programme and they drive down to the federal prison for drug addiction at Lexington, Kentucky. When they arrive, Miles has to commit himself voluntarily since he hasn't been convicted of a criminal offence. He can't bring himself to do this and leaves with his father. Red Rodney is an inmate at Lexington at this time, hears that Miles is checking in and rushes to greet him only to find that Miles has left.
Miles returns to New York and moves into Jackie McLean's apartment on 21st Street between Sixth and Seventh Avenues.

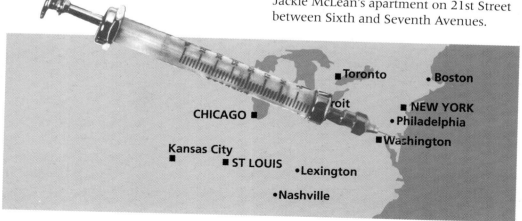

JANUARY	FEBRUARY	MARCH
TUES 1	FRI 1	SAT 1
WED 2	SAT 2	SUN 2
THUR 3	SUN 3	MON 3
FRI 4	MON 4	TUES 4
SAT 5	TUES 5	WED 5
SUN 6	WED 6	THUR 6
MON 7	THUR 7	FRI 7
TUES 8	FRI 8	SAT 8
WED 9	SAT 9	SUN 9
THUR 10	SUN 10	MON 10
FRI 11	MON 11	TUES 11
SAT 12	TUES 12	WED 12
SUN 13	WED 13	THUR 13
MON 14	THUR 14	FRI 14
TUES 15	FRI 15	SAT 15
WED 16	SAT 16	SUN 16
THUR 17	SUN 17	MON 17
FRI 18	MON 18	TUES 18
SAT 19	TUES 19	WED 19
SUN 20	WED 20	THUR 20
MON 21	THUR 21	FRI 21
TUES 22	FRI 22	SAT 22
WED 23	SAT 23	SUN 23
THUR 24	SUN 24	MON 24
FRI 25	MON 25	TUES 25
SAT 26	TUES 26	WED 26
SUN 27	WED 27	THUR 27
MON 28	THUR 28	FRI 28
TUES 29	FRI 29	SAT 29
WED 30		SUN 30
THUR 31		MON 31

On 23 February 1952, the London *Melody Maker* runs this story:

Poll-topper Miles has been at a standstill since back in 1950

says LEONARD FEATHER in this Pen Portrait

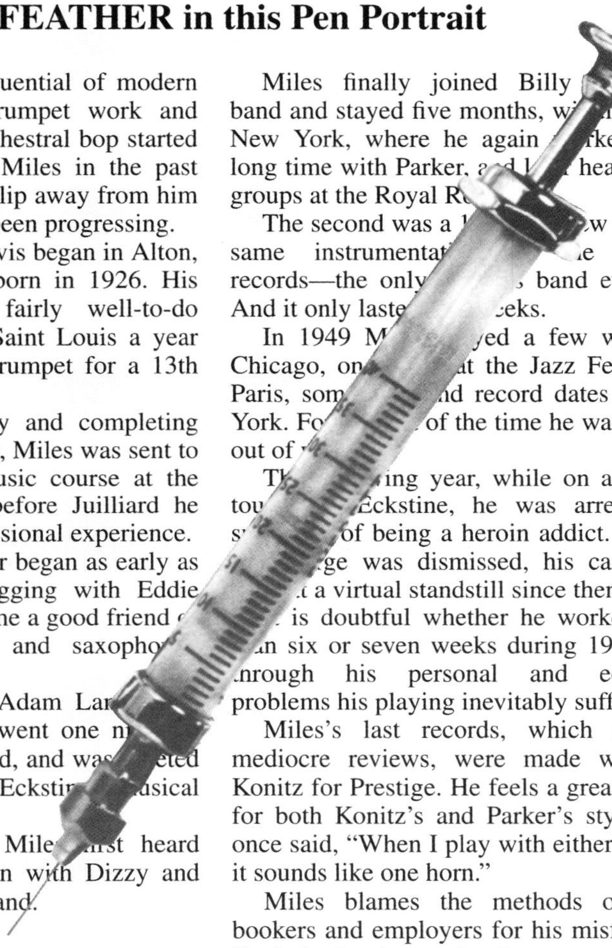

ONE of the most influential of modern jazzmen, through his trumpet work and through the school of orchestral bop started by his Capitol records, Miles in the past year has seen his career slip away from him while his imitators have been progressing.

The story of Miles Davis began in Alton, Illinois, where he was born in 1926. His father, a respectable, fairly well-to-do dentist, moved to East Saint Louis a year later. He gave Miles a trumpet for a 13th birthday present.

After studying locally and completing his high school education, Miles was sent to New York to take a music course at the Juilliard Institute. But before Juilliard he had acquired some professional experience.

His professional career began as early as 1941, when he was gigging with Eddie Randall's band. He became a good friend of trumpeter Clark Terry and saxopho Sonny Stitt.

Later, working with Adam La Springfield, Illinois, he went one n visit Billy Eckstine's band, and was by Dizzy, who was then Eckstin usical director.

This was the night Miles st heard Charlie Parker. He sat in with Dizzy and Bird but didn't join the band.

Dial sessions

During his study period in New York, Miles worked around 52nd Street with Coleman Hawkins, Bird and Eddie (Lockjaw) Davis. Then he went home, ran into Benny Carter in St. Louis, and joined Benny to get a trip to California.

Miles stayed in California about eight months, leaving Carter after a few weeks. He was unemployed most of the time, but made some dates with Bird, including the famous Dial sessions.

Miles finally joined Billy Eckstine's band and stayed five months, winding up in New York, where he again worked for a long time with Parker, and later headed two groups at the Royal R

The second was a band with the same instrumenta e Capitol records—the only band ever had. And it only laste eeks.

In 1949 M yed a few weeks in Chicago, on at the Jazz Festival in Paris, som d record dates in New York. Fo of the time he was mostly out of

Th ing year, while on a concert tou Eckstine, he was arrested on s of being a heroin addict. Though ge was dismissed, his career has a virtual standstill since then.

is doubtful whether he worked more n six or seven weeks during 1951. And hrough his personal and economic problems his playing inevitably suffered.

Miles's last records, which received mediocre reviews, were made with Lee Konitz for Prestige. He feels a great affinity for both Konitz's and Parker's styles, and once said, "When I play with either of them it sounds like one horn."

Miles blames the methods of talent bookers and employers for his misfortunes. He feels they have ruined many great artists through their lack of respect for musicians, and says he would like to go to Europe to spend several months out of each year with his wife and children.

His favourite writers are Gil Evans, John Lewis and Gerry Mulligan. He would like to record some more of their stuff (they were responsible for the Capitol sides).

His all-time preferences on trumpet include the late Freddie Webster, Louis Armstrong and Dizzy.

TUES	**1**	THUR	**1**
WED	**2**	FRI	**2**
THUR	**3**	SAT	**3**
FRI	**4**	SUN	**4**
SAT	**5**	MON	**5**
SUN	**6**	TUES	**6**
MON	**7**	WED	**7**
TUES	**8**	THUR	**8**
WED	**9**	FRI	**9**
THUR	**10**	SAT	**10**
FRI	**11**	SUN	**11**
SAT	**12**	MON	**12**
SUN	**13**	TUES	**13**
MON	**14**	WED	**14**
TUES	**15**	THUR	**15**
WED	**16**	FRI	**16**
THUR	**17**	SAT	**17**
FRI	**18**	SUN	**18**
SAT	**19**	MON	**19**
SUN	**20**	TUES	**20**
MON	**21**	WED	**21**
TUES	**22**	THUR	**22**
WED	**23**	FRI	**23**
THUR	**24**	SAT	**24**
FRI	**25**	SUN	**25**
SAT	**26**	MON	**26**
SUN	**27**	TUES	**27**
MON	**28**	WED	**28**
TUES	**29**	THUR	**29**
WED	**30**	FRI	**30**
		SAT	**31**

Down Beat reports:

Miles Davis back in town (25lbs heavier) and working Birdland as a single.

FRIDAY 25 APRIL 1952

Miles Davis broadcasts with a pick-up group from Birdland in New York City.
MILES DAVIS (trumpet), DON ELLIOTT (vibes), CHUCK WAYNE (guitar), BERYL BOOKER (piano), CLYDE LOMBARDI (bass), CONNIE KAY (drums)
Lady Be Good / All The Things You Are / The Squirrel

SATURDAY 26 APRIL 1952

Miles Davis broadcasts with a pick-up group from Birdland in New York City.
MILES DAVIS (trumpet), DON ELLIOTT (vibes), CHUCK WAYNE (guitar), BERYL BOOKER (piano), CLYDE LOMBARDI (bass), CONNIE KAY (drums)
Lady Be Good / It Could Happen To You / Wee Dot / Theme

THURSDAY 1 MAY 1952

The Miles Davis Sextet open at Birdland in New York City.

FRIDAY 2 MAY 1952

The Miles Davis Sextet broadcast from Birdland in New York City.
MILES DAVIS (trumpet), JACKIE McLEAN (alto sax), DON ELLIOTT (vibes/mellophone), GIL COGGINS (piano), CONNIE HENRY (bass), CONNIE KAY (drums)
Theme / Evans (Out Of The Blue) / Confirmation / Theme

SATURDAY 3 MAY 1952

The Miles Davis Sextet broadcast from Birdland in New York City.
MILES DAVIS (trumpet), JACKIE McLEAN (alto sax), DON ELLIOTT (vibes/mellophone), GIL COGGINS (piano), CONNIE HENRY (bass), CONNIE KAY (drums)
Wee Dot / The Chase / It Could Happen To You / Evans / Opmet

WEDNESDAY 7 MAY 1952

The Miles Davis Sextet close at Birdland in New York City.

Opposite page: The Symphony Sid package show o stage at the Hi-Hat in Boston. L to r: Don Ellio Percy Heath, Symphony Sid, Phil Urso, Kenr Clarke, Milt Jackson and Miles Davi

Boppers Bring Big Business As Sid Heads Traveling Uni

Boston—With seven weeks of almost solid bookings set, Sympho Sid's modern jazz entourage is proving itself commercially, as w as musically, one of the season's major jazz phenomena.

Sid, while shepherding his troubadours through an excellent wee at the Hi-Hat here, expressed great admiration for the booking wiz- ardry of Billy Shaw. At last count, Billy had set the unit to open New Haven's Storyville, to play a week in a new club in Niagara, followe by stays in Montreal and Toron to, Chicago, Detroit, Columbus, Youngstown, Pittsburgh and At- lantic City with frequent one- nighters to fill in gaps in the tour.

Personnel changes are still tak- ing place. J. J. Johnson returned to the group after Boston, replac- ing Don Elliott; altoist Jackie Mc- Lean took over from tenor Phil Urso and, by the end of June in Toronto, Sid intends to have Max Roach on drums with John Lewis coming in on piano. The latter move will allow Milt Jackson full vibe time since Milt doubles now.

Percy Heath, Kenny Clarke and Milt fused into a tremendous rhythm section here with the front line energized by Miles Davis' intensely imaginative horn. Sid introduces each number with a minimum of verbiage, though he occasionally orates tartly at the overcommercialism of disc jockeys afraid or too square to play jazz.

Sid is convinced of the salability, let alone the durability of modern jazz, when properly booked and presented. And his grosses prove it.

—nat

TRUMPET
Non-Pressure System ...ilding breath control, ...d flexibility, ...elect...

HUR	1
RI	2
AT	3
UN	4
MON	5
UES	6
WED	7
HUR	8
RI	9
AT	10
UN	11
MON	12
UES	13
WED	14
HUR	15
RI	16
AT	17
UN	18
MON	19
UES	20
WED	21
HUR	22
RI	23
AT	24
SUN	25
MON	26
UES	27
WED	28
HUR	29
RI	30
SAT	31

FRIDAY 9 MAY 1952

Recording session by the Miles Davis Sextet for Blue Note in New York City.

MILES DAVIS (trumpet), JACKIE MCLEAN (alto sax), J. J. JOHNSON (trombone), GIL COGGINS (piano), OSCAR PETTIFORD (bass), KENNY CLARKE (drums)

Dear Old Stockholm / Chance It / Donna (2 takes) / *Woodyn' You* (2 takes) / *Yesterdays* (JJJ, JML out) / *How Deep Is The Ocean* (JJJ, JML out)

The resulting LP is issued as *Miles Davis Vol 1*.

MONDAY 12 MAY 1952

Miles joins the touring *Jumping With Symphony Sid* package show emceed by disc jockey Symphony Sid Torin. They open at the Hi-Hat in Boston for a one-week engagement. The group comprises Miles Davis (trumpet), Don Elliott (mellophone), Phil Urso (tenor sax), Milt Jackson (piano/vibes), Percy Heath (bass) and Kenny Clarke (drums).

SUNDAY 18 MAY 1952

Miles and the *Jumping With Symphony Sid* package close at the Hi-Hat in Boston.

MONDAY 19 MAY 1952

Miles and the *Jumping With Symphony Sid* package open at the Storyville Club in New Haven for a one-week engagement. The group now comprises Miles Davis (trumpet), J. J. Johnson (trombone), Jackie McLean (alto sax), Milt Jackson (piano/vibes), Percy Heath (bass) and Kenny Clarke (drums).

SUNDAY 25 MAY 1952

Miles and the *Jumping With Symphony Sid* package close at the Storyville Club in New Haven.

MONDAY 26 MAY 1952

Miles and the *Jumping With Symphony Sid* package open at the Colonial Tavern in Toronto for a one-week engagement.

Opening night is Miles' 26th birthday.

SATURDAY 31 MAY 1952

Miles and the *Jumping With Symphony Sid* package close at the Colonial Tavern in Toronto. The package then does a series of one-nighters in the Midwest, with Zoot Sims (tenor sax) replacing Jackie McLean.

SUN **1**	TUES **1**	FRI **1**
MON **2**	WED **2**	SAT **2**
TUES **3**	THUR **3**	SUN **3**
WED **4**	FRI **4**	MON **4**
THUR **5**	SAT **5**	TUES **5**
FRI **6**	SUN **6**	WED **6**
SAT **7**	MON **7**	THUR **7**
SUN **8**	TUES **8**	FRI **8**
MON **9**	WED **9**	SAT **9**
TUES **10**	THUR **10**	SUN **10**
WED **11**	FRI **11**	MON **11**
THUR **12**	SAT **12**	TUES **12**
FRI **13**	SUN **13**	WED **13**
SAT **14**	MON **14**	THUR **14**
SUN **15**	TUES **15**	FRI **15**
MON **16**	WED **16**	SAT **16**
TUES **17**	THUR **17**	SUN **17**
WED **18**	FRI **18**	MON **18**
THUR **19**	SAT **19**	TUES **19**
FRI **20**	SUN **20**	WED **20**
SAT **21**	MON **21**	THUR **21**
SUN **22**	TUES **22**	FRI **22**
MON **23**	WED **23**	SAT **23**
TUES **24**	THUR **24**	SUN **24**
WED **25**	FRI **25**	MON **25**
THUR **26**	SAT **26**	TUES **26**
FRI **27**	SUN **27**	WED **27**
SAT **28**	MON **28**	THUR **28**
SUN **29**	TUES **29**	FRI **29**
MON **30**	WED **30**	SAT **30**
	THUR **31**	SUN **31**

THURSDAY 12 JUNE 1952

Miles and the *Jumping With Symphony Sid* package open at Weekes Café in Atlantic City for a one-week engagement. Jimmy Heath replaces Zoot Sims on tenor saxophone.

WEDNESDAY 18 JUNE 1952

Miles and the *Jumping With Symphony Sid* package close at Weekes Café in Atlantic City.

MONDAY 23 JUNE 1952

Miles and the *Jumping With Symphony Sid* package open in Youngstown, Ohio for a one-week engagement.

SUNDAY 29 JUNE 1952

Miles and the *Jumping With Symphony Sid* package close in Youngstown, Ohio.

TUESDAY 1 JULY 1952

Miles and the *Jumping With Symphony Sid* package open at the Ebony Club in Cleveland for a one-week engagement.

SUNDAY 6 JULY 1952

Miles and the *Jumping With Symphony Sid* package close at the Ebony Club in Cleveland.

FRIDAY 11 JULY 1952

Miles and the *Jumping With Symphony Sid* package open at the Apollo Theatre in Harlem for a one-week engagement.

THURSDAY 17 JULY 1952

Miles and the *Jumping With Symphony Sid* package close at the Apollo Theatre in Harlem.

THURSDAY 24 JULY 1952

Miles and the Symphony Sid All-Stars, including Jimmy Heath, J. J. Johnson, Milt Jackson, Percy Heath and Kenny Clarke, open at Le Downbeat at 263 W54th Street in New York City for a two-week engagement.

WEDNESDAY 6 AUGUST 1952

Miles and the Symphony Sid All-Stars close at Le Downbeat.

Opposite page: The Symphony Sid All Stars at the Apollo. In the centre are Percy and Jimmy Heath. Clockwise from top left are: Kenny Clarke, Percy Heath and J. J. Johnson, Symphony Sid Torin, J. J. Johnson and Jimmy Heath, Milt Jackson and Miles Davis. Le Downbeat was short-lived, but the building remains, now housing a bar called Ye Olde Tripple Inn.

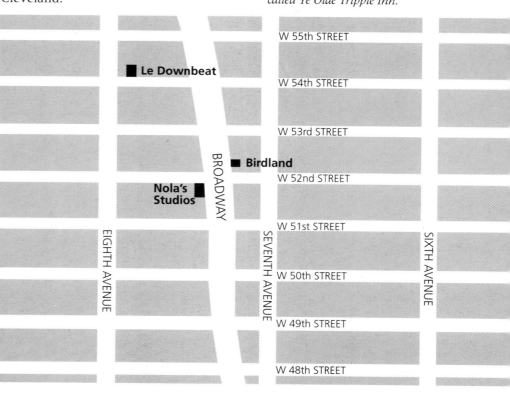

MON	1	WED	1	SAT	1
TUES	2	THUR	2	SUN	2
WED	3	FRI	3	MON	3
THUR	4	SAT	4	TUES	4
FRI	5	SUN	5	WED	5
SAT	6	MON	6	THUR	6
SUN	7	TUES	7	FRI	7
MON	8	WED	8	SAT	8
TUES	9	THUR	9	SUN	9
WED	10	FRI	10	MON	10
THUR	11	SAT	11	TUES	11
FRI	12	SUN	12	WED	12
SAT	13	MON	13	THUR	13
SUN	14	TUES	14	FRI	14
MON	15	WED	15	SAT	15
TUES	16	THUR	16	SUN	16
WED	17	FRI	17	MON	17
THUR	18	SAT	18	TUES	18
FRI	19	SUN	19	WED	19
SAT	20	MON	20	THUR	20
SUN	21	TUES	21	FRI	21
MON	22	WED	22	SAT	22
TUES	23	THUR	23	SUN	23
WED	24	FRI	24	MON	24
THUR	25	SAT	25	TUES	25
FRI	26	SUN	26	WED	26
SAT	27	MON	27	THUR	27
SUN	28	TUES	28	FRI	28
MON	29	WED	29	SAT	29
TUES	30	THUR	30	SUN	30
		FRI	31		

WEDNESDAY 24 SEPTEMBER 1952

Down Beat reviews Miles' latest record release:

MILES DAVIS
** **Woody'n'You**
** **Dear Old Stockholm**
The Gillespie original, and the traditional Swedish air brought over here by Stan Getz, afford solo opportunities for J.J. Johnson and altoist Jackie McLean, both of whom cut Miles on these sides. Neither opus, however, gets the feeling of the tunes as well as the original versions. Rhythm is by 'Gil' Coggins and Kenny Clarke with Oscar Pettiford, who has a solo on *Woody'n'*.
(**Blue Note 15595.**)

SATURDAY 15 NOVEMBER 1952

Miles appears at a midnight jam session concert at the Howard Theatre in Washington. Also appearing are Max Roach, J. J. Johnson, Ed Safranski and many more.

Below: Max Roach and Miles on the stage of the Howard Theatre in Washington D.C. during a midnight concert.

MON	**1**	THUR	**1**	SUN	**1**
TUES	**2**	FRI	**2**	MON	**2**
WED	**3**	SAT	**3**	TUES	**3**
THUR	**4**	SUN	**4**	WED	**4**
FRI	**5**	MON	**5**	THUR	**5**
SAT	**6**	TUES	**6**	FRI	**6**
SUN	**7**	WED	**7**	SAT	**7**
MON	**8**	THUR	**8**	SUN	**8**
TUES	**9**	FRI	**9**	MON	**9**
WED	**10**	SAT	**10**	TUES	**10**
THUR	**11**	SUN	**11**	WED	**11**
FRI	**12**	MON	**12**	THUR	**12**
SAT	**13**	TUES	**13**	FRI	**13**
SUN	**14**	WED	**14**	SAT	**14**
MON	**15**	THUR	**15**	SUN	**15**
TUES	**16**	FRI	**16**	MON	**16**
WED	**17**	SAT	**17**	TUES	**17**
THUR	**18**	SUN	**18**	WED	**18**
FRI	**19**	MON	**19**	THUR	**19**
SAT	**20**	TUES	**20**	FRI	**20**
SUN	**21**	WED	**21**	SAT	**21**
MON	**22**	THUR	**22**	SUN	**22**
TUES	**23**	FRI	**23**	MON	**23**
WED	**24**	SAT	**24**	TUES	**24**
THUR	**25**	SUN	**25**	WED	**25**
FRI	**26**	MON	**26**	THUR	**26**
SAT	**27**	TUES	**27**	FRI	**27**
SUN	**28**	WED	**28**	SAT	**28**
MON	**29**	THUR	**29**		
TUES	**30**	FRI	**30**		
WED	**31**	SAT	**31**		

WEDNESDAY 3 DECEMBER 1952

Down Beat reviews Miles' latest release:

> **MILES DAVIS**
> ** Dig? (I & II)**
> Here we have some six minutes of *Sweet Georgia Brown*, extracted from Miles' LP. Miles, altoist Jack McLean, tenor Sonny Rollins are not helped a bit by the rude, unswinging drumming of Art Blakey. (**Prestige 777.**)

Miles is 2nd to Maynard Ferguson in the *Down Beat* trumpet poll.

THURSDAY 8 JANUARY 1953

Miles Davis gigs for a couple of weeks at Le Downbeat in New York City with Charlie Parker, Milt Jackson, Don Abney, Chuck Wayne and others.

FRIDAY 30 JANUARY 1953

Miles Davis Sextet recording session for Prestige at the WOR Studios in New York City features Charlie Parker on tenor sax. The session is produced by Ira Gitler.
MILES DAVIS (trumpet), CHARLIE PARKER (tenor sax), SONNY ROLLINS (tenor sax), WALTER BISHOP (piano), PERCY HEATH (bass) PHILLY JOE JONES (drums)
Compulsion / The Serpent's Tooth (2 takes) / *Round About Midnight* (SR out)

WEDNESDAY 11 FEBRUARY 1953

Down Beat reviews Miles' latest record release:

> **MILES DAVIS**
> *Dear Old Stockholm / Woody'n'You / Yesterdays / Chance It / Donna / How Deep Is The Ocean*
> **Album Rating: *****
> Miles' environment here: J.J. Johnson, trombone; Jackie McLean, alto; Gil Coggins, piano; Kenny Clarke, drums; Oscar Pettiford, bass. Swingingest sides are *Donna*, a comely McLean variant on *Georgia Brown*, and *Chance It*, an old opus by Oscar also known as *Something For You* and *Max Is Making Wax*. Though Miles' articulation and intonation are still sometimes bothersome, his two slow solo sides, *Yesterdays* and *Ocean*, are long on ideas. J.J., McLean, and especially Oscar have some good solos. (**Blue Note 5013.**)

THURSDAY 19 FEBRUARY 1953

Recording session by the Miles Davis Septet for Prestige at the WOR Studios in New York City. The session is produced by Ira Gitler.
MILES DAVIS (trumpet), SONNY TRUITT (trombone), AL COHN (tenor sax), ZOOT SIMS (tenor sax), JOHN LEWIS (piano), LEONARD GASKIN (bass) KENNY CLARKE (drums)
Tasty Pudding (ST out) / *Willie The Wailer* (ST out) / *Floppy* / *For Adults Only* (ST out)

SATURDAY 21 FEBRUARY 1953

Miles appears at a midnight jam session concert at the Howard Theatre in Washington. Also appearing are Max Roach, Allen Eager, Joe Theimer, Terry Swope and many more.

Left: Charlie Parker playing tenor saxophone at the Miles Davis Sextet recording session for Prestige.

SUN	**1**	WED	**1**
MON	**2**	THUR	**2**
TUES	**3**	FRI	**3**
WED	**4**	SAT	**4**
THUR	**5**	SUN	**5**
FRI	**6**	MON	**6**
SAT	**7**	TUES	**7**
SUN	**8**	WED	**8**
MON	**9**	THUR	**9**
TUES	**10**	FRI	**10**
WED	**11**	SAT	**11**
THUR	**12**	SUN	**12**
FRI	**13**	MON	**13**
SAT	**14**	TUES	**14**
SUN	**15**	WED	**15**
MON	**16**	THUR	**16**
TUES	**17**	FRI	**17**
WED	**18**	SAT	**18**
THUR	**19**	SUN	**19**
FRI	**20**	MON	**20**
SAT	**21**	TUES	**21**
SUN	**22**	WED	**22**
MON	**23**	THUR	**23**
TUES	**24**	FRI	**24**
WED	**25**	SAT	**25**
THUR	**26**	SUN	**26**
FRI	**27**	MON	**27**
SAT	**28**	TUES	**28**
SUN	**29**	WED	**29**
MON	**30**	THUR	**30**
TUES	**31**		

WEDNESDAY 8 APRIL 1953

Down Beat reviews Miles' latest album release:

MILES DAVIS
** **Bluing**
* **Blue Room**
*** **Out Of The Blue**

Blue Period is the title of this LP, and it was certainly that for us, as we thought back to Miles' great Capitol sides and reflected how sadly that great promise, that exceptional talent, has been betrayed.

The first 23 bars of *Blue Room* are simple and beautiful, and Miles gets through them without a fluff. By bar 32 you find yourself muttering "Damn, if only he could have made it through the chorus." After an awkward pause as if the take had ended, Sonny Rollins' tenor takes over for 16 bars that sound as if they were patched on from another take. *Out of the Blue* is not blues, but a string of choruses on the changes of *Get Happy* with a long, long solo by Miles divided between moments of inspiration and others of vacuum. This is the most effective performance of the three.

The entire second side is occupied by nine minutes of desultory blues blowing by Miles, Rollins, Jackie McLean's alto, and Walter Bishop's piano. Where it aims at relaxation it merely reaches lethargy, winding up with complete chaos when the front line goofs, Art Blakey is left playing by himself, and Miles is heard commentating, something to the effect that they'd better make another take. Alas, they didn't. Informality on records is one thing; sloppiness is another. (**Prestige 140.**)

MONDAY 20 APRIL 1953

Recording session by the Miles Davis Sextet for Blue Note in New York City.

MILES DAVIS (trumpet), J.J. JOHNSON (trombone), JIMMY HEATH (tenor sax), GIL COGGINS (piano), PERCY HEATH (bass) ART BLAKE (drums)

Tempus Fugit (2 takes) / *Enigma* / *Ray's Idea* (2 takes) / *Kelo* / *C.T.A.* (2 takes) / *I Waited For You* (JJJ, JH out)

VED **1**
HUR **2**
RI **3**
AT **4**
UN **5**
MON **6**
UES **7**
VED **8**
HUR **9**
RI **10**
AT **11**
UN **12**
MON **13**
UES **14**
VED **15**
HUR **16**
RI **17**
AT **18**
UN **19**
MON **20**
UES **21**
VED **22**
HUR **23**
RI **24**
AT **25**
UN **26**
MON **27**
UES **28**
VED **29**
HUR **30**

TUESDAY 28 APRIL 1953

Miles Davis and his Band open at the Club Tijuana in Baltimore
for a one-week engagement. Sonny Rollins is billed on tenor,
but Jimmy Heath deputises for the week.

*Opposite page: Miles at the April 20th
recording session for Blue Note. Also visible
are Jimmy Heath and his brother Percy.*

FRI	1
SAT	2
SUN	3
MON	4
TUES	5
WED	6
THUR	7
FRI	8
SAT	9
SUN	10
MON	11
TUES	12
WED	13
THUR	14
FRI	15
SAT	16
SUN	17
MON	18
TUES	19
WED	20
THUR	21
FRI	22
SAT	23
SUN	24
MON	25
TUES	26
WED	27
THUR	28
FRI	29
SAT	30
SUN	31

SUNDAY 3 MAY 1953

Miles Davis and his Band close at the Club Tijuana in Baltimore.

THURSDAY 7 MAY 1953

Miles Davis Band opens at Le Downbeat on W54th Street in New York City.

WEDNESDAY 13 MAY 1953

Miles Davis Band closes at Le Downbeat on W54th Street in New York City.

SATURDAY 16 MAY 1953

Miles deputises for Dizzy Gillespie with Dizzy's Band in a broadcast from Birdland.
MILES DAVIS (trumpet), SAHIB SHIHAB (baritone sax), WADE LEGGE (piano), LOUIS HACKNEY (bass), AL JONES (drums), CANDIDO (conga), JOE CARROLL (vocal)
I Got Rhythm (vJC) / *Move* / *Tenderly* / *A Night In Tunisia* / *Dig* / *Lullaby Of Birdland*

TUESDAY 19 MAY 1953

Recording session by the Miles Davis Quartet for Prestige in New York City. The producer is Ira Gitler.
MILES DAVIS (trumpet), JOHN LEWIS (piano), PERCY HEATH (bass) MAX ROACH (drums)
When Lights Are Low / *Tune Up* / *Miles Ahead*
CHARLIE MINGUS (piano) replaces John Lewis
Smooch

SATURDAY 23 MAY 1953

Miles and Charlie Parker guest with Dizzy Gillespie's Band in a broadcast from Birdland.
MILES DAVIS (trumpet), DIZZY GILLESPIE (trumpet), CHARLIE PARKER (alto sax), SAHIB SHIHAB (baritone sax), WADE LEGGE (piano), LOUIS HACKNEY (bass), AL JONES (drums), JOE CARROLL (vocal)
The Bluest Blues / *On The Sunny Side Of The Street*

TUESDAY 26 MAY 1953

Miles' 27th birthday.

MON	**1**	WED	**1**
UES	**2**	THUR	**2**
VED	**3**	FRI	**3**
HUR	**4**	SAT	**4**
RI	**5**	SUN	**5**
AT	**6**	MON	**6**
JN	**7**	TUES	**7**
MON	**8**	WED	**8**
UES	**9**	THUR	**9**
VED	**10**	FRI	**10**
HUR	**11**	SAT	**11**
RI	**12**	SUN	**12**
AT	**13**	MON	**13**
JN	**14**	TUES	**14**
ION	**15**	WED	**15**
UES	**16**	THUR	**16**
VED	**17**	FRI	**17**
HUR	**18**	SAT	**18**
RI	**19**	SUN	**19**
AT	**20**	MON	**20**
JN	**21**	TUES	**21**
ION	**22**	WED	**22**
UES	**23**	THUR	**23**
VED	**24**	FRI	**24**
HUR	**25**	SAT	**25**
RI	**26**	SUN	**26**
AT	**27**	MON	**27**
JN	**28**	TUES	**28**
ION	**29**	WED	**29**
UES	**30**	THUR	**30**
		FRI	**31**

Before the Birdland job as a guest with Dizzy's band, Miles is finding jobs very scarce, but he has an ally in drummer and fellow junkie Philly Joe Jones:

MILES AND I HAD BEEN BARNSTORMING AROUND THE COUNTRY. WHEN WE GOT IN A CITY WHERE WE HAD A GIG, I'D GET THERE FIRST AND FIND ANOTHER HORN PLAYER, A PIANO PLAYER AND A BASS PLAYER. IN THOSE DAYS WE WERE REALLY PUTTING THE MUSIC TOGETHER. WE'D GET ON THE PLANE AND HE'D HUM THE ARRANGEMENTS WE'D PLAY. WHEN I GOT THE MUSICIANS TOGETHER, HE NEVER HAD MUCH TO SAY TO THEM EXCEPT 'HI'. HE'D HAVE ME TALK TO THEM … IT GOT TO BE A DRAG, BECAUSE EVERY TOWN WE'D PLAY, I'D TRY TO FIND THE MUSICIANS THAT WERE THE CREAM OF THE CROP, BUT THEY WOULDN'T BE WORTH SHIT. WE FINALLY HAD TO SIT DOWN AND HASH OVER THE MUSICIANS THAT WE BOTH KNEW WHO COULD REALLY PLAY. WE HAD IT ALL IN OUR MINDS WHAT WE WERE GOING TO DO.

Opposite page: Miles sits in with Charlie Parker at Birdland, where Parker is alternating with the Dizzy Gillespie band. Also visible are Curly Russell (bass) and Art Taylor (drums).

Around the time of this appearance at Birdland, Miles becomes starkly aware of the depths to which he has sunk when, standing outside Birdland nodding and dishevelled, he has two $100 bills stuffed into his pocket by Max Roach. Acutely embarrassed, Miles spends the money on a bus ride home to East St. Louis.

WEDNESDAY 17 JUNE 1953
Down Beat reviews Miles' latest album release:

MILES DAVIS
Tasty Pudding / Floppy / Willie The Wailer / For Adults Only
Rating: **

Miles Davis Plays The Compositions Of Al Cohn, it says here, and sure enough he does. Surrounding Miles with Sonny Truitt's trombone, Al Cohn's and Zoot Sims' tenors, plus John Lewis, Kenny Clarke, and Leonard Gaskin, Prestige has evidently endeavoured here to recapture some of the glory that was Capitol's, and Miles', when he last recorded with his own organized band some four years ago.

Alas, Al and the guys aren't equal to the task. These are fair swing arrangements with nothing startling to offer in new sounds or new harmonic directions. There are some superior samples of what Barry Ulanov described so vividly as Miles' "eggshell trumpet"; there are good solos by others, too; but Klook's drums get in the way at times, and the ensembles just don't make it. As a theme, *Adults* is the only attractive item of the four, and it's still nothing to gas you.

As genuine admirers of Little Willie and of Cohn, we wish we could feel more than two stars for this set, but it just doesn't succeed in what it evidently set out to do. (**Prestige 154.**)

SAT	**1**	TUES	**1**
SUN	**2**	WED	**2**
MON	**3**	THUR	**3**
TUES	**4**	FRI	**4**
WED	**5**	SAT	**5**
THUR	**6**	SUN	**6**
FRI	**7**	MON	**7**
SAT	**8**	TUES	**8**
SUN	**9**	WED	**9**
MON	**10**	THUR	**10**
TUES	**11**	FRI	**11**
WED	**12**	SAT	**12**
THUR	**13**	SUN	**13**
FRI	**14**	MON	**14**
SAT	**15**	TUES	**15**
SUN	**16**	WED	**16**
MON	**17**	THUR	**17**
TUES	**18**	FRI	**18**
WED	**19**	SAT	**19**
THUR	**20**	SUN	**20**
FRI	**21**	MON	**21**
SAT	**22**	TUES	**22**
SUN	**23**	WED	**23**
MON	**24**	THUR	**24**
TUES	**25**	FRI	**25**
WED	**26**	SAT	**26**
THUR	**27**	SUN	**27**
FRI	**28**	MON	**28**
SAT	**29**	TUES	**29**
SUN	**30**	WED	**30**
MON	**31**		

AUGUST 1953

After nearly three months in East St. Louis, bored and still shooting dope, Miles is relieved to hear from Max Roach. Max is to take Shelly Manne's place in Howard Rumsey's Lighthouse All Stars and he and Charlie Mingus are driving out to Los Angeles together. They plan to stay over in East St. Louis and visit Miles who is delighted and invites them to stay at his father's farm in Millstadt. They have a great time and Miles realises how much he misses being on the scene. He decides to go with them to Los Angeles.

When they arrive in Los Angeles, Max takes up his job at the Lighthouse and Miles just hangs out, occasionally sitting in with The Lighthouse All-Stars. He meets Chet Baker for the first time during a session at the Lighthouse and is photographed with him and the All-Stars trumpet man, Rolf Ericson (*above*). Miles also meets, and is attracted to, dancer Frances Taylor.

THURSDAY 10 SEPTEMBER 1953

Miles opens at the Downbeat in San Francisco instead of the scheduled Gerry Mulligan group. Gerry is in jail on a narcotics charge. Miles arrives without a horn and uses a local group consisting of Kenny Drew (piano), Addison Farmer (bass) and George Walker (drums). The engagement is for four weeks, alternating with Sidney Bechet's group.

HUR	1		SUN	1
I	2		MON	2
AT	3		TUES	3
UN	4		WED	4
ON	5		THUR	5
JES	6		FRI	6
ED	7		SAT	7
HUR	8		SUN	8
I	9		MON	9
AT	10		TUES	10
UN	11		WED	11
ON	12		THUR	12
JES	13		FRI	13
ED	14		SAT	14
HUR	15		SUN	15
I	16		MON	16
AT	17		TUES	17
UN	18		WED	18
ON	19		THUR	19
JES	20		FRI	20
ED	21		SAT	21
HUR	22		SUN	22
I	23		MON	23
AT	24		TUES	24
UN	25		WED	25
ON	26		THUR	26
JES	27		FRI	27
ED	28		SAT	28
HUR	29		SUN	29
I	30		MON	30
AT	31			

WEDNESDAY 7 OCTOBER 1953

Miles closes at the Downbeat in San Francisco.

OCTOBER 1953

From San Francisco, Miles travels to Chicago for an engagement at Nob-Hill.

nob - hill
5228 LAKE PARK
Presents
BIG DOUBLE REVUE
MILES DAVIS
(Nations Number One Trumpet Star)
plus
GENE AMMONS
(AMERICA'S NUMBER ONE SAX STAR)
LEFTY BATES and his new Jazz Combo
WE SPECIALIZE IN SUNDAY COCKTAIL PARTIES
CLUBS & ORGANIZATIONS (At No Extra Cost)
For information, call Benny White, HY. 3-9535

nob - hill
5228 LAKE PARK
Presents
AMERICA'S NO 1 TRUMPET STAR
MILLS DAVIS
WINNER OF DOWNBEAT & METRONONE POLL
FIRST CHICAGO APPEARANCE IN 3 YEARS
PLUS LEFTY BATES COMBO
WE SPECIALIZE IN SUNDAY COCKTAIL PARTIES
CLUBS & ORGANIZATIONS
(At No Extra Cost)
For information, call Benny White, HY. 3-9535'

!5 October 1953:

MILES DAVIS AT NOB HILL

All you dance lovers, Nob Hill, 5228 Lake Park Ave., is currently featuring one of the nation's most versatile trumpet players, Miles Davis, who was the winner of several national awards. This will be his first Chicago appearance in three years.

Miles will feature an all request program nitely so the patrons of the club can hear him play his latest disc hits in person. Miles, a favorite of the juke box lovers, should be just what the patrons have been waiting for, this big attraction plus Lefty Bates and his new Jazz band should really keep the club jumping nightly. The Monday jam session will be loaded with guest stars welcoming this guest artist to Chicago.

THURSDAY 19 NOVEMBER 1953

Miles is still in Chicago in the middle of November when he is featured at Nob-Hill with tenor saxophone star Ben Webster.

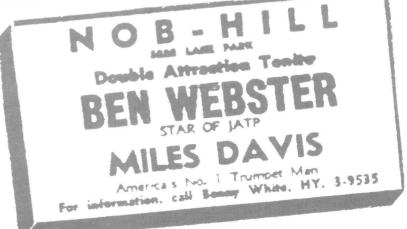

NOB - HILL
5228 LAKE PARK
Double Attraction Tonite
BEN WEBSTER
STAR OF JATP
MILES DAVIS
America's No. 1 Trumpet Man
For information, call Benny White, HY. 3-9535

TUES	1	FRI	1
WED	2	SAT	2
THUR	3	SUN	3
FRI	4	MON	4
SAT	5	TUES	5
SUN	6	WED	6
MON	7	THUR	7
TUES	8	FRI	8
WED	9	SAT	9
THUR	10	SUN	10
FRI	11	MON	11
SAT	12	TUES	12
SUN	13	WED	13
MON	14	THUR	14
TUES	15	FRI	15
WED	16	SAT	16
THUR	17	SUN	17
FRI	18	MON	18
SAT	19	TUES	19
SUN	20	WED	20
MON	21	THUR	21
TUES	22	FRI	22
WED	23	SAT	23
THUR	24	SUN	24
FRI	25	MON	25
SAT	26	TUES	26
SUN	27	WED	27
MON	28	THUR	28
TUES	29	FRI	29
WED	30	SAT	30
THUR	31	SUN	31

Again, Miles returns to his father's farm in Millstadt determined to break his habit. This time he really wants it. He is locked up in the family guest house for two weeks to kick the habit cold turkey. Miles later recalls:

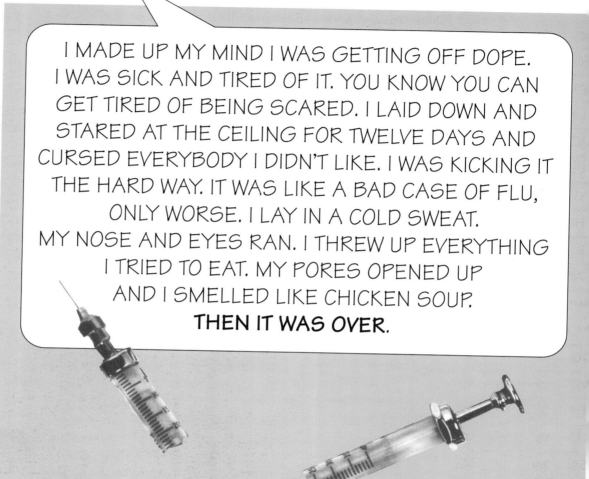

I MADE UP MY MIND I WAS GETTING OFF DOPE. I WAS SICK AND TIRED OF IT. YOU KNOW YOU CAN GET TIRED OF BEING SCARED. I LAID DOWN AND STARED AT THE CEILING FOR TWELVE DAYS AND CURSED EVERYBODY I DIDN'T LIKE. I WAS KICKING IT THE HARD WAY. IT WAS LIKE A BAD CASE OF FLU, ONLY WORSE. I LAY IN A COLD SWEAT. MY NOSE AND EYES RAN. I THREW UP EVERYTHING I TRIED TO EAT. MY PORES OPENED UP AND I SMELLED LIKE CHICKEN SOUP. **THEN IT WAS OVER.**

To recuperate and to keep away from old connections, Miles decides to go to Detroit where there is a large contingent of top-class jazz musicians. He appears regularly throughout his time in Detroit at the Bluebird Inn where Billy Mitchell leads the house band which includes Tommy Flanagan on piano and Elvin Jones on drums. Other local musicians who come to sit in include Donald Byrd, Curtis Fuller, Barry Harris, Thad Jones, Yusef Lateef and Betty Carter.

At the end of the year, Miles has slipped way down the list in the *Down Beat* trumpet poll which is won by Chet Baker.

WEDNESDAY 27 JANUARY 1954
Down Beat reviews Miles' latest EP release:

MILES DAVIS Blue Haze
When Lights Are Low / Tune Up / Miles Ahead / Smooch
Rating: ****
Miles couldn't have asked for a more musically background than that provided by John Lewis, Max Roach and Percy Heath last May. His own playing is consistently interesting but it's too bad he had so large an intonation problem on the date. Most absorbing tune thematically is Charlie Mingus' *Smooch*. The rating is higher than it would ordinarily be thanks to the accompaniment. (**Prestige PREP 1326**)

ION	**1**	MON	**1**
UES	**2**	TUES	**2**
VED	**3**	WED	**3**
HUR	**4**	THUR	**4**
RI	**5**	FRI	**5**
AT	**6**	SAT	**6**
JN	**7**	SUN	**7**
ION	**8**	MON	**8**
UES	**9**	TUES	**9**
VED	**10**	WED	**10**
HUR	**11**	THUR	**11**
RI	**12**	FRI	**12**
AT	**13**	SAT	**13**
JN	**14**	SUN	**14**
ION	**15**	MON	**15**
UES	**16**	TUES	**16**
VED	**17**	WED	**17**
HUR	**18**	THUR	**18**
RI	**19**	FRI	**19**
AT	**20**	SAT	**20**
JN	**21**	SUN	**21**
ION	**22**	MON	**22**
UES	**23**	TUES	**23**
VED	**24**	WED	**24**
HUR	**25**	THUR	**25**
RI	**26**	FRI	**26**
AT	**27**	SAT	**27**
JN	**28**	SUN	**28**
		MON	**29**
		TUES	**30**
		WED	**31**

FEBRUARY 1954

Miles returns to New York City, finally free of his addiction and ready to concentrate exclusively on his music. He checks into the Arlington Hotel on 25th Street and calls Alfred Lion of Blue Note and Bob Weinstock of Prestige to tell them he is ready to make records. Pianist Horace Silver is living at the Arlington and Miles recruits him for the upcoming record date. They spend a lot of time in Horace's room playing and composing together.

SATURDAY 6 MARCH 1954

Recording session by the Miles Davis Quartet for Blue Note in New York City.
MILES DAVIS (trumpet), HORACE SILVER (piano), PERCY HEATH (bass), ART BLAKEY (drums)
Well You Needn't / Lazy Susan / The Leap / Weirdo / Take Off / It Never Entered My Mind

Below: Clifford Brown (left) visits Miles and Horace Silver at the 6 March recording session for Blue Note.

MONDAY 15 MARCH 1954

Recording session by the Miles Davis Quartet for Prestige at the 31st Street Studios in New York City. The producer is Bob Weinstock.
MILES DAVIS (trumpet), HORACE SILVER (piano), PERCY HEATH (bass), ART BLAKEY (drums)
Four / That Old Devil Called Love / Blue Haze
This is the first recording session of the new three-year contract Miles has signed with Prestige. Ira Gitler is at the session and recalls Miles turning down the lights on *Blue Haze* to create atmosphere.

57

THUR	**1**	SAT	**1**
FRI	**2**	SUN	**2**
SAT	**3**	MON	**3**
SUN	**4**	TUES	**4**
MON	**5**	WED	**5**
TUES	**6**	THUR	**6**
WED	**7**	FRI	**7**
THUR	**8**	SAT	**8**
FRI	**9**	SUN	**9**
SAT	**10**	MON	**10**
SUN	**11**	TUES	**11**
MON	**12**	WED	**12**
TUES	**13**	THUR	**13**
WED	**14**	FRI	**14**
THUR	**15**	SAT	**15**
FRI	**16**	SUN	**16**
SAT	**17**	MON	**17**
SUN	**18**	TUES	**18**
MON	**19**	WED	**19**
TUES	**20**	THUR	**20**
WED	**21**	FRI	**21**
THUR	**22**	SAT	**22**
FRI	**23**	SUN	**23**
SAT	**24**	MON	**24**
SUN	**25**	TUES	**25**
MON	**26**	WED	**26**
TUES	**27**	THUR	**27**
WED	**28**	FRI	**28**
THUR	**29**	SAT	**29**
FRI	**30**	SUN	**30**
		MON	**31**

SATURDAY 3 APRIL 1954

Recording session by the Miles Davis Quintet for Prestige in New York City. The producer is Bob Weinstock.
MILES DAVIS (trumpet), DAVE SCHILDKRAUT (alto sax), HORACE SILVER (piano), PERCY HEATH (bass), KENNY CLARKE (drums)
Solar / You Don't Know What Love Is (DS out) / *Love Me Or Leave Me / I'll Remember April*

THURSDAY 15 APRIL 1954

Miles Davis All Stars open at Birdland for a two-week engagement opposite Dinah Washington and the Earl Hines Band.

WEDNESDAY 21 APRIL 1954

Dinah Washington closes at Birdland but Miles Davis All Stars and the Earl Hines Band stay on for another week.

Down Beat reports:

Miles Davis, blowing well, had a swinging group at Birdland for two weeks with Kenny Clarke, Lucky Thompson, Percy Heath and Horace Silver.

WEDNESDAY 28 APRIL 1954

The Miles Davis All Stars close at Birdland.

THURSDAY 29 APRIL 1954

Recording session by the Miles Davis All Star Sextet for Prestige in Hackensack, New Jersey.
MILES DAVIS (trumpet), JAY JAY JOHNSON (trombone), LUCKY THOMPSON (tenor sax), HORACE SILVER (piano), PERCY HEATH (bass), KENNY CLARKE (drums)
Blue'n'Boogie / Walkin'
Ira Gitler remembers the rehearsals for this session taking place at a concert in a record store (see page 63).

TUESDAY 4 MAY 1954

The Miles Davis Quartet open at Basin Street i New York City for a two-week engagement opposite Flip Phillips and Slim Gaillard.

WEDNESDAY 12 MAY 1954

The Miles Davis All Stars close at Basin Street in New York City.

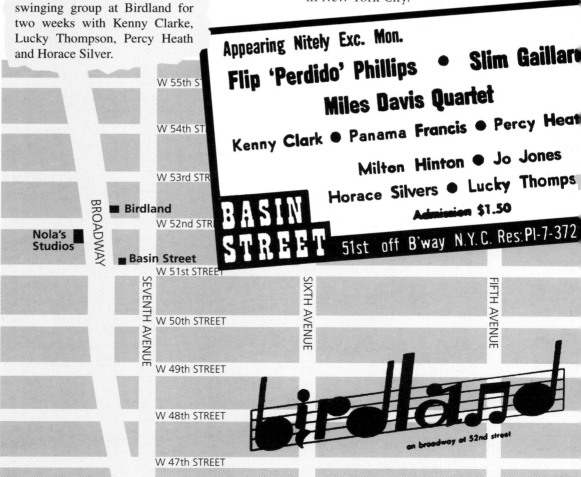

THURSDAY 13 MAY 1954
The Miles Davis All Stars open at Birdland in New York City for a two-week engagement opposite Chet Baker Quartet and Dizzy Gillespie.

WEDNESDAY 26 MAY 1954
Miles' 28th birthday.
The Miles Davis All Stars close at Birdland in New York City.

Down Beat reviews Miles' performance at Birdland:

Miles Davis, Chet Baker; Birdland, New York

Chet Baker's New York debut was successful in terms of the crowds he attracted to Birdland. Musically, his unit might have sounded more impressive if it hadn't been for the strikingly contrasting presence on the same bill of a Miles Davis band that made the Bakermen sound rather frail and, I'm afraid, a little dull.

Both Chet and Miles were working under disadvantages. While Miles had Lucky Thompson on tenor, Chet had to carry the entire front line himself (wouldn't it have been wiser to bring another horn along?) and he was nervous. "He can't be that afraid of Birdland" said an increduous bassist, who then went over to ask him. It turned out that Chet *was* rather frightened.

Miles, on the other hand, had worked only rarely in the last year, and at the beginning of the date, his lips weren't yet in shape, so there were some cracked notes and several near misses in execution.

What was most immediately apparent was the difference in rhythm sections. In Chet's unit, drummer Bob Neel was just adequate, bassist Carson Smith has a good tone and is steady, and Russ Freeman, while no major jazz pianist yet, has individually intriguing conception at times.

But as a section, Baker's rhythm entourage was static compared with the swinging, often elated rapport among Percy Heath, Kenny Clarke, and Horace Silver in Miles' unit. And man for man, Miles' men were also easily superior. Even Freeman was pallid compared with Silver in both ideas and beat, and Smith and Neel could take lessons from Heath and Clarke.

As for the leaders, Baker's tone is distinctive, his conception erratic. He is least consistent on up-tempos and is best on ballads on which he usually creates an effective mood. But even on these he is not always able to sustain long tones, and in general, his execution is spotty.

What he lacks, as do the members of his unit, is a sufficient range of dynamics and a mature sense of structure. This is evident both in their playing and in their choice of "originals" that are usually just underdeveloped sketches of small thematic strength. And if they deeply enjoy what they play, it is not at all apparent.

Miles, largely though his own fault, has not yet fulfilled his great early promise. He now may be on the way ahead again. As the week ended and his embouchure strengthened, he was often the Miles of old in quality of conception with a new, drivingly emotional way of playing ("souling" as one musician put it). On a ballad like *It Never Entered My Mind*, he cut Chet at his own specialty. For one thing, Miles' harmonic awareness, let alone his phrasing, is considerably keener, And on middle and up-tempo numbers, Miles, even when he occasionally fluffed, was a wholly alive, stimulating voice.

What is most important is that Miles' whole band kept building on each number, rarely letting it slide into a routine succession of choruses. And Miles isn't afraid to try for some startlingly imaginative patterns, even when they don't always work out. In short, where Miles and his band plunged in and swam, Chet and his men mostly went wading.

AT   1
JN   2
ON   3
JES 4
ED   5
HUR 6
I   7
AT   8
JN   9
ON 10
JES 11
ED 12
HUR 13
I   14
AT 15
JN 16
ON 17
JES 18
ED 19
HUR 20
I   21
AT 22
JN 23
ON 24
JES 25
ED 26
HUR 27
I   28
AT 29
JN 30
ON 31

TUES	1
WED	2
THUR	3
FRI	4
SAT	5
SUN	6
MON	7
TUES	8
WED	9
THUR	10
FRI	11
SAT	12
SUN	13
MON	14
TUES	15
WED	16
THUR	17
FRI	18
SAT	19
SUN	20
MON	21
TUES	22
WED	23
THUR	24
FRI	25
SAT	26
SUN	27
MON	28
TUES	29
WED	30

In May, Capitol release eight of the Nonet recordings on a 10″ LP called Birth of the Cool.
Down Beat reviews the album in its 2 June issue:

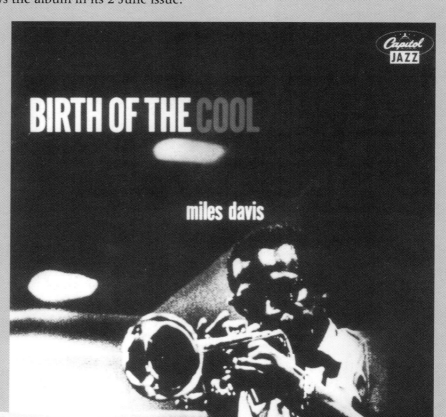

MILES DAVIS: Birth of the Cool

Jeru / Moon Dreams / Venus de Milo / Deception / Godchild / Rocker / Israel / Rouge
Rating: *****

Not only has Capitol reissued four of the important Davis-Mulligan-Evans 1949 new directional experiments, but also included in this LP are four others that have never been released before. Three of them were cut in 1950—Gerry Mulligan's *Rocker*, Miles Davis' *Deception*, and an arrangement of Johnny Mercer's *Moon Dreams*, the last half of which is of unusually rich textural interest. The personnel on those three had Miles, J.J. Johnson, Lee Konitz, Mulligan, John Lewis, Al McKibbon, Max Roach, John Barber (tuba), and Gunther Schuller (French horn).

The other new recording, Lewis' *Rouge*, was recorded in 1949 on the same date as *Israel*. On that session, Sandy Siegelstein was on French horn; Nelson Boyd, bass; and Kenny Clarke, drums, with the rest of the personnel the same. The band changes on the *Jeru/Godchild* date were Kai Winding, trombone; Junior Collins, French horn; Al Haig, piano, and Joe Schulman, bass.

The four heard here for the first time are just as absorbing as the other results of these collaborations (not all of which are included in this LP). The unusual instrumentation—for that time—was skilfully utilized by the arrangers to provide new ensemble colorations and a unity of complexly-knit sound that has influenced modern jazz ever since. And with all the paper work, the sides swing with a lightness and crispness of attack that will keep them alive for many years. Not everything worked out perfectly at these sessions, but so large a percentage of the searching was successful that these are among the major historical guideposts in recorded jazz. (**Capitol LP H-459**)

SUNDAY 13 JUNE 1954
Miles plays a one-nighter at the Open Door in
Greenwich Village, accompanied by Horace Silver,
Percy Heath and Kenny Clarke.

Bob Reisner presents
THE GREATEST IN MODERN JAZZ
MILES DAVIS
TRUMPET
HORACE SILVER—Piano
KENNY CLARKE—Drums
PERCY HEATH—Bass
SUNDAY, JUNE 13
9.00 P. M. to 1 A. M.
OPEN DOOR
55 WEST 3rd STREET

TUES	**1**
WED	**2**
THUR	**3**
FRI	**4**
SAT	**5**
SUN	**6**
MON	**7**
TUES	**8**
WED	**9**
THUR	**10**
FRI	**11**
SAT	**12**
SUN	**13**
MON	**14**
TUES	**15**
WED	**16**
THUR	**17**
FRI	**18**
SAT	**19**
SUN	**20**
MON	**21**
TUES	**22**
WED	**23**
THUR	**24**
FRI	**25**
SAT	**26**
SUN	**27**
MON	**28**
TUES	**29**
WED	**30**

WEDNESDAY 16 JUNE 1954
Down Beat reviews Miles' new Prestige album:

MILES DAVIS: Blue Haze
When Lights Are Low / Tune Up / Miles Ahead / Smooch / Four / That Ole Devil Called Love / Blue Haze
Rating: ***

First four were made in May, 1953, with John Lewis, Percy Heath, and Max Roach and were reviewed as an EP (*Down Beat*, Jan. 27). Second side was recorded in January of this year with Horace Silver, Percy Heath, and Art Blakey. Though there are small lapses in intonation and execution throughout, Miles blows interestingly for the most part, but he apparently needs the stimulus of at least one other horn to improvise at his best.

His most cohesive work here is on Charlie Mingus' *Smooch* and on the simple blues, *Blue Haze*, where he comes on in spots like Rex Stewart. Miles has rarely sounded as warmly relaxed as on *Haze*. Rhythm sections on both dates acquitted themselves with distinction.
(**Prestige PRLP 161**)

MONDAY 21 JUNE 1954
Birdland is jammed and crowds gathered outside as Miles is reunited with Charlie Parker for a Monday night jam session.

TUESDAY 22 JUNE 1954
Miles Davis Quintet, featuring Sonny Rollins, open at the Club Tijuana in Baltimore for a one-week engagement.

MONDAY 28 JUNE 1954
Miles Davis Quintet close at the Club Tijuana in Baltimore.

TUESDAY 29 JUNE 1954
Recording session by the Miles Davis Quintet for Prestige in Hackensack, New Jersey.
MILES DAVIS (trumpet), SONNY ROLLINS (tenor sax), HORACE SILVER (piano), PERCY HEATH (bass), KENNY CLARKE (drums)
Airegin / Oleo / But Not For Me (2 takes) / *Doxy*

July		August		September	
THUR	1	SUN	1	WED	1
FRI	2	MON	2	THUR	2
SAT	3	TUES	3	FRI	3
SUN	4	WED	4	SAT	4
MON	5	THUR	5	SUN	5
TUES	6	FRI	6	MON	6
WED	7	SAT	7	TUES	7
THUR	8	SUN	8	WED	8
FRI	9	MON	9	THUR	9
SAT	10	TUES	10	FRI	10
SUN	11	WED	11	SAT	11
MON	12	THUR	12	SUN	12
TUES	13	FRI	13	MON	13
WED	14	SAT	14	TUES	14
THUR	15	SUN	15	WED	15
FRI	16	MON	16	THUR	16
SAT	17	TUES	17	FRI	17
SUN	18	WED	18	SAT	18
MON	19	THUR	19	SUN	19
TUES	20	FRI	20	MON	20
WED	21	SAT	21	TUES	21
THUR	22	SUN	22	WED	22
FRI	23	MON	23	THUR	23
SAT	24	TUES	24	FRI	24
SUN	25	WED	25	SAT	25
MON	26	THUR	26	SUN	26
TUES	27	FRI	27	MON	27
WED	28	SAT	28	TUES	28
THUR	29	SUN	29	WED	29
FRI	30	MON	30	THUR	30
SAT	31	TUES	31		

Despite being free of drugs, Miles is still finding it difficult to obtain regular club work for his group. He has another year of scuffling ahead before his reputation is restored.

WEDNESDAY 28 JULY 1954

Down Beat reports:

NYC Record Store Begins Free Jazz Concert Series

New York—In recent weeks, pleased customers at the Record Collectors Shop on 47th Street have been able to hear hours of Miles Davis, Art Farmer, and Charlie Parker for free. Not on the demonstration machines—but in live Thursday night concerts.

It's a uniquely effective move—with application possibilities all over the country—to advertise the extensive jazz department at the Shop. For 17 years, the Record Collectors Shop was primarily a classical operation, but like many other record retailers, owner-violist Herman Lemberg has been discovering that even when the rest of the record field is in a temporary decline, "jazz pays the rent."

So far the concerts have been resolutely low-pressure in atmosphere. No records are sold the night of the concerts. There is no pitch at any time during the evening concerning the buying of records. "In short," says Lemberg, "those nights, we hide the cash register."

When Miles Davis opened the series, about 175 people sat in bemused but orderly rows inside the store and 100 clustered about outside. Succeeding attendance has also been good, and depending on the availability of talent, Lemberg would like to have a session every week. As of now, he intends to continue through the summer and into the fall with some possibility of a live chamber music series to parallel the jazz concerts at the shop.

The musicians are pleased with this extra source of jobs—especially because Lemberg pays quite comfortably above scale. And for Lemberg, paying the musicians and a small amount of advertising comprise his overhead. Since he charges no admission for the concerts, he doesn't have to get involved in tax and other legalistic problems.

Ink Spots Again In Union Dispute

Hollywood — The jurisdictional friction which has been breaking out from time to time between the American Federation of Musicians and the entertainment guilds, got hot again as the American Federation of Television and Radio Artists tried for the second time to bar the Ink Spots from a guest appearance. This time it was from Art Linkletter's *Houseparty* (a CBS simulcast).

Three members of the present-day Ink Spots (the original unit minus falsetto-voiced Bill Kenny) are AFM card-holders. Two are members of AGVA (American Guild of Variety Artists). AFTRA, which tried to bar the same group from the Spade Cooley show here last year, claims they should join its roster if they play radio or television. In the recent issue, the AFM's Jimmy Petrillo threatened to pull all of his members from the show if AFTRA persisted. The Ink Spots played the show.

Atcher Heads Tiffany C&W Department

Chicago—Tiffany records has expanded its operations to include a country-western department. Heading the new division is Bob Atcher, slated to make his bow on Tiffany wax this month.

The firm's initial c&w disc, cut by Captain Stubby and the Buccaneers, already has been released.

FRI **1**	MON **1**	WED **1**
SAT **2**	TUES **2**	THUR **2**
SUN **3**	WED **3**	FRI **3**
MON **4**	THUR **4**	SAT **4**
TUES **5**	FRI **5**	SUN **5**
WED **6**	SAT **6**	MON **6**
THUR **7**	SUN **7**	TUES **7**
FRI **8**	MON **8**	WED **8**
SAT **9**	TUES **9**	THUR **9**
SUN **10**	WED **10**	FRI **10**
MON **11**	THUR **11**	SAT **11**
TUES **12**	FRI **12**	SUN **12**
WED **13**	SAT **13**	MON **13**
THUR **14**	SUN **14**	TUES **14**
FRI **15**	MON **15**	WED **15**
SAT **16**	TUES **16**	THUR **16**
SUN **17**	WED **17**	FRI **17**
MON **18**	THUR **18**	SAT **18**
TUES **19**	FRI **19**	SUN **19**
WED **20**	SAT **20**	MON **20**
THUR **21**	SUN **21**	TUES **21**
FRI **22**	MON **22**	WED **22**
SAT **23**	TUES **23**	THUR **23**
SUN **24**	WED **24**	FRI **24**
MON **25**	THUR **25**	SAT **25**
TUES **26**	FRI **26**	SUN **26**
WED **27**	SAT **27**	MON **27**
THUR **28**	SUN **28**	TUES **28**
FRI **29**	MON **29**	WED **29**
SAT **30**	TUES **30**	THUR **30**
SUN **31**		FRI **31**

FRIDAY 24 DECEMBER 1954

Recording session by the Miles Davis Quintet for Prestige at Rudy Van Gelder's Studio in Hackensack, New Jersey. MILES DAVIS (trumpet), MILT JACKSON (vibes), THELONIOUS MONK (piano), PERCY HEATH (bass), KENNY CLARKE (drums) *Bags' Groove* (2 takes) / *Bemsha Swing / Swing Spring / The Man I Love* (2 takes)

This historic session, produced by Bob Weinstock, is notorious for the alleged friction between Miles and Monk.

Ira Gitler later broaches the subject in h sleeve notes for the album:

Legend had it, for a while, that Miles Monk during a disagreement over whetl Monk should 'lay out' or not. ('Laying o is the equivalent of 'strolling' where pianist refrains from chording and the solo is backed only by bass and drums.) I kno there was no fight during the time I was the studio although there were verl exchanges. When I asked Monk about t alleged fisticuffs that some inside-hipst had confronted me with, he chuckle "Miles'd got killed if he hit me". In an event, things were not serene when I le towards the dinner hour (the session ha started somewhere between two and three the afternoon) and not much had bee accomplished. I had my doubts as whether anything would. Later that night, Minton's, I saw Kenny Clarke wh answered my "How did it go?" with "Mile sure is a beautiful cat", which was his wa of saying that despite the obstacles, Mile had seen it through and produced somethin extraordinary and lasting.

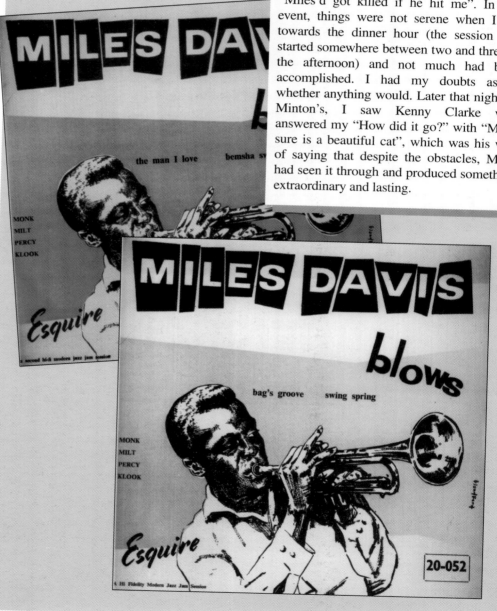

AT	**1**	TUES	**1**	TUES	**1**
UN	**2**	WED	**2**	WED	**2**
ON	**3**	THUR	**3**	THUR	**3**
JES	**4**	FRI	**4**	FRI	**4**
ED	**5**	SAT	**5**	SAT	**5**
UR	**6**	SUN	**6**	SUN	**6**
	7	MON	**7**	MON	**7**
T	**8**	TUES	**8**	TUES	**8**
N	**9**	WED	**9**	WED	**9**
ON	**10**	THUR	**10**	THUR	**10**
JES	**11**	FRI	**11**	FRI	**11**
ED	**12**	SAT	**12**	SAT	**12**
UR	**13**	SUN	**13**	SUN	**13**
	14	MON	**14**	MON	**14**
T	**15**	TUES	**15**	TUES	**15**
N	**16**	WED	**16**	WED	**16**
ON	**17**	THUR	**17**	THUR	**17**
ES	**18**	FRI	**18**	FRI	**18**
ED	**19**	SAT	**19**	SAT	**19**
UR	**20**	SUN	**20**	SUN	**20**
	21	MON	**21**	MON	**21**
T	**22**	TUES	**22**	TUES	**22**
N	**23**	WED	**23**	WED	**23**
ON	**24**	THUR	**24**	THUR	**24**
ES	**25**	FRI	**25**	FRI	**25**
ED	**26**	SAT	**26**	SAT	**26**
UR	**27**	SUN	**27**	SUN	**27**
	28	MON	**28**	MON	**28**
T	**29**			TUES	**29**
N	**30**			WED	**30**
ON	**31**			THUR	**31**

MARCH 1955

Miles is at the Hi-Hat in Boston for a week as a single with local musicians Jay Migliori (tenor sax), Al Walcott (piano), Jimmy Woode (bass) and Jimmy Zitano (drums). He does well and is held over for a further week.

9 MARCH 1955

Down Beat reviews the Blue Note album:

12 MARCH 1955

Charlie Parker dies in Baroness Nica de Koenigswarter's apartment at the Stanhope Hotel in New York City.

**CHARLIE PARKER
1920–1955**

MILES DAVIS, Vol 3
Take Off; It Never Entered My Mind; Well, You Needn't; Lazy Susan; Wierdo; The Leap
Rating: ****
In this recital, Miles is excellently accompanied by Horace Silver, Percy Heath, and Art Blakey. The first and last three originals are by Miles. One of the two best originals of the set, however, is Thelonious Monk's characteristically quizzical *Well, You Needn't*. The Rodgers and Hart *Mind* is taken slowly with a deliberate simplicity that is somewhat more stolid than lyrical. The other four line-patterns are good vehicles for extended variation by Miles, particularly the haunting, blues-filled *Wierdo*.

It would have helped to further sustain the interest of the date if there had been at least one other horn, but the rating remains high for the strongly alive rhythm section and for Miles, who blows with imaginative and tonal style — a style unmistakably and influentially his own. A very attractive cover design.
(Blue Note BLP 5040)

FRI	**1**	SUN	**1**
SAT	**2**	MON	**2**
SUN	**3**	TUES	**3**
MON	**4**	WED	**4**
TUES	**5**	THUR	**5**
WED	**6**	FRI	**6**
THUR	**7**	SAT	**7**
FRI	**8**	SUN	**8**
SAT	**9**	MON	**9**
SUN	**10**	TUES	**10**
MON	**11**	WED	**11**
TUES	**12**	THUR	**12**
WED	**13**	FRI	**13**
THUR	**14**	SAT	**14**
FRI	**15**	SUN	**15**
SAT	**16**	MON	**16**
SUN	**17**	TUES	**17**
MON	**18**	WED	**18**
TUES	**19**	THUR	**19**
WED	**20**	FRI	**20**
THUR	**21**	SAT	**21**
FRI	**22**	SUN	**22**
SAT	**23**	MON	**23**
SUN	**24**	TUES	**24**
MON	**25**	WED	**25**
TUES	**26**	THUR	**26**
WED	**27**	FRI	**27**
THUR	**28**	SAT	**28**
FRI	**29**	SUN	**29**
SAT	**30**	MON	**30**
		TUES	**31**

MONDAY 18 APRIL 1955

Miles Davis and his new group featuring Sonny Rollins (tenor sax), Red Garland (piano), Paul Chambers (bass) and Philly Joe Jones (drums) open at the Blue Note in Philadelphia for a one-week engagement.

SUNDAY 24 APRIL 1955

Miles Davis and his new group close at the Blue Note in Philadelphia.

FRIDAY 13 MAY 1955

Miles appears at the Stuyvesant Casino in New York City with Kai Winding, George Wallington, Charlie Mingus, Don Elliott and Philly Joe Jones.

SATURDAY 14 MAY 1955

Miles appears at the Grand Ballroom of the Paramount Hotel in New York City with Kai Winding, George Wallington, Charlie Mingus, Don Elliott and Philly Joe Jones.

THURSDAY 26 MAY 1955

Miles' 29th birthday.

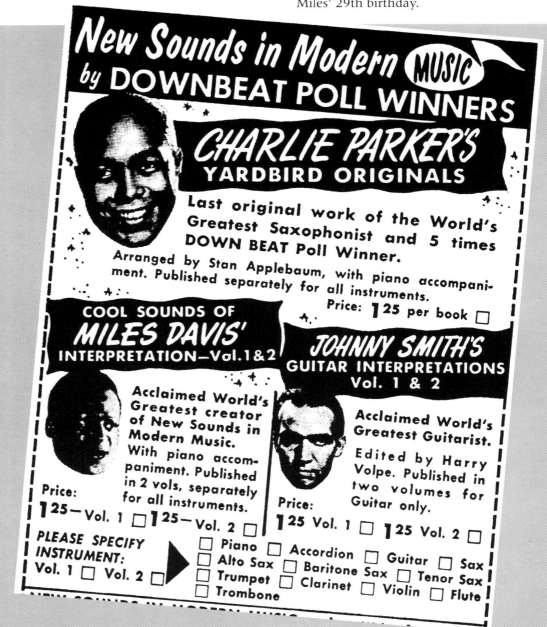

ED **1**
UR **2**
3
T **4**
N **5**
ON **6**
ES **7**
ED **8**
UR **9**
10
T **11**
N **12**
ON **13**
ES **14**
ED **15**
UR **16**
17
T **18**
N **19**
ON **20**
ES **21**
ED **22**
UR **23**
24
T **25**
N **26**
ON **27**
ES **28**
ED **29**
UR **30**

TUESDAY 7 JUNE 1955

Recording session by the Miles Davis Quartet for Prestige at Rudy Van Gelder's studio in Hackensack, New Jersey. Bob Weinstock is the producer.

MILES DAVIS (trumpet), RED GARLAND (piano), OSCAR PETTIFORD (bass), PHILLY JOE JONES (drums)
I Didn't / Will You Still Be Mine? / Green Haze / I See Your Face Before Me / A Night In Tunisia / A Gal In Calico

The album is issued as *The Musings of Miles* (Prestige LP 7007)

Ira Gitler is at the session to obtain background for the sleeve notes.
He interviews Miles in a car outside the studio.

… I asked Miles who his current favorites were. On his own instrument he quickly named Art Farmer and Clifford Brown as the new stars and Kenny Dorham as one who has come into his own. Then he spoke lovingly of Dizzy Gillespie. "Diz is it … whenever I want to learn something I go and listen to Diz." In the piano department two Philadelphia boys, Red Garland (heard to good advantage in this LP) and Ray Bryant were mentioned along with Horace Silver, Hank Jones and Carl Perkins "a cat on the Coast who plays bass notes with his elbow", The talk shifted to saxophone and to Sonny Rollins and Hank Mobley who are carrying on the tradition of Charlie Parker. This naturally started us talking about Bird. Miles credited his most wonderful experiences in jazz to his years with Bird. He stared slowly ahead "Like Max [Roach] said, 'New York isn't New York anymore without Bird'".

Max's name being mentioned directed the conversation to drummers. "Art Blakey and Philly Joe Jones; Max for brushes." Miles is very conscious of drummers. Many times he will sit down between the drummer and bass player and just listen to what the drummer is doing. You might even say that listening to drummers is a hobby with Miles. His real hobby, however, is boxing and he concerns himself with two aspects—spectator and participator. As a spectator he is not merely a TV fan. You'll find him at Madison Square Garden or St. Nick's when he is in New York and similar arenas in other cities when there is a good match on tap. His personal fistic activity is confined to working out on the light punching bag in various gyms. Anything more would be dangerous. One stiff right cross to the "chops" and this LP might have been delayed indefinitely.

FRI	**1**
SAT	**2**
SUN	**3**
MON	**4**
TUES	**5**
WED	**6**
THUR	**7**
FRI	**8**
SAT	**9**
SUN	**10**
MON	**11**
TUES	**12**
WED	**13**
THUR	**14**
FRI	**15**
SAT	**16**
SUN	**17**
MON	**18**
TUES	**19**
WED	**20**
THUR	**21**
FRI	**22**
SAT	**23**
SUN	**24**
MON	**25**
TUES	**26**
WED	**27**
THUR	**28**
FRI	**29**
SAT	**30**
SUN	**31**

SATURDAY 9 JULY 1955

Recording session by the Miles Davis Quintet for Charlie Mingus' Debut label in New York City.
MILES DAVIS (trumpet), BRITT WOODMAN (trombone), TEDDY CHARLES (vibes), CHARLIE MINGUS (bass), ELVIN JONES (drums)
Nature Boy / Alone Together / There Is No You / Easy Living
The album is issued as *Blue Moods* on Debut 120.

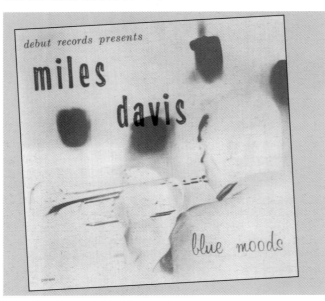

Around this time Miles takes the quintet into the newly opened Café Bohemia in New York City.

WEDNESDAY 13 JULY 1955

The Miles Davis Quintet broadcast from the Café Bohemia in New York City.
MILES DAVIS (trumpet), SONNY ROLLINS (tenor sax), RED GARLAND (piano), PAUL CHAMBERS (bass) PHILLY JOE JONES (drums)
Bye Bye Blackbird / Walkin'

SUNDAY 17 JULY 1955

Miles appears as part of an All Star group at the Newport Jazz Festival in Newport, Rhode Island and is a great success. The All Star group is sandwiched between the headline attractions of Count Basie's Orchestra and the Dave Brubeck Quartet. *Down Beat* reports:

> Then it was time for Duke Ellington, who emceed the Sunday affair, to introduce Miles Davis, Zoot Sims, Gerry Mulligan, Thelonious Monk, Percy Heath, and Connie Kay. They opened with *Hackensack*, on which Miles played thrillingly and indicated that his comeback is in full stride. Heath, too, shone, as did all members on the ensuing *Now's TheTime*. It was Miles, however, who captured most ears.

Burt Goldblatt is also there and, in his book *Newport Jazz Festival – the illustrated history*, writes:

> It was a completely unscheduled appearance. Miles, in a white jacket and black bow tie, looked the antithesis of what the critics had intimated he had been going through for the past couple of years. He had shaken off the junk and personal problems that had led the jazz establishment to write him off.
>
> Accompanied by Gerry Mulligan on baritone, Zoot Sims on tenor, Thelonious Monk on piano, Percy Heath on bass, and Connie Kay on drums, Miles opened with a driving, emotional assault, "Hackensack." The tempo and smouldering intensity of Miles's solo was like spontaneous combustion, which spread to the rest of the sextet. For about ten minutes they held that audience by the throat.
>
> Members of the press were uneasy. After all, this was someone they had written off. George Avakian remembers, "Miles came out on that stage like a walk-on. He blew *so* beautifully!"
>
> Miles and the sextet continued the set with "'Round About Midnight." Miles played with great emotion. His solo, particularly after the bridge, had a clarity and austerity that were to mark much of his later work. He got at something more than the truth. The audience sat spellbound. He concluded with "Now's the Time," which he had first recorded with Bird in 1945. The audience gave the group a standing ovation. Miles left the stage as quietly as he had come on. Later, in response to the critical acclaim for his Newport performance, he was quoted as saying, "I don't know what all those cats were talking about. I played the way I always play." Despite his disclaimers, Newport was a turning point in his career.

George Avakian, of Columbia Records, hears Miles a Newport and is determined to sign him to record for Columbia.

MONDAY 18 JULY 1955

Miles Davis, Bud Shank and a local rhythm section open at the Blue Note in Philadelphia for a one-wee engagement.

SUNDAY 24 JULY 1955

Miles Davis and Bud Shank close at the Blue Note in Philadelphia.

Opposite page: Miles on stage at the Newport Jazz Festival 1955, with Percy Heath (bass) and Gerry Mulligan.

RI **1**

AT **2**

UN **3**

ON **4**

JES **5**

VED **6**

HUR **7**

RI **8**

AT **9**

UN **10**

ION **11**

JES **12**

VED **13**

HUR **14**

RI **15**

AT **16**

UN **17**

ION **18**

JES **19**

VED **20**

HUR **21**

RI **22**

AT **23**

UN **24**

ION **25**

JES **26**

VED **27**

HUR **28**

RI **29**

AT **30**

UN **31**

MON	**1**
TUES	**2**
WED	**3**
THUR	**4**
FRI	**5**
SAT	**6**
SUN	**7**
MON	**8**
TUES	**9**
WED	**10**
THUR	**11**
FRI	**12**
SAT	**13**
SUN	**14**
MON	**15**
TUES	**16**
WED	**17**
THUR	**18**
FRI	**19**
SAT	**20**
SUN	**21**
MON	**22**
TUES	**23**
WED	**24**
THUR	**25**
FRI	**26**
SAT	**27**
SUN	**28**
MON	**29**
TUES	**30**
WED	**31**

FRIDAY 5 AUGUST 1955

Recording session by the Miles Davis Sextet for Prestige at Rudy Van Gelder's studio in Hackensack, New Jersey.

MILES DAVIS (trumpet), JACKIE MCLEAN (alto sax), MILT JACKSON (vibes), RAY BRYANT (piano), PERCY HEATH (bass) ART TAYLOR (drums)

Dr Jackle / Minor March / Bitty Ditty (JML out) / *Blues Changes* (JML out)

After recording two numbers, Jackie McLean and Miles have a disagreement and Jackie walks out. The album is issued as *Milt and Miles* (Prestige LP 7034)

WEDNESDAY 10 AUGUST 1955

Down Beat reviews Miles' latest album release:

MILES DAVIS ALL STARS Vol 1
Bags' Groove; Swing Spring
Rating: *

Volume 1 of the *Miles Davis All Stars* has one tune to a side. Milt Jackson's *Bags' Groove* goes 11¼ minutes and Miles' new original, *Swing Spring*, lasts about 10¾. The all-stars are Milt Jackson, Percy Heath, Kenny Clarke, and Thelonious Monk. The outstanding soloist is Jackson, and the rhythm section moves well with Heath and Clarke being an especial gas.

Miles has his moments (e.g. the final choruses on *Groove*), but I've heard him in more incandescent form. And Monk has known more fruitful hours (much of his lengthy exercise in understatement on *Groove* strikes me as valuable only if it's meant to be a parody). All in all, both tunes lasted too long and not enough care was given to organizing the session. Good recording quality. (**Prestige LP 196**)

WEDNESDAY 24 AUGUST 1955

Miles Davis is placed equal first with Dizzy Gillespie in the trumpet section of the *Down Beat* Critics Poll.

HUR	**1**
RI	**2**
AT	**3**
UN	**4**
ON	**5**
JES	**6**
ED	**7**
HUR	**8**
RI	**9**
AT	**10**
UN	**11**
ON	**12**
JES	**13**
ED	**14**
HUR	**15**
RI	**16**
AT	**17**
UN	**18**
ON	**19**
JES	**20**
ED	**21**
HUR	**22**
RI	**23**
AT	**24**
UN	**25**
ON	**26**
JES	**27**
ED	**28**
HUR	**29**
RI	**30**

SEPTEMBER 1955

Sonny Rollins signs himself into Lexington to try to kick his drug habit. Miles hires John Gilmore from Sun Ra's Arkestra as a replacement, but he doesn't work out.

MONDAY 5 SEPTEMBER 1955

The Miles Davis Quintet, with John Gilmore on tenor saxophone, opens at the Blue Note in Philadelphia for a one-week engagement.

SATURDAY 10 SEPTEMBER 1955

The Miles Davis Quintet closes at the Blue Note in Philadelphia.

MONDAY 26 SEPTEMBER 1955

Philly Joe Jones telephones John Coltrane and tells him to join the band in Baltimore the next day.

TUESDAY 27 SEPTEMBER 1955

The classic Miles Davis Quintet with Miles Davis (trumpet), John Coltrane (tenor sax), Red Garland (piano), Paul Chambers (bass) and Philly Joe Jones (drums) make their debut at Club Las Vegas in Baltimore where they open a one-week engagement.

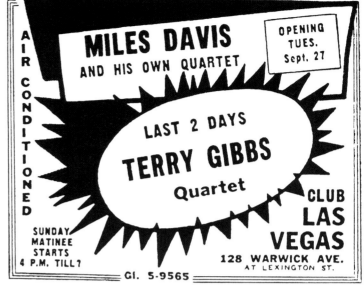

MILES DAVIS   JOHN COLTRANE

RED GARLAND   PAUL CHAMBERS   PHILLY JOE JONES

THE CLASSIC **MILES DAVIS** QUINTET

SAT	**1**
SUN	**2**
MON	**3**
TUES	**4**
WED	**5**
THUR	**6**
FRI	**7**
SAT	**8**
SUN	**9**
MON	**10**
TUES	**11**
WED	**12**
THUR	**13**
FRI	**14**
SAT	**15**
SUN	**16**
MON	**17**
TUES	**18**
WED	**19**
THUR	**20**
FRI	**21**
SAT	**22**
SUN	**23**
MON	**24**
TUES	**25**
WED	**26**
THUR	**27**
FRI	**28**
SAT	**29**
SUN	**30**
MON	**31**

SUNDAY 2 OCTOBER 1955
The Miles Davis Quintet close at Club Las Vegas in Baltimore.

MONDAY 3 OCTOBER 1955
Naima Grubbs travels to Baltimore and she and John Coltrane are married.

WEDNESDAY 5 OCTOBER 1955
The Miles Davis Quintet open a one-week engagement in Detroit.

MONDAY 10 OCTOBER 1955
The Miles Davis Quintet close in Detroit.

THURSDAY 13 OCTOBER 1955
The Miles Davis Quintet open a two-week engagement at Birdland in New York City. Jeri Southern and the Terry Gibbs Quartet are also on the bill. Nat Hentoff reviews the show in *Down Beat*:

Jeri Southern, Miles Davis, Terry Gibbs; Birdland, NYC

Jeri Southern's first Birdland appearance in six years was as welcome as a warm, sunny day in the dead of winter. It is the largely indescribable quality of personality that is Jeri's primary power. She comes through as a girl who feels music sensitively and who doesn't dig distorting it for quick commercial gain. Equally effective is her sound, and her attention to lyrics so that there is no mistaking the story contours of each song.

There are very few singers like Jeri who make it equally well at Birdland and the Blue Angel and still remain uniquely themselves. Her choice of numbers is uniformly intelligent and apt for her particular style with a song. On one set, she caressed *You'd Better Go Now*, moved into a darkly effective *Black Is the Colour of My True Love's Hair*, then jumped lightly through *This Can't Be Love, Something I Dreamed Last Night* and *Something Wonderful* created other moods, chiefly a marked reluctance on the part of the audience to hear the set end.

Miles Davis' band made for a generally effective complementary billing with Jeri. Miles himself had not played as consistently and strongly in a New York club in some time, but the band as a whole is not cohesive yet.

Terry Gibbs' quartet was the third unit on the bill, and swung all the way with bassist Herman Wright, drummer Jerry Segal, and the attractive—and always moving—Terry Pollard. Gibbs himself so obviously enjoys playing that he communicates much of that enjoyment to the audience.

All in all, this was as good a bill as Birdland has had in some time—always excepting, of course, Count Basie.

SATURDAY 15 OCTOBER 1955
Miles appears at an 8.30pm concert at Carnegie Hall for the benefit of Israel's Red Cross.

WEDNESDAY 26 OCTOBER 1955
The Miles Davis Quintet close at Birdland in New York City.

THURSDAY 27 OCTOBER 1955
The Miles Davis Quintet open a two-week engagement at Café Bohemia in New York City.

AT **1**

UN **2**

MON **3**

UES **4**

WED **5**

THUR **6**

RI **7**

AT **8**

UN **9**

MON **10**

UES **11**

WED **12**

THUR **13**

RI **14**

AT **15**

UN **16**

MON **17**

UES **18**

WED **19**

THUR **20**

RI **21**

AT **22**

UN **23**

MON **24**

UES **25**

WED **26**

THUR **27**

RI **28**

AT **29**

UN **30**

MON **31**

Below: Miles on stage at Birdland.

SAT	**1**
SUN	**2**
MON	**3**
TUES	**4**
WED	**5**
THUR	**6**
FRI	**7**
SAT	**8**
SUN	**9**
MON	**10**
TUES	**11**
WED	**12**
THUR	**13**
FRI	**14**
SAT	**15**
SUN	**16**
MON	**17**
TUES	**18**
WED	**19**
THUR	**20**
FRI	**21**
SAT	**22**
SUN	**23**
MON	**24**
TUES	**25**
WED	**26**
THUR	**27**
FRI	**28**
SAT	**29**
SUN	**30**
MON	**31**

THURSDAY 27 OCTOBER 1955
Recording session by the Miles Davis Quintet for Columbia at their studio at 799 Seventh Avenue in New York City. The producer is Teo Macero.
MILES DAVIS (trumpet), JOHN COLTRANE (tenor sax), RED GARLAND (piano), PAUL CHAMBERS (bass), PHILLY JOE JONES (drums)
Two Bass Hit (5 takes) / *Ah-Leu-Cha* (5 takes) / *Billy Boy* (MD, JC out, 3 takes) / *Little Melonae* (4 takes) / *Budo* (6 takes)
All the issued tracks are edited from the various takes.

This is Miles' first recording session for Columbia who have persuaded Miles to sign with them, despite having a year to run on his Prestige contract. A deal is worked out whereby Columbia can begin recording Miles but are unable to release the recordings until after the completion of his contractual obligations to Prestige, which calls for four more albums.
George Avakian, Columbia's jazz producer, is a regular in the audience at Café Bohemia during the quintet's engagement.

WEDNESDAY 2 NOVEMBER 1955

Miles and his comeback is the subject of a long *Down Beat* article by Nat Hentoff.

miles

A Trumpeter In The Midst Of A Big
Comeback Makes A Very Frank
Appraisal Of Today's Jazz Scene

By Nat Hentoff

NOVEMBER 2, 1955

The same issue also contains a review of Miles' latest record release:

MILES DAVIS: The Musings of Miles
Will You Still be Mine?; I See Your Face Before Me; I Didn't; A Gal in Calico; A Night in Tunisia; Green Haze

Rating: *****

Miles' first 12" LP enlists the aid of bassist Oscar Pettiford, Philadelphia pianist Red Garland, and drummer Philly Jo Jones. The two originals, both by Miles, are sparely built but intriguing. Pettiford is solid; Jones has a lot of fire along with taste and works very well behind Miles; Garland is good but has a frequently idle left hand on middle and up tempos that thereby takes a dimension away from most of his choruses. Miles is fine, and plays with so much heart and intelligently original conception that he's consistently cooking. Dig, for example, his simple lyrically effective muted work on *Face*, the way he renews *Tunisia*, and the blues-deep warmth of his horn in *Haze*. Good, informative notes by Ira Gitler. **(Prestige 12" LP 7007)**

AFTER A TIME of confusion and what appeared to be a whirlpool of troubles, Miles Davis is moving rapidly again toward the forefront of the modern jazz scene. He has just signed a contract guaranteeing him 20 weeks a year in Birdland. He has been added to the three-and-a-half-week all-star Birdland tour that begins Feb. 5, and there are reports—at present unconfirmed and denied by Prestige—that Miles may leave Prestige for one of the major record companies.

Miles already had shown clearly this year how important a jazz voice he still is by his July performance at the Newport festival, a performance that caused Jack Tracy to write: "Miles played thrillingly and indicated that his comeback is in full stride." A few weeks later, Miles surprised the international jazz audience by tying Dizzy for first place in the *Down Beat* Critics' poll.

......

SO MILES is now in the most advantageous position of his career thus far. He has the bookings, the record outlet, and he has the group that he's been eager to assemble for some months. As of this writing, on drums there's Philly Joe Jones, described by Miles as "the best drummer around today." On bass is the young Detroit musician, Paul Chambers, who's recently been working with George Wallington at the Bohemia and of whose ability Miles says only "Whew! He really drives a band. He never stops." On piano is Red Garland from Philadelphia. The tenor is Sonny Rollins, for whom Miles has deep respect. Miles has been trying to convince Sonny to leave Chicago and go on the road with him and finally, to Miles' great delight, he has succeeded.

"I want this group," says Miles, "to sound the way Sonny plays, the way all of the men in it play individually—different from anyone else in jazz today. We've got that quality individually; now we have to work on getting the group to sound that way collectively. As we get to work regularly, something will form up and we'll get a style."

WEDNESDAY 9 NOVEMBER 1955

Charlie Mingus, concerned by Miles' attitude as expressed in a couple of *Down Beat* articles, writes an open letter to Miles which is published in *Down Beat*.

An Open Letter

From Charlie Mingus

To Miles Davis

Parker and Monk

. . . With Love . . .

FOUR EDITIONS of *Down Beat* come to my mind's eye—Bird's *Blindfold Test*, mine, Miles', and Miles' recent "comeback story" as I sit down and attempt to honestly write my thoughts in an open letter to Miles Davis. (I discarded numerous "mental" letters before this writing, but one final letter formed last night as I looked through some pictures of Bird that Bob Parent had taken at a Village session.) If a picture needs to go with this story, it should be this picture of Bird, standing and looking down at Monk with more love than I think we'll ever find in this jazz business!

Jazz wasn't a business with Bird. That's probably why his scope could be so broad as to dig Monk, as I do, and even to dig the way Mingus writes presently. Perhaps even Teo. Some cats seem so hungry to make money with what they call jazz that they're scratching at those few eyes that focus on the least likely subjects—and this doesn't exclude some of our jazz critics. But back to the subject.

Bird's love, so warmly obvious in this picture, was again demonstrated in his *Blindfold Test*. But dig my own *Blindfold Test!* See what I mean? And more recently, dig Miles' comeback story. How is Miles going to act when he *gets* back and gets going again? Will it be like a gig in Brooklyn not too long ago with Max, Monk, and me when he kept telling Monk to "lay out" because his chords were all wrong? Or even at a more recent record date when he cursed, laid out, argued, and threatened Monk and asked Bob Weinstock why he hired such a nonmusician and would Monk lay out on his trumpet solos? What's happening to us disciples of Bird? Or would Miles think I'm presuming too much to include myself as one?

IT SEEMS SO HARD for some of us to grow up mentally just enough to realize that there are other persons of flesh and bone, just like us, on this great, big earth. And if they don't even stand still, move, or "swing," they are as right as we are, even if they are as wrong as hell by our standards. Yes, Miles, I am apologizing for my stupid *Blindfold Test*. I can do it gladly because I'm learning a little something. No matter how much they try to say that Brubeck doesn't swing—or whatever else they're stewing or whoever else they're brewing—it's factually unimportant.

Not because Dave made *Time* magazine—and a dollar—but mainly because Dave honestly thinks he's swinging. He feels a certain pulse and plays a certain pulse which gives him pleasure and a sense of exaltation because he's sincerely doing something the way

he, Dave Brubeck, feels like doing it. And as you said in your story, Miles, "if a guy makes you pat your foot, and if you feel it down your back, etc.," then Dave is the swingingest *by your own definition*, Miles, because at Newport and elsewhere Dave had the whole house patting its feet and even clapping its hands.

Incidentally, since Duke Ellington has conducted several compositions without tempo, music to which it is not possible to pat your foot except by following his baton out of tempo, would you say, Miles, that Duke was not playing jazz on these compositions? Or is it safe for me to wager that foot-patting Miles digs Duke's invisible foot-patting music in a nonjazzical ad lib sense? The lack of foot-patting *should* make Duke kick less for us, according to your definition of swing. But I believe that foot-*patable* or footless, Duke's music, with or without tempo, manages to get down Miles' back and ring jazz bells for him. Just like Duke, Bartok, Schoenberg, or Bird ring other bells for me.

I KNOW MILES and his cult of self-esteemed creators, who are convinced of their clan's mystical powers of secret formula swinging, and they're cool as long as they are together to pat each other on the back. These self-appointed prophets should get together and lead the way as they miss those couple notes Miles speaks of while trying not to play the same old cliches, a fault that all but Bird is guilty of in the past era. Let them pave the way for whoever will follow.

Dave is content. So are Tristano, Duke, Max, etc.—and me, too. Miles' explorers would be very important to jazz if they all missed in the same places, and more important to new development in counterpoint when and if they missed in different places and remembered to do it the same place on the same tune. And especially if it all happened on a Thursday night at 1:15 a.m. at Minton's and for no reason at all.

Miles, don't you remember that *Mingus Fingers* was written in 1945 when I was a youngster, 22 years of age, who was studying and doing his damndest to write in the Ellington tradition? Miles, that was 10 years ago when I weighed 185. Those clothes are worn and don't fit me any more. I'm a man; I weigh 215; I think my *own way*. I don't think like you and my music isn't meant just for the patting of feet and going down backs. When and if I feel gay and carefree, I write or play that way. When I feel angry I write or play that way—or when I'm happy, or depressed, *even*.

JUST BECAUSE I'm playing jazz I don't forget about *me*. I play or write *me*, the way I feel, through jazz, er whatever. Music is, or was, a language of the emotions. If someone has been escaping reality, I don't expect him to dig my music, and I would begin to worry about my writing if such a person began to really like it. My music is alive and it's about the living and the dead, about good and evil. It's angry, yet it's real because it *knows* it's angry.

I know you're making a comeback, Miles, and I'm with you more than you know. You're playing the greatest *Miles* I've ever heard, and I'm sure you already know that you're one of America's truly great jazz stylists. You're often fresh in a creative sense and, if anything, you underevaluate yourself—on the outside—and so with other associates in the art. Truly, Miles, I love you and want you to know you're needed here, but you're too important a person in jazz to be less than extra careful about what you say about other musicians who are *also trying* to create.

Too many people believe everything you say, so be sure you're saying what you really mean. You can check that by saying it personally to the musician in question to see how it will feel in print. Go easy on those stepping stones on your way to the highest mountain peak. You might step on as many people as I did, and you're starting a little late—in years. So, easy! It's a long trip back from even a tiny hill once you think yourself there.

REMEMBER ME, MILES? I'm Charles. Yeah, Mingus! You read third trumpet on my California record dates 11 years ago on the recommendation of Lucky Thompson. So easy, young man. Easy on those stepping stones.

When I played at Newport, you came near the very end of the concert. You couldn't have heard any of my music as it was played in the first half of our concert. Except for *Non-Sectarian*, which was the closing number and was a piece written to be conducted by a

drummer's baton, instead of a patting foot on a bass drum with an equally loud foot-patted sock cymbal. As I reloud here, it was chosen last by the member, it was chosen last by the musicians, who wanted to leave it as a parting thought to the audience. And if the composition wasn't good, then don't worry about my ability to fool all the people who seemed to enjoy it, if fooling is what you think I'm doing—or Teo, either, for that matter, who didn't win all those scholarships by *fooling* anybody.

If you should get around to answering this open letter, Miles, there is one thing I would like to know concerning what you said to Nat Hentoff about all the tunes you've recorded in the last two years. Why did you continue to record, session after session, when you now say you don't like them except for two LPs? I wonder if you forgot the names of *those* tunes; also, how a true artist can allow all this music, which even he himself doesn't like, to be sold to the jazz public. Or even accept payment for a job which you yourself say wasn't well done.

You blithely put down California cats for copying New York cliches and for playing "too clean," but the really bad thing was commenting on music that you never heard—mine and Teo's. You really should listen to *Eulogy for Rudy Williams*, or Thad Jones playing my composition, *Portrait*, with strings, or Teo's *Abstractions*.

Good luck on your comeback, Miles.

Forbes, Thornhill Go To Anthony

New York—Don Forbes, singer with the Les Elgart orchestra who has been making a splash in band singing ranks of late, is leaving Elgart to work as a single. Fred Benson, of Ray Anthony Enterprises, signed the singer to a managerial pact.

Also joining the Anthony ranks is Claude Thornhill, whose band is being reactivated for nationwide tours. At presstime, it looked as if Thornhill would be added to the long list of bands now recording for Capitol.

Readers' Help Asked By Parker Biographer

New York—Bob Reisner, jazz lecturer and curator of the Institute of Jazz Studies, is writing a Charlie Parker biography, for which he would be most happy to receive any material. Anyone having information on Bird can write to Reisner at 135 W. 16th St., New York, N. Y.

November 30, 1955

UES	**1**
VED	**2**
HUR	**3**
RI	**4**
AT	**5**
UN	**6**
MON	**7**
UES	**8**
VED	**9**
HUR	**10**
RI	**11**
AT	**12**
UN	**13**
MON	**14**
UES	**15**
VED	**16**
HUR	**17**
RI	**18**
AT	**19**
UN	**20**
MON	**21**
UES	**22**
VED	**23**
HUR	**24**
RI	**25**
AT	**26**
UN	**27**
MON	**28**
UES	**29**
VED	**30**

WEDNESDAY 9 NOVEMBER 1955

The Miles Davis Quintet close at Café Bohemia in New York City.

WEDNESDAY 16 NOVEMBER 1955

Recording session by the Miles Davis Quintet for Prestige at Rudy Van Gelder's Studio in Hackensack, New Jersey.

MILES DAVIS (trumpet), JOHN COLTRANE (tenor sax), RED GARLAND (piano), PAUL CHAMBERS (bass), PHILLY JOE JONES (drums)

Stablemates / How Am I To Know? / Just Squeeze Me / There Is No Greater Love (JC out) / *Miles' Theme / S'posin'*

These recordings are issued as *Miles* on Prestige LP 7014.

FRIDAY 18 NOVEMBER 1955

The Miles Davis Quintet open at Basin Street in New York City for a two-night engagement. Also on the bill are the Erroll Garner Trio, Johnny Smith Quartet and singer Beverly Kenny.

During opening night, the quintet appear live on a TV broadcast from the Basin Street Club, *The Steve Allen Tonight Show*:

MILES DAVIS (trumpet), JOHN COLTRANE (tenor sax), RED GARLAND (piano), PAUL CHAMBERS (bass), PHILLY JOE JONES (drums), STEVE ALLEN (announcer/interviewer)

announcement / *Max Is Making Wax* / interview / *It Never Entered My Mind*

SATURDAY 19 NOVEMBER 1955

The Miles Davis Quintet close at Basin Street in New York City.

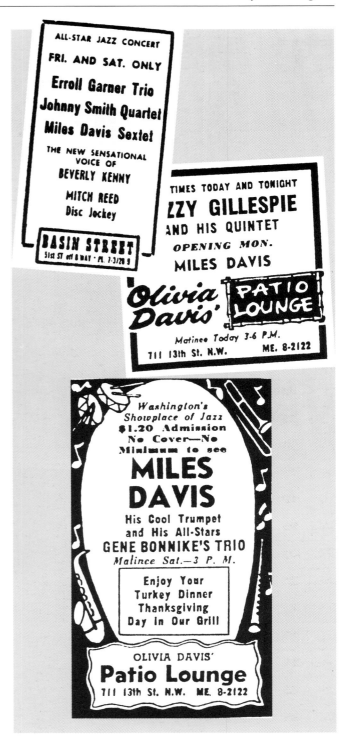

MONDAY 21 NOVEMBER 1955

The Miles Davis Quintet open at Olivia Davis' Patio Lounge in Washington, D.C. for a one-week engagement.

SUNDAY 27 NOVEMBER 1955

The Miles Davis Quintet close at Olivia Davis' Patio Lounge in Washington, D.C.

THUR	**1**
FRI	**2**
SAT	**3**
SUN	**4**
MON	**5**
TUES	**6**
WED	**7**
THUR	**8**
FRI	**9**
SAT	**10**
SUN	**11**
MON	**12**
TUES	**13**
WED	**14**
THUR	**15**
FRI	**16**
SAT	**17**
SUN	**18**
MON	**19**
TUES	**20**
WED	**21**
THUR	**22**
FRI	**23**
SAT	**24**
SUN	**25**
MON	**26**
TUES	**27**
WED	**28**
THUR	**29**
FRI	**30**
SAT	**31**

MONDAY 5 DECEMBER 1955
The Miles Davis Quintet opens at the Blue Note in Philadelphia for a one-week engagement.

THURSDAY 8 DECEMBER 1955
The Miles Davis Quintet broadcast from the Blue Note Club in Philadelphia.
MILES DAVIS (trumpet), JOHN COLTRANE (tenor sax), RED GARLAND (piano), PAUL CHAMBERS (bass), PHILLY JOE JONES (drums)
Tune Up / Walkin'

SATURDAY 10 DECEMBER 1955
The Miles Davis Quintet closes at the Blue Note in Philadelphia.

WEDNESDAY 21 DECEMBER 1955
The Miles Davis Quintet open at Birdland (formerly the Beige Room) in the Pershing Hotel in Chicago for a two-week engagement.

TODAY—AS FOR OVER A HUNDRED YEARS...

The best play Besson!

MILES DAVIS
Hear the great Prestige LP
"THE MUSINGS OF MILES"

For over one hundred years
Besson (Paris) and Besson (London) brasses
have been acclaimed by the world's foremost
artists as the ultimate in quality and performance.
Ask your favorite artist or dealer to
tell you the Besson story today!

UN	1	WED	1
MON	2	THUR	2
UES	3	FRI	3
VED	4	SAT	4
HUR	5	SUN	5
RI	6	MON	6
AT	7	TUES	7
UN	8	WED	8
MON	9	THUR	9
UES	10	FRI	10
VED	11	SAT	11
HUR	12	SUN	12
RI	13	MON	13
AT	14	TUES	14
UN	15	WED	15
MON	16	THUR	16
UES	17	FRI	17
VED	18	SAT	18
HUR	19	SUN	19
RI	20	MON	20
AT	21	TUES	21
UN	22	WED	22
MON	23	THUR	23
UES	24	FRI	24
VED	25	SAT	25
HUR	26	SUN	26
RI	27	MON	27
AT	28	TUES	28
UN	29	WED	29
MON	30		
UES	31		

TUESDAY 3 JANUARY 1956

The Miles Davis Quintet close at Birdland in Chicago.

FRIDAY 6 JANUARY 1956

The Miles Davis Quintet open at Jazz City in Los Angeles for a two-week engagement.

THURSDAY 19 JANUARY 1956

The Miles Davis Quintet close at Jazz City in Los Angeles.

TUESDAY 24 JANUARY 1956

The Miles Davis Quintet open at the Blackhawk in San Francisco for a two-week engagement.

SUNDAY 5 FEBRUARY 1956

The Miles Davis Quintet close at the Blackhawk in San Francisco.

After the Blackhawk engagement Miles and the quintet drive back to Los Angeles for a return engagement at Jazz City.

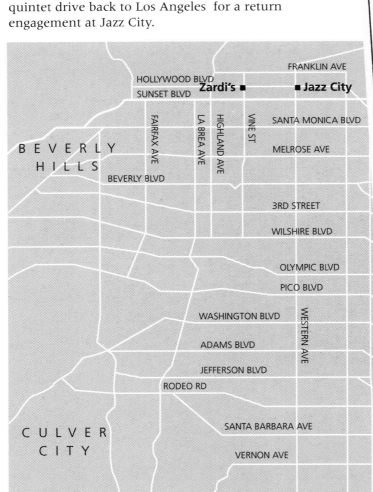

THUR	1	SUN	1
FRI	2	MON	2
SAT	3	TUES	3
SUN	4	WED	4
MON	5	THUR	5
TUES	6	FRI	6
WED	7	SAT	7
THUR	8	SUN	8
FRI	9	MON	9
SAT	10	TUES	10
SUN	11	WED	11
MON	12	THUR	12
TUES	13	FRI	13
WED	14	SAT	14
THUR	15	SUN	15
FRI	16	MON	16
SAT	17	TUES	17
SUN	18	WED	18
MON	19	THUR	19
TUES	20	FRI	20
WED	21	SAT	21
THUR	22	SUN	22
FRI	23	MON	23
SAT	24	TUES	24
SUN	25	WED	25
MON	26	THUR	26
TUES	27	FRI	27
WED	28	SAT	28
THUR	29	SUN	29
FRI	30	MON	30
SAT	31		

THURSDAY 1 MARCH 1956
or FRIDAY 2 MARCH 1956

Paul Chambers, John Coltrane and Philly Joe Jones, along with Kenny Drew (piano) record for Jazz West in Los Angeles. The recordings are issued under Paul Chamber's name as *Chamber's Music*.

WEDNESDAY 7 MARCH 1956

The Miles Davis Quintet open at Birdland in the Pershing Hotel in Chicago for a one-week engagement. The club is being sued by Birdland in New York and, after a brief period as Chicago's ? Show Lounge, changes its name to Budland.

FRIDAY 16 MARCH 1956

Recording session by the Miles Davis All Stars for Prestige at Rudy Van Gelder's studio in Hackensack, New Jersey.
MILES DAVIS (trumpet), SONNY ROLLINS (tenor sax), TOMMY FLANAGAN (piano), PAUL CHAMBERS (bass), ART TAYLOR (drums)
In Your Own Sweet Way / No Line / Vierd Blues
The recordings are paired with the 30 January 1953 session and issued by Prestige as *Collectors' Items* on LP 7044.

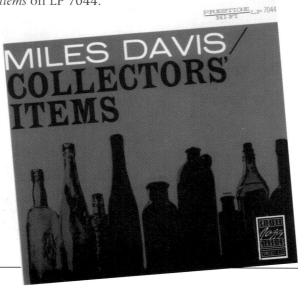

TUESDAY 27 MARCH 1956

The Miles Davis Quintet close at Birdland in th Pershing Hotel in Chicago.

MONDAY 9 APRIL 1956

The Miles Davis Quintet open at the Oyster Barrel in Quebec for a one-week engagement.

SUNDAY 15 APRIL 1956

The Miles Davis Quintet close at the Oyster Barrel in Quebec.

MONDAY 16 APRIL 1956

The Miles Davis Quintet open at Storyville in Boston for a one-week engagement.

FRIDAY 20 APRIL 1956

Paul Chambers, John Coltrane and Philly Joe Jones, along with Pepper Adams, Curtis Fuller and Roland Alexander record for Transition Records in Boston. The recordings are issued as *Jazz In Transition*. In the evening Chambers, Coltrane and Jones rejoin the Miles Davis Quintet at Storyville in Boston.

SUNDAY 22 APRIL 1956

The Miles Davis Quintet close at Storyville in Boston.

THURSDAY 3 MAY 1956

The Miles Davis Quintet open at Café Bohemia in New York City for a one-week engagement opposite Charles Mingus' Jazz Workshop.

MONDAY 7 MAY 1956

Paul Chambers, John Coltrane and Philly Joe Jones record with the Elmo Hope Sextet for Prestige at Rudy Van Gelder's Studio in Hackensack, New Jersey. Also on the session are Donald Byrd, Hank Mobley and Elmo Hope. The recordings are issued as *Informal Jazz.*

WEDNESDAY 9 MAY 1956

The Miles Davis Quintet close at Café Bohemia in New York City.

FRIDAY 11 MAY 1956

Recording session by the Miles Davis Quintet for Prestige in Hackensack, New Jersey.
MILES DAVIS (trumpet), JOHN COLTRANE (tenor sax), RED GARLAND (piano), PAUL CHAMBERS (bass), PHILLY JOE JONES (drums)
In Your Own Sweet Way / Diane / Trane's Blues / Something I Dreamed Last Night (JC out) / *It Could Happen To You / Woody'n You / Ahmad's Blues* (MD, JC out) / *The Surrey With The Fringe On Top / It Never Entered My Mind / When I Fall In Love* (JC out) / *Salt Peanuts / Four / The Theme I / The Theme II*
These recordings are issued on 3 LPs – *Workin'* (Prestige LP 7166), *Steamin'* (Prestige LP 7200) and *Relaxin'* (Prestige LP 7129).

THURSDAY 24 MAY 1956

John Coltrane, Red Garland, Paul Chambers and Philly Joe Jones record with Sonny Rollins for Prestige at Rudy Van Gelder's Studio in Hackensack, New Jersey. The recordings are issued as *Tenor Madness* by the Sonny Rollins Quartet + John Coltrane.

FRIDAY 25 MAY 1956

The Miles Davis Quintet open at Café Bohemia.

SATURDAY 26 MAY 1956

Miles' 30th birthday.

WEDNESDAY 30 MAY 1956

Down Beat reviews Miles' latest album release:

The New Miles Davis Quintet
Squeeze Me; There Is No Greater Love; How Am I To Know?; S'posin'; The Theme; Stablemates
Rating:****
The New Miles Davis Quintet is the unit with which he's been travelling for several months — tenor John Coltrane, pianist Red Garland, bassist Paul Chambers, and drummer Philly Joe Jones. Miles is in wonderfully cohesive form here, blowing with characteristically personal, eggshell tone, muted on the standards, open on the originals. And he continues to grow in his searching quality of being able to get so inside a song that he makes it fit him as if to order without injuring the essence of the work as first written. Coltrane, as Ira Gitler notes accurately, "is a mixture of Dexter Gordon, Sonny Rollins, and Sonny Stitt." But so far there's very little Coltrane. His general lack of individuality lowers the rating.

Garland plays some of his best choruses on record here, combining imaginative sensitivity with relaxed light-fingered swing. Chambers lays down a support that could carry an army band. His tone is full and never flabby and his time is right. He has only one solo, a building one on *The Theme*. His bass is somewhat over-recorded in places.

Philly Joe is pulsatingly crisp as usual, and has apparently curbed a previous tendency to play too loudly too often. The last, uniquely attractive original, is by Philadelphian Benny Golson. A very good set, particularly worth absorbing for Miles. He himself deserves five.
(Prestige 12" LP 7014)

FRI	1	SUN	1
SAT	2	MON	2
SUN	3	TUES	3
MON	4	WED	4
TUES	5	THUR	5
WED	6	FRI	6
THUR	7	SAT	7
FRI	8	SUN	8
SAT	9	MON	9
SUN	10	TUES	10
MON	11	WED	11
TUES	12	THUR	12
WED	13	FRI	13
THUR	14	SAT	14
FRI	15	SUN	15
SAT	16	MON	16
SUN	17	TUES	17
MON	18	WED	18
TUES	19	THUR	19
WED	20	FRI	20
THUR	21	SAT	21
FRI	22	SUN	22
SAT	23	MON	23
SUN	24	TUES	24
MON	25	WED	25
TUES	26	THUR	26
WED	27	FRI	27
THUR	28	SAT	28
FRI	29	SUN	29
SAT	30	MON	30
		TUES	31

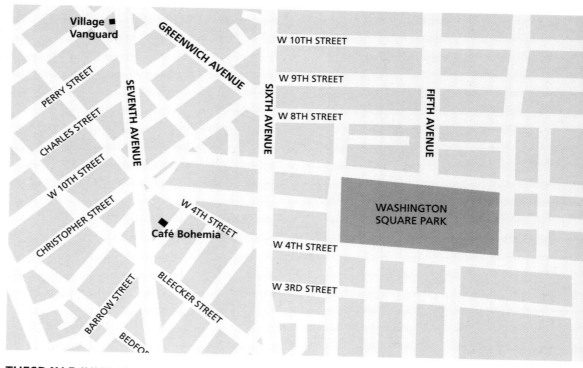

TUESDAY 5 JUNE 1956

Recording session by the Miles Davis Quintet for Columbia at the 30th Street Studios in New York City.
MILES DAVIS (trumpet), JOHN COLTRANE (tenor sax), RED GARLAND (piano), PAUL CHAMBERS (bass), PHILLY JOE JONES (drums)
Dear Old Stockholm (6 takes) / *Bye Bye Blackbird* (3 takes) / *Tadd's Delight* (5 takes)

SUNDAY 10 JUNE 1956

The Miles Davis Quintet close at Café Bohemia in New York City.

TUESDAY 19 JUNE 1956

The Miles Davis Quintet open at the Crown Propeller in Chicago for a three-week engagement.

CROWN PROPELLER 868 E. 63RD ST.
NOW PLAYING
MILES DAVIS And Band
PAULA GREER

CLIFFORD BROWN 1930–1956

TUESDAY 26 JUNE 1956

Clifford Brown and Richie Powell of the Clifford Brown-Max Roach Quintet are killed in an auto crash.

SATURDAY 7 JULY 1956

The Miles Davis Quintet close at the Crown Propeller in Chicago.

FRIDAY 13 JULY 1956

The Miles Davis Quintet open at Peacock Alley in St Louis for a 9-day engagement.

SATURDAY 21 JULY 1956

The Miles Davis Quintet close at Peacock Alley in St Louis.

VED	**1**	SAT	**1**
HUR	**2**	SUN	**2**
RI	**3**	MON	**3**
AT	**4**	TUES	**4**
UN	**5**	WED	**5**
MON	**6**	THUR	**6**
UES	**7**	FRI	**7**
VED	**8**	SAT	**8**
HUR	**9**	SUN	**9**
RI	**10**	MON	**10**
AT	**11**	TUES	**11**
UN	**12**	WED	**12**
MON	**13**	THUR	**13**
UES	**14**	FRI	**14**
VED	**15**	SAT	**15**
HUR	**16**	SUN	**16**
RI	**17**	MON	**17**
AT	**18**	TUES	**18**
UN	**19**	WED	**19**
MON	**20**	THUR	**20**
UES	**21**	FRI	**21**
VED	**22**	SAT	**22**
HUR	**23**	SUN	**23**
RI	**24**	MON	**24**
AT	**25**	TUES	**25**
UN	**26**	WED	**26**
MON	**27**	THUR	**27**
UES	**28**	FRI	**28**
VED	**29**	SAT	**29**
HUR	**30**	SUN	**30**
RI	**31**		

FRIDAY 17 AUGUST 1956

Red Garland and Paul Chambers, with Art Taylor on drums, record *A Garland of Red* (LP7064) for Prestige in New York City.

FRIDAY 31 AUGUST 1956

The Miles Davis Quintet open at Café Bohemia in New York City opposite Bud Powell for a four-week engagement.

FRIDAY 7 SEPTEMBER 1956

John Coltrane, Red Garland and Paul Chambers record *Tenor Conclave* for Prestige at Rudy Van Gelder's Studio in Hackensack, New Jersey. Al Cohn, Hank Mobley, Zoot Sims and Art Taylor are also on the session.

MONDAY 10 SEPTEMBER 1956

Recording session by the Miles Davis Quintet for Columbia at the 30th Street Studio in New York City.
MILES DAVIS (trumpet), JOHN COLTRANE (tenor sax), RED GARLAND (piano), PAUL CHAMBERS (bass), PHILLY JOE JONES (drums)
All Of You (3 takes) / *Sweet Sue, Just You* (8 takes) / *'Round Midnight*
All Of You and *Sweet Sue* are edits from various takes.
The recordings are issued as *Round About Midnight* on Columbia CL 949.

SATURDAY 15 SEPTEMBER 1956

The Miles Davis Quintet broadcast on Mutual's *Bandstand USA*, live from the Café Bohemia.
MILES DAVIS (trumpet), JOHN COLTRANE (tenor sax), RED GARLAND (piano), PAUL CHAMBERS (bass), PHILLY JOE JONES (drums)
Well, You Needn't / It Never Entered My Mind (JC out)

FRIDAY 21 SEPTEMBER 1956

John Coltrane, Paul Chambers and Philly Joe Jones record *Whims of Chambers* for Blue Note at Rudy Van Gelder's Studio in Hackensack, New Jersey. Donald Byrd, Horace Silver and Kenny Burrell are also on the session.

THURSDAY 27 SEPTEMBER 1956

The Miles Davis Quintet close at Café Bohemia in New York City.

MON	1
TUES	2
WED	3
THUR	4
FRI	5
SAT	6
SUN	7
MON	8
TUES	9
WED	10
THUR	11
FRI	12
SAT	13
SUN	14
MON	15
TUES	16
WED	17
THUR	18
FRI	19
SAT	20
SUN	21
MON	22
TUES	23
WED	24
THUR	25
FRI	26
SAT	27
SUN	28
MON	29
TUES	30
WED	31

MONDAY 1 OCTOBER 1956

The Miles Davis Quintet open at Storyville in Boston for a one-week engagement opposite the Australian Jazz Quintet.

SATURDAY 6 OCTOBER 1956

The Miles Davis Quintet broadcast on Mutual's *Bandstand USA*, live from Storyville in Boston.

SUNDAY 7 OCTOBER 1956

The Miles Davis Quintet close at Storyville in Boston.

MONDAY 15 OCTOBER 1956

The Miles Davis Quintet open at Café Bohemia in New York City for a two-week engagement opposite the Randy Weston Quartet.

During this engagement, Miles rows with Coltrane who leaves the band. Sonny Rollins fills in, but Miles relents and brings back Coltrane who plays alongside Rollins for a few nights. However, the arguments continue and, by the last few nights at the Bohemia, Rollins is the only saxophonist and Coltrane is back home in Philadelphia.

WEDNESDAY 17 OCTOBER 1956

Down Beat reviews Miles' latest album release:

MILES DAVIS
Dr Jackle; Bitty Ditty; Minor March; Changes
Rating: ****

A basic personnel of Miles, Milt Jackson, Percy Heath, Arthur Taylor, and pianist Ray Bryant becomes a sextet on the first and third tracks with altoist Jackie McLean. Both are his tunes. *Bitty* is by Thad Jones, and Bryant contributed *Changes*.

In contrast to many current sets that emphasize written frameworks and/or extended form, these conversations are in the tradition of improvised solo jazz with practically all the responsibility on the soloist, however fetching be the starting lines and sequence of changes.

Bags' statements are as close to "pure" elemental jazz as the Hot 5 Louis. Nothing he plays is extraneous or self-consciously rhetorical; it's all part of the swinging marrow of his jazz self-expression. Miles, more reflective, is less abandoned than Bags but no less hot-from-the-inside. McLean has the least solo space, and blows what he has with jagged warmth.

Bryant is impressive here, playing with logic, imagination, heat, and force. Rhythm section is steady. Bags is fine all the way through; Miles flows particularly in his muted solo in the oddly melancholy *Changes*, but also has intense personal reflections of value elsewhere. A no-frills, this-is-my-story collection, the LP is recommended. (**Prestige 12" LP 7034**)

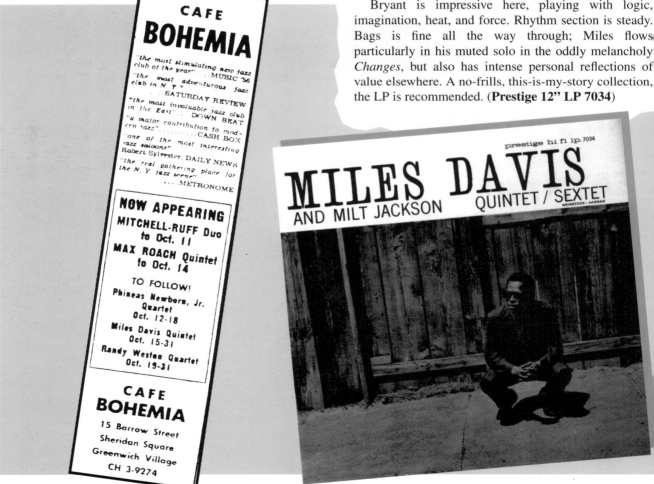

SATURDAY 20 OCTOBER 1956

Miles is principal soloist in a recording session by the Brass Ensemble of the Jazz and Classical Music Society for Columbia in New York City.

MILES DAVIS, BERNIE GLOW, ARTHUR STRUTTER, JOE WILDER (trumpet), JIM BUFFINGTON (french horn), URBIE GREEN, J. J. JOHNSON (trombone), MILT HINTON (bass), OSIE JOHNSON (drums), DICK HOROWITZ (percussion), JOHN LEWIS (composer/arranger), GUNTHER SCHULLER (conductor)

Three Little Feelings

TUESDAY 23 OCTOBER 1956

Miles is principal soloist in a recording session by the Brass Ensemble of the Jazz and Classical Music Society for Columbia in New York City.

MILES DAVIS, (flugelhorn), BERNIE GLOW, ARTHUR STRUTTER, JOE WILDER (trumpet), JIM BUFFINGTON (french horn), URBIE GREEN, J. J. JOHNSON (trombone), MILT HINTON (bass), OSIE JOHNSON (drums), J. J. JOHNSON (composer/arranger), GUNTHER SCHULLER (conductor)

Jazz Suite For Brass

FRIDAY 26 OCTOBER 1956

Recording session by the Miles Davis Quintet for Prestige at Rudy Van Gelder's Studio in Hackensack, New Jersey.

MILES DAVIS (trumpet), JOHN COLTRANE (tenor sax), RED GARLAND (piano), PAUL CHAMBERS (bass), PHILLY JOE JONES (drums)

If I Were A Bell / Well You Needn't / 'Round About Midnight / Half Nelson / You're My Everything / I Could Write A Book / Oleo / Airegin / Tune Up / When Lights Are Low / Blues By Five / My Funny Valentine (JC out)

This is the second of two marathon sessions for Prestige and completes Miles' contract with the company. Four LPs are issued over the next five years with the music from this session being used on *Cookin'* (LP 7094) and *Relaxin'* (LP 7129).

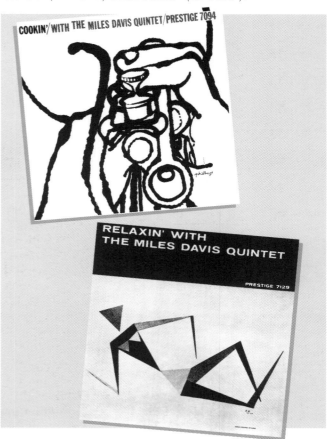

It seems likely that after this session John Coltrane returns to Philadelphia, leaving Sonny Rollins to play out the last two nights of the Café Bohemia engagement.

WEDNESDAY 31 OCTOBER 1956

The Miles Davis Quintet close at Café Bohemia in New York City. Miles dissolves the quintet and travels to Europe for a tour with the Birdland All Stars.

THUR	**1**
FRI	**2**
SAT	**3**
SUN	**4**
MON	**5**
TUES	**6**
WED	**7**
THUR	**8**
FRI	**9**
SAT	**10**
SUN	**11**
MON	**12**
TUES	**13**
WED	**14**
THUR	**15**
FRI	**16**
SAT	**17**
SUN	**18**
MON	**19**
TUES	**20**
WED	**21**
THUR	**22**
FRI	**23**
SAT	**24**
SUN	**25**
MON	**26**
TUES	**27**
WED	**28**
THUR	**29**
FRI	**30**

THURSDAY 1 NOVEMBER 1956

Miles arrives in Paris to join the Birdland All Stars.

English jazz writer Alun Morgan flies to Paris to hear Miles:

I flew over the day before and booked into a hotel in the Rue-des-Saintes Pères. About eleven that evening Tony Hall and I walked over to the Club St. Germain, pushed through the velvet curtain at the bottom of the stairs and saw Miles at the bar, a handsome young man of slight build wearing a smart grey suit. In the far corner of the room Don Byas was weaving his way through a ballad with Raymond Fol feeding chords, and Jean-Marie Ingrande marking time. Someone introduced us. "This is Alun Morgan, a jazz writer from England." Miles turned, his face expressionless. As he gripped my hand he looked at me with a wide-eyed, unwavering gaze. Suddenly his face broke into a quick, warm smile. "Hi, Alun."

Sitting there at the bar Miles was completely relaxed. He spoke slowly and with a deep, hoarse voice. A throat ailment had impaired his speech and for the same reason he wore a cravat instead of a tie. Few musicians like or want to talk about music but Miles answered questions with patience and courtesy. "You know that record of *Blue Room*, made in 1951, Miles? What happened there? Did you play piano and trumpet on that or what?" The trumpeter smiled. "Hell man, I was playing badly on that date. I was… you know." He made a gesture which clarified the point. I edged closer. "Have you heard of Al Haig recently? Someone told me he was in Miami." The grin again. "That cat's been *all* over. Canada and everywhere. I saw him in New York just before I left. He was talking with Dizzy. Maybe he's going to join the band." No, he couldn't extend his stay in Europe. No, he wouldn't be visiting London. "I've got to get back home after this tour. I've got four guys depending on me back there. I've got the best rhythm section in the world right now. Philly Joe Jones is just great and you know that Coltrane is the best since Bird." How much say did he have in the release of his records on Prestige? His eyes opened wider in apparent amazement. "I *could* go down to see Weinstock and throw a fit or something, but it usually works out okay."

The velvet curtains parted and admitted Milt Jackson, Connie Kay, Kenny Clarke, Percy Heath, Bud Powell and Bud's wife, Buttercup. Their delight at meeting Miles was obvious. "Hi, Dave." They pummelled each other good naturedly, arms were thrown around shoulders. Bud stood slightly apart and looked sad. The conversation flowed and laughter came easily. Later the hum of conversation was stilled. Someone said "Bud's going to play" in a kind of shocked half-whisper; there was Bud up on the stand with Pierre Michelot and Al Levitt. No one had noticed him leave the circle around the bar. All talking ceased as Bud went into a fast *Nice Work If You Can Get It* which began to degenerate into chaos before the end of the first chorus. A kind of paralysis seemed to have seized the pianist's hands and the more he tried to fight his way free the more inaccurate became his fingering. Four choruses and it was all over. Bud stood up quickly, bowed, mopped his face with a handkerchief and began his uncertain walk back to the bar. Half-way his interest became focused on a girl sitting at a table. He stopped and stared at her with a slightly puzzled smile. Time stood still in that hot, smoky atmosphere and it was an age before Buttercup led her husband back to the silent circle of embarrassed musicians. Miles broke the tension by flinging a comforting arm around Bud's shoulders. "You know man, you shouldn't try to play when you're juiced like that." Within a few minutes the room was normal. Byas was back on the stand and a French musician was amusing Miles with a story in between gusts of laughter. "So there we were, walking down the Champs Elysées smoking. You know, I mean *smoking*. And this gendarme…"

At about three the following morning Tony Hall, Stevie Wise (she's now Lady Listowel) and I were hurrying through the deserted streets to the Mars Club when we met Miles strolling along the pavement with Sinatra-like nonchalance. He hailed us. "Hey Stevie, where do I live?"

"Don't you know the name of your hotel?"

Miles considered. "No," he said slowly. "But wherever it is I'm in room 215", and he continued his nocturnal perambulation.

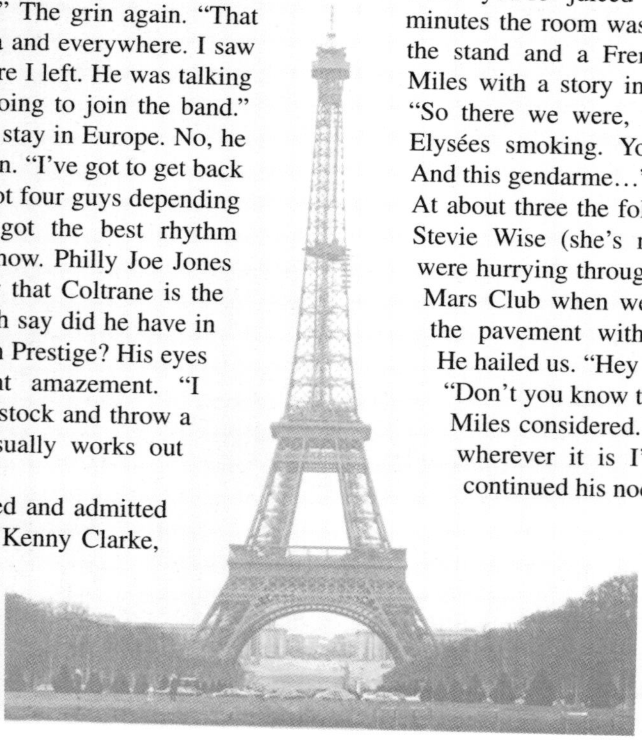

UR	1
	2
T	3
N	4
ON	5
ES	6
ED	7
UR	8
	9
T	10
N	11
ON	12
ES	13
ED	14
UR	15
	16
T	17
N	18
ON	19
ES	20
ED	21
UR	22
	23
T	24
N	25
ON	26
ES	27
ED	28
UR	29
	30

FRIDAY 2 NOVEMBER 1956

The Birdland All Stars in Europe tour gets underway with a reception at the American Embassy in Paris, followed by the opening concert at the Salle Pleyel. The cast includes Miles Davis, Lester Young, Bud Powell, the Modern Jazz Quartet and a French rhythm section. Miles plays four tunes at each of the two concerts backed by Rene Urtrégér (piano), Pierre Michelot (bass) and Christian Garros (drums). Miles renews his friendship with Juliette Greco and, after the concert, they visit the Club St Germain to see Don Byas.

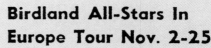

Birdland All-Stars In Europe Tour Nov. 2-25

New York—The Birdland All-Stars European tour begins Nov. 2 in Paris and ends Nov. 25 in Lyons. The cast includes the Modern Jazz Quartet, Miles Davis, Bud Powell, Lester Young, and a French rhythm section. Amsterdam, Brussels, Dusseldorf, Berlin, Mannheim, Frankfurt, Hamburg, Munich, and Freiburg will be visited until Nov. 12.

The Scandinavian countries will be covered from Nov. 13-18, while Zurich, Geneva, and Basel are on the schedule from Nov. 19-21. There are dates in Italy Nov. 22 and 23 and then the final two days in France.

Paris Bash Greets Birdland Troupe

Paris—The arrival of the touring Birdland '56 troupe with the Modern Jazz Quartet, Miles Davis, Bud Powell, and Lester Young was marked by an unprecedented reception at the Theatre de L'Ambassade. Organized and financed by the American embassy (William Weld, cultural attache) and arranged in conjunction with the L'Academie du Jazz, the event featured a concert by Le Jazz Group de Paris in honor of the visitors.

Andre Hodeir, music director of the Jazz Group de Paris, led his unit in *Jordu, Milano, Parisian Thoroughfare,* and his own *Paradoxe II.* Classical composer Georges Auric presented Oscars du Disque de Jazz awards to Milt Jackson and to John Lewis.

The two Birdland '56 concerts in Paris were so successful that a third was scheduled for Nov. 17.

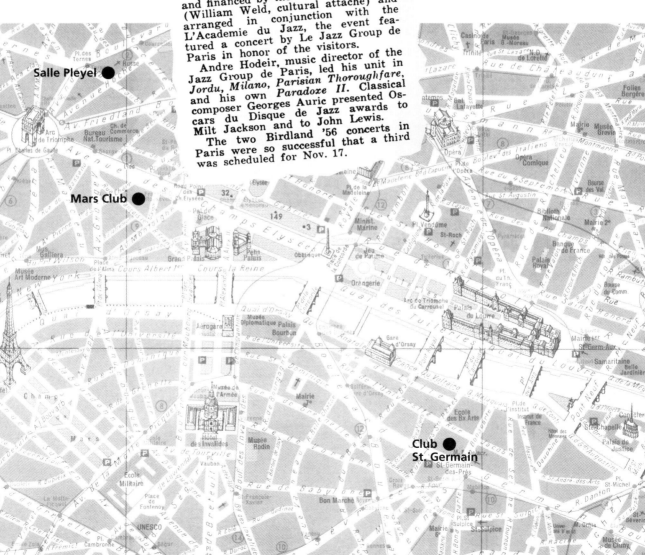

THUR	1
FRI	2
SAT	3
SUN	4
MON	5
TUES	6
WED	7
THUR	8
FRI	9
SAT	10
SUN	11
MON	12
TUES	13
WED	14
THUR	15
FRI	16
SAT	17
SUN	18
MON	19
TUES	20
WED	21
THUR	22
FRI	23
SAT	24
SUN	25
MON	26
TUES	27
WED	28
THUR	29
FRI	30

SATURDAY 3 NOVEMBER 1956

The Birdland All Stars in Europe package appears at the Salle Pleyel in Paris.

SUNDAY 4 NOVEMBER 1956

The Birdland All Stars in Europe package appears in Haarlem and Amsterdam in the Netherlands.

MONDAY 5 NOVEMBER 1956

The Birdland All Stars in Europe package appears in Brussels, Belgium.

TUESDAY 6 NOVEMBER 1956

The Birdland All Stars in Europe package appears in Düsseldorf, Germany.

WEDNESDAY 7 NOVEMBER 1956

The Birdland All Stars in Europe package appears at the Sportpalast in Berlin, Germany.

THURSDAY 8 NOVEMBER 1956

The Birdland All Stars in Europe package appears in Mannheim, Germany.

FRIDAY 9 NOVEMBER 1956

The Birdland All Stars in Europe package appears in Frankfurt, Germany.

SATURDAY 10 NOVEMBER 1956

The Birdland All Stars in Europe package appears in Hamburg, Germany.

SUNDAY 11 NOVEMBER 1956

The Birdland All Stars in Europe package appears in Munich, Germany.

MONDAY 12 NOVEMBER 1956

The Birdland All Stars in Europe package appears at the Stadthalle in Freiburg, Germany. Part of the concert is shown on television.

MILES DAVIS (trumpet), RENÉ URTREGER (piano), PIERRE MICHELOT (bass), CHRISTIAN GARROS (drums)
Tune Up / What's New
All Star Jam Session: MILES DAVIS (trumpet), LESTER YOUNG (tenor sax), MILT JACKSON (vibes), JOHN LEWIS (piano), PERCY HEATH (bass), CONNIE KAY (drums)
How High The Moon
All Stars with Kurt Edelhagen Orchestra: MILES DAVIS (trumpet), LESTER YOUNG (tenor sax), MILT JACKSON (vibes), JOHN LEWIS (piano), PERCY HEATH (bass), CONNIE KAY (drums)
Lester Leaps In

MORRIS LEVY
PRESENTEERT
BIRDLAND '56
The Modern Jazz Quartet
MILT JACKSON (VIBRAFOON) — JOHN LEWIS (PIANO) — PERCY HEATH (BAS) — CONNIE KAY (DRUMS)
Een keuze zal gemaakt worden uit o.m.:
Variaties „God rest ye merry gentlemen" – Fontessa – Concorde – Angel Eyes – La Ronde
Softly as a morning sunrise – Versailles – Django
Miles Davis
EN
Lester Young
maken een keuze uit o.m.:
Pennies From Heaven – Lester leaps in – Three little words – Symphony Sid
Polka dots and moonbeams – I didn't know what time it was – Lullaby of Birdland
Bud Powell
maakt een keuze uit o.m.:
Parisian Thoroughfare – So sorry please – Celia – Strictly confidential – Oblivion – Un poco loco
Trio René Urtréger
RENÉ URTRÉGER (PIANO) — CHRISTIAN GARROS (DRUMS) — PIERRE MICHELOT (BAS)
NAAR NEDERLAND GEBRACHT DOOR:
JAZZ-IMPRESARIAAT PAUL ACKET, ADELHEIDSTRAAT 5 · 's-GRAVENHAGE, TELEFOON 72 25 46 | HET NEDERLANDS THEATERBUREAU, HUYGENSSTRAAT 20 · 's-GRAVENHAGE, TELEFOON 11 28 54

MJQ Will Join In Schuller Premiere

Freiburg, Germany — The Modern Jazz Quartet, the Kurt Edelhagen orchestra, and German jazz harpist Johnny Teupen will join Nov. 12 in the world premiere of a new work by Gunther Schuller, *Transformation*.

Schuller's work was commissioned by the Sudwestfunk, the German southwestern radio station in Baden-Baden that covers a large part of Germany. The Nov. 12 concert, incidentally, commemorates the 1,000th jazz broadcast on Sudwestfunk by Joachim Berendt, a leading German jazz critic and organizer.

Also on the program will be Lester Young, Miles Davis, and Bud Powell as well as other sections by the Edelhagen orchestra and harpist Teupen. The concert will be broadcast Dec. 1.

HUR	**1**
I	**2**
AT	**3**
UN	**4**
ON	**5**
JES	**6**
ED	**7**
HUR	**8**
I	**9**
AT	**10**
UN	**11**
ON	**12**
JES	**13**
ED	**14**
HUR	**15**
I	**16**
AT	**17**
UN	**18**
ON	**19**
JES	**20**
ED	**21**
HUR	**22**
I	**23**
AT	**24**
UN	**25**
ON	**26**
JES	**27**
ED	**28**
HUR	**29**
I	**30**

MILES DAVIS

Miles Davis mag zonder twijfel de belangrijkste trompettist in de moderne jazz genoemd worden. Men kan zeggen dat practisch allen die dit instrument in het moderne idioom bespelen in meerdere of mindere mate door Miles Davis zijn beïnvloed. Het hoogtepunt van diens muzikale carrière wordt gevormd door de nu haast legendarische opnamen in 1949 en '50 ("Israël", "Venus de Milo", "Jeru" etc.) met een orkest dat helaas alleen in de platenstudio heeft bestaan, maar desondanks voor de moderne jazz van grote betekenis is geweest. De dertien opnamen die de Miles Davis Band maakte zijn hierom zo belangrijk, daar we deze eensdeels als eindpunt mogen zien van de vernieuwingen die de bop bracht, maar tegelijkertijd ook als uitgangspunt voor alles wat er na die tijd in de jazz zou gaan gebeuren. Historisch gezien dus eenzelfde positie als die de King Oliver Band in 1928 innam. Miles Davis' trompetspel geeft, hoewel op oudere opnamen technisch soms niet altijd even gaaf, steeds blijk van een .... ideeënrijkdom. Daarbij komt dan nog een eigenschap die alleen de beste jazz-.... ... tempo. Uit recente opnamen blijkt, dat het spel van .... gaande lijn beweegt.

BUD P....

De pianist Bud Powell b....
de bop betrokken is ge....
wist hij zich reeds vroe....
1943-'44 bij het orkest v....
slechts deel uit van kle....
namen, die hij maakte....
componist blijken ("Wa....
Door de trio-opnamen,....
zijn, leren we hem ken....
fraaie improvisaties w....
gekozen harmonieën v....
moderne pianisten, di....
wordt Bud Powell, de....
rijke spel beïnvloedd....
moderne jazz-pianiste....

Morris Levy's
BIRDLAND '56

THE MODERN JAZZ QUARTET

THUR	**1**
FRI	**2**
SAT	**3**
SUN	**4**
MON	**5**
TUES	**6**
WED	**7**
THUR	**8**
FRI	**9**
SAT	**10**
SUN	**11**
MON	**12**
TUES	**13**
WED	**14**
THUR	**15**
FRI	**16**
SAT	**17**
SUN	**18**
MON	**19**
TUES	**20**
WED	**21**
THUR	**22**
FRI	**23**
SAT	**24**
SUN	**25**
MON	**26**
TUES	**27**
WED	**28**
THUR	**29**
FRI	**30**

Above: Miles and Lester Young take a bow in Stockholm.
Right: Backstage in Stockholm, Miles looks on as Milt Jackson displays his piano technique.
Opposite page: Miles solos in Stockholm while (inset) Lester Young joins him for a swinging 'Lady Be Good'.

TUESDAY 13 NOVEMBER 1956
The Birdland All Stars in Europe package appears at the Konserthuset in Stockholm, Sweden.

WEDNESDAY 14 NOVEMBER 1956
The Birdland All Stars in Europe package appears at the KB-Hallen in Copenhagen, Denmark.

FRIDAY 16 NOVEMBER 1956
The Birdland All Stars in Europe package appears in Lille, France.

UR **1**
2
T **3**
N **4**
ON **5**
ES **6**
ED **7**
UR **8**
9
T **10**
N **11**
ON **12**
ES **13**
ED **14**
UR **15**
16
T **17**
N **18**
ON **19**
ES **20**
ED **21**
UR **22**
23
T **24**
N **25**
ON **26**
ES **27**
ED **28**
UR **29**
30

THUR	1
FRI	2
SAT	3
SUN	4
MON	5
TUES	6
WED	7
THUR	8
FRI	9
SAT	10
SUN	11
MON	12
TUES	13
WED	14
THUR	15
FRI	16
SAT	17
SUN	18
MON	19
TUES	20
WED	21
THUR	22
FRI	23
SAT	24
SUN	25
MON	26
TUES	27
WED	28
THUR	29
FRI	30

SATURDAY 17 NOVEMBER 1956
The Birdland All Stars in Europe package appears at the Salle Pleyel in Paris, France.

SUNDAY 18 NOVEMBER 1956
The Birdland All Stars in Europe package appears in Strasbourg, France.

MONDAY 19 NOVEMBER 1956
The Birdland All Stars in Europe package appears at the Kongreßhaus in Zurich, Switzerland. Part of the concert is privately taped.
Miles Davis (trumpet), René Urtreger (piano), Pierre Michelot (bass), Christian Garros (drums)
Four

TUESDAY 20 NOVEMBER 1956
The Birdland All Stars in Europe package appears at the Victoria Hall in Geneva, Switzerland.

WEDNESDAY 21 NOVEMBER 1956
The Birdland All Stars in Europe package appears at the Musiksaal in Basle, Switzerland.

THURSDAY 22 NOVEMBER 1956
The Birdland All Stars in Europe package appears at the Teatro di via Manzoni in Turin, Italy.

FRIDAY 23 NOVEMBER 1956
The Birdland All Stars in Europe package appears at the Teatro Nuovo in Turin, Italy.

SATURDAY 24 NOVEMBER 1956
The Birdland All Stars in Europe package appears in Marseilles, France.

SUNDAY 25 NOVEMBER 1956
The Birdland All Stars in Europe package play the final concert of the tour in Lyons, France.

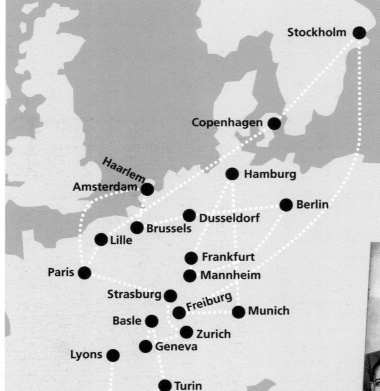

SATURDAY 1 DECEMBER 1956

The Miles Davis Quintet, with John Coltrane back on tenor sax, open at Olivia Davis' Patio Lounge in Washington for a two-week engagement opposite Max Roach's group.

FRIDAY 14 DECEMBER 1956

The Miles Davis Quintet close at Olivia Davis' Patio Lounge in Washington.

FRIDAY 21 DECEMBER 1956

The Miles Davis Quintet open at the Crown Propeller in Chicago for a one-week engagement.

WEDNESDAY 26 DECEMBER 1956

Down Beat reviews Miles' latest album release:

MILES DAVIS: Collector's Items
The Serpent's Tooth (2 takes); 'Round About Midnight; Compulsion; No Line; Vierd Blues; In Your Own Sweet Way
Rating: **** 1/2

Collector's Items is in two parts. The first side was cut in January, 1953, and is released for the first time. It's the session with Charlie Parker on tenor that Sonny Rollins talked about in the Nov. 28 *Down Beat*. Sonny is also present on tenor with a cooking rhythm section of Philly Joe Jones, Walter Bishop, and Percy Heath. The most arresting track is the mournful *Midnight* which has Bird's best tenor and Miles' best trumpet of the date.

For the rest, his tenor work is inevitably intriguing and forceful, and I wish there had been more recorded examples of his work on the horn after he had been playing it for some months (on this date, he has a new tenor that was christened on the date). Sonny also plays with heat. Miles is in good if not outstanding form, and Philly Joe is somewhat too loud in places. Bird is called Charlie Chan on the envelope.

The newer session (the last three tracks) has better Miles; considerably improved Rollins (with fuller, warmer tone and more cohesive idea structuring), and a superior rhythm section of Tommy Flanagan, Paul Chambers, and Art Taylor. Flanagan also solos with flowing distinction. Miles wrote the first two, and the third is Dave Brubeck's. The improvement in Prestige's recorded sound in three years, incidentally, is illuminating.

Vierd is a fine demonstration of the continuing, freshening, earthy validity of the blues in modern jazz with Sonny blowing one of his most eloquent choruses

THURSDAY 27 DECEMBER 1956

The Miles Davis Quintet close at the Crown Propeller in Chicago.

on record. The track has superb Miles and another excellent Flanagan solo. Miles treats the Brubeck ballad with sensitive intentness. Sonny is less lyrical, but his solo is built interestingly. And Flanagan, one of the few younger pianists with a quality of touch and lyricism akin to Hank Jones; speaks briefly. An important record. **(Prestige 12" LP 7044)**

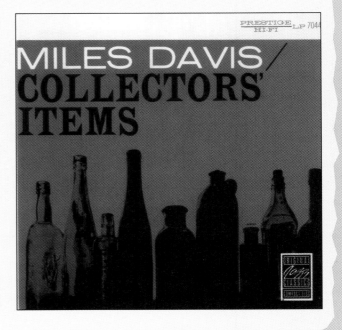

TUES	**1**	FRI	**1**
WED	**2**	SAT	**2**
THUR	**3**	SUN	**3**
FRI	**4**	MON	**4**
SAT	**5**	TUES	**5**
SUN	**6**	WED	**6**
MON	**7**	THUR	**7**
TUES	**8**	FRI	**8**
WED	**9**	SAT	**9**
THUR	**10**	SUN	**10**
FRI	**11**	MON	**11**
SAT	**12**	TUES	**12**
SUN	**13**	WED	**13**
MON	**14**	THUR	**14**
TUES	**15**	FRI	**15**
WED	**16**	SAT	**16**
THUR	**17**	SUN	**17**
FRI	**18**	MON	**18**
SAT	**19**	TUES	**19**
SUN	**20**	WED	**20**
MON	**21**	THUR	**21**
TUES	**22**	FRI	**22**
WED	**23**	SAT	**23**
THUR	**24**	SUN	**24**
FRI	**25**	MON	**25**
SAT	**26**	TUES	**26**
SUN	**27**	WED	**27**
MON	**28**	THUR	**28**
TUES	**29**		
WED	**30**		
THUR	**31**		

SATURDAY 5 JANUARY 1957

The Miles Davis Quintet open at Jazz City in Los Angeles for a three-week engagement.

SATURDAY 19 JANUARY 1957

Red Garland, Paul Chambers and Philly Joe Jones record *Art Pepper Meets the Rhythm Section* with Art Pepper for Contemporary in Los Angeles.

Art Pepper meets The Rhythm Section
(Red Garland, Paul Chambers, Philly Joe Jones)
Contemporary 7532

TUESDAY 22 JANUARY 1957

Paul Chambers records for Xanadu in Los Angeles. Jack Montrose, Bill Perkins, Paul Moer and Mel Lewis are also on the album which is released as *The East/West Controversy*.

Late in January the Miles Davis Quintet close at Jazz City in Los Angeles and move up the coast to San Francisco.

FRIDAY 25 JANUARY 1957

The Miles Davis Quintet open at the Blackhawk in San Francisco opposite Dave Brubeck for a two-week engagement.

THURSDAY 7 FEBRUARY 1957

The Miles Davis Quintet close at the Blackhawk in San Francisco.

FRIDAY 15 FEBRUARY 1957

The Miles Davis Quintet appear at the Syria Mosque, Pittsburgh for a concert with the Ted Heath Band.

F 1
AT 2
UN 3
ON 4
JES 5
ED 6
HUR 7
I 8
AT 9
UN 10
ON 11
JES 12
ED 13
HUR 14
I 15
AT 16
UN 17
ON 18
JES 19
ED 20
HUR 21
I 22
AT 23
UN 24
ON 25
JES 26
ED 27
HUR 28
I 29
AT 30
UN 31

Miles Davis Trio Hits Chicago On Long Jaunts

Miles Davis brings his quintet to the Preview's Modern Jazz Room Wednesday, for a two-week stay.

Only 30 years old, Miles was a teen-aged trumpet prodigy, touring with jazz greats Dizzy Gillespie and Charlie Parker in the short-lived Billy Eckstine Band in the early 40's. Since then, he has become one of the most influential trumpet stylists in the jazz field.

His quintet, which has been together for two years, is a close-knit, integrated, driving group. It features John Coltrane, Paul Chambers, "Philly Joe" Jones not to be confused with Jo Jones, and Red Garland.

Also featured at the Modern Jazz Room is The Versitones trio. Johnny Greenwood is the featured vocalist with the trio. Herb Stubbs plays the conga drum, and Roni Chapman plays the guitar. Johnny and Herb are from Trinidad and Roni is from Barbados. All are in their 20's.

MILES DAVIS QUITS JAZZ

From Leonard Feather

NEW YORK, Wednesday—Miles Davis said in Chicago that he will pack away his horn as an active performer in the jazz world at the end of his current engagement in the Windy City's Modern Jazz Room.

Now 30 years old, Miles started playing professionally when he was 13 for $3 a week, and his combo now earns up to $700 a night.

"I've had it," he told reporters. "This is no sudden decision. I've been thinking about it for a long time and after I close here I'm calling it quits."

He said he had no immediate plans but revealed that he had a record company offer for $200 a week as musical director, and another offer of a teaching post.

WEDNESDAY 6 MARCH 1957
The Miles Davis Quintet open at Preview's Modern Jazz Room in Chicago for a two-week engagement.

TUESDAY 19 MARCH 1957
The Miles Davis Quintet close at Preview's Modern Jazz Room in Chicago.

FRIDAY 22 MARCH 1957
John Coltrane and Paul Chambers record *Interplay for Two Trumpets and Two Tenors* for Prestige at Rudy Van Gelder's studio in Hackensack, New Jersey. Webster Young, Idrees Sulieman, Bobby Jaspar, Mal Waldron, Kenny Burrell and Art Taylor are also on the session.

TUESDAY 26 MARCH 1957
The Miles Davis Quintet open at the Comedy Club in Baltimore for a one-week engagement.

MON	1
TUES	2
WED	3
THUR	4
FRI	5
SAT	6
SUN	7
MON	8
TUES	9
WED	10
THUR	11
FRI	12
SAT	13
SUN	14
MON	15
TUES	16
WED	17
THUR	18
FRI	19
SAT	20
SUN	21
MON	22
TUES	23
WED	24
THUR	25
FRI	26
SAT	27
SUN	28
MON	29
TUES	30

MONDAY 1 APRIL 1957
The Miles Davis Quintet close at the Comedy Club in Baltimore.

FRIDAY 5 APRIL 1957
The Miles Davis Quintet open a three-week engagement at Café Bohemia, New York City opposite The Jazz Messengers.

SATURDAY 6 APRIL 1957
John Coltrane and Paul Chambers record *A Blowing Session* with the Johnny Griffin Septet for Blue Note at Rudy Van Gelder's studio in Hackensack, New Jersey. Lee Morgan, Johnny Griffin, Hank Mobley, Wynton Kelly and Art Blakey are also on the session.

MONDAY 8 APRIL 1957
The Ronnell Bright Trio replace The Jazz Messengers at Café Bohemia.

SATURDAY 13 APRIL 1957
The Miles Davis Quintet star in an all star concert presented by Al 'Jazzbo' Collins at Town Hall in New York City.

CAFE BOHEMIA
"the most invaluable jazz club in the East" . . . . —Down Beat
Now thru April 14
MILES DAVIS quintet
RONNELL BRIGHT trio
April 15 - 28
MILES DAVIS quintet
LEE KONITZ quintet
Cafe Bohemia
15 Barrow St.
just off Sheridan Square
for reservations CH 3-9274

NEW YORK AREA
2 — NIGHTS of JAZZ — 2
at TOWN HALL
123 West 43rd St., N.Y.C.

Sat. Apr. 13 & Sat. Apr. 20
2 SHOWS NIGHTLY — 8:30 & 11:30 p.m.

— Al 'Jazzbo' Collins presents —
MILES DAVIS & His Great Band
DON ELLIOTT ★ TONY SCOTT
BOB BROOKMEYER ★ LEE KONITZ
ROY ELDRIDGE ★ COLEMAN HAWKINS
AL COHN ★ BUCK CLAYTON
THELONIOUS MONK ★ MILT HINTON
HERBIE MANN ★ MAT MATHEWS
JO JONES ★ GEO. WALLINGTON
JIMMY RUSHING and many others.

All Seats Reserved $2   Box office or mail
Best Seats Available Now

Between shows at Town Hall, the quintet still manage their regular stints at the club and to broadcast on Mutual's *Bandstand USA*, live from the Café Bohemia. *The Theme / Woody'n You / Walkin' / All Of You* (incomplete)

SUNDAY 14 APRIL 1957
Paul Chambers records with the Sonny Rollins Quintet for Blue Note at Rudy Van Gelder's Studio in Hackensack, New Jersey. J. J. Johnson, Horace Silver, Thelonious Monk and Art Blakey are also on the session which is issued as *Sonny Rollins Volume 2* on BLP 1558.

MONDAY 15 APRIL 1957
The Lee Konitz Quintet replace Ronnell Bright at Café Bohemia.

TUESDAY 16 APRIL 1957

John Coltrane records one track with Thelonious Monk and Wilbur Ware for Riverside at the Reeves Sound Studio in New York City.

THURSDAY 18 APRIL 1957

John Coltrane records with the Prestige All Stars at Rudy Van Gelder's Studio in Hackensack, New Jersey. Also on the session are Idrees Sulieman, Tommy Flanagan, Kenny Burrell, Doug Watkins and Louis Hayes. The recordings are issued as *The Cats* on Prestige New Jazz LP 8217.

FRIDAY 19 APRIL 1957

John Coltrane records with the Mal Waldron Sextet for Prestige at Rudy Van Gelder's Studio in Hackensack, New Jersey. Also on the session are Bill Hardman, Jackie McLean, Mal Waldron, Julian Euell and Art Taylor. The recordings are issued as *Mal 2* on Prestige LP 7111.

SATURDAY 20 APRIL 1957

John Coltrane records with the Prestige All Stars at Rudy Van Gelder's Studio in Hackensack, New Jersey. Also on the session are Cecil Payne, Pepper Adams, Mal Waldron, Doug Watkins and Art Taylor. The recordings are issued as *Modern Jazz Survey–Baritones and French Horns* on Prestige LP 16-6.

The Miles Davis Quintet star in a repeat of the all star concert presented by Al 'Jazzbo' Collins at Town Hall in New York City.

SUNDAY 28 APRIL 1957

The Miles Davis Quintet close at Café Bohemia, New York City. Miles finally loses patience and fires John Coltrane and Philly Joe Jones. The problems caused by their drug habits are affecting the band and Miles brings in Sonny Rollins and Art Taylor to replace them.

ON 1
ES 2
ED 3
UR 4
5
T 6
N 7
ON 8
ES 9
ED 10
UR 11
12
T 13
N 14
ON 15
ES 16
ED 17
UR 18
19
T 20
N 21
ON 22
ES 23
ED 24
UR 25
26
T 27
N 28
ON 29
ES 30

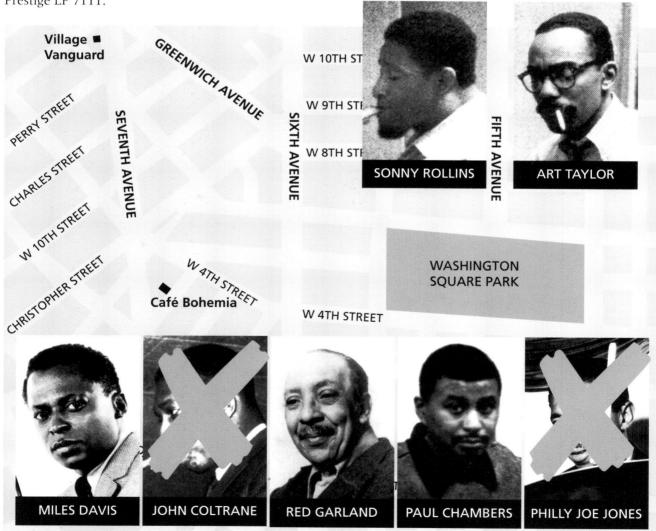

SONNY ROLLINS

ART TAYLOR

Village Vanguard

GREENWICH AVENUE

W 10TH ST

W 9TH ST

W 8TH ST

PERRY STREET

SEVENTH AVENUE

SIXTH AVENUE

FIFTH AVENUE

CHARLES STREET

W 10TH STREET

CHRISTOPHER STREET

W 4TH STREET

Café Bohemia

W 4TH STREET

WASHINGTON SQUARE PARK

MILES DAVIS

JOHN COLTRANE

RED GARLAND

PAUL CHAMBERS

PHILLY JOE JONES

WED **1**

THUR **2**

FRI **3**

SAT **4**

SUN **5**

MON **6**

TUES **7**

WED **8**

THUR **9**

FRI **10**

SAT **11**

SUN **12**

MON **13**

TUES **14**

WED **15**

THUR **16**

FRI **17**

SAT **18**

SUN **19**

MON **20**

TUES **21**

WED **22**

THUR **23**

FRI **24**

SAT **25**

SUN **26**

MON **27**

TUES **28**

WED **29**

THUR **30**

FRI **31**

MONDAY 6 MAY 1957

Recording session by Miles Davis with the Gil Evans Orchestra for Columbia in New York City.
MILES DAVIS (flugelhorn), BERNIE GLOW, ERNIE ROYAL, LOUIS MUCCI, TAFT JORDAN, JOHN CARISI (trumpet), FRANK REHAK, JIMMY CLEVELAND, JOE BENNETT (trombone), TOM MITCHELL (bass trombone), WILLIE RUFF, TONY MIRANDA, JIM BUFFINGTON (french horn), BILL BARBER (tuba), LEE KONITZ (alto sax), DANNY BANK (bass clarinet), ROMEO PENQUE, SID COOPER, EDWIN CAINE (clarinet/flute), PAUL CHAMBERS (bass), ART TAYLOR (drums), GIL EVANS (arranger/conductor)
The Maids Of Cadiz / The Duke

FRIDAY 10 MAY 1957

Recording session by Miles Davis with the Gil Evans Orchestra for Columbia in New York City.
MILES DAVIS (flugelhorn), BERNIE GLOW, ERNIE ROYAL, LOUIS MUCCI, TAFT JORDAN, JOHN CARISI (trumpet), FRANK REHAK, JIMMY CLEVELAND, JOE BENNETT (trombone), TOM MITCHELL (bass trombone), WILLIE RUFF, TONY MIRANDA, JIM BUFFINGTON (french horn), BILL BARBER (tuba), LEE KONITZ (alto sax), DANNY BANK (bass clarinet), ROMEO PENQUE, SID COOPER, EDWIN CAINE (clarinet/flute), PAUL CHAMBERS (bass), ART TAYLOR (drums), GIL EVANS (arranger/conductor)
My Ship / Miles Ahead

Below: Miles and Gil Evans in discussion during a recording session for the ground-breaking album "Miles Ahead".

ED **1**
UR **2**
3
T **4**
N **5**
ON **6**
ES **7**
ED **8**
UR **9**
10
T **11**
N **12**
ON **13**
ES **14**
ED **15**
UR **16**
17
T **18**
N **19**
ON **20**
ES **21**
ED **22**
UR **23**
24
T **25**
N **26**
ON **27**
ES **28**
ED **29**
UR **30**
31

THURSDAY 23 MAY 1957

Recording session by Miles Davis with the Gil Evans Orchestra for Columbia in New York City.
MILES DAVIS (flugelhorn), BERNIE GLOW, ERNIE ROYAL, LOUIS MUCCI, TAFT JORDAN, JOHN CARISI (trumpet), FRANK REHAK, JIMMY CLEVELAND, JOE BENNETT (trombone), TOM MITCHELL (bass trombone), WILLIE RUFF, TONY MIRANDA, JIM BUFFINGTON (french horn), BILL BARBER (tuba), LEE KONITZ (alto sax), DANNY BANK (bass clarinet), ROMEO PENQUE, SID COOPER, EDWIN CAINE (clarinet/flute), PAUL CHAMBERS (bass), ART TAYLOR (drums), GIL EVANS (arranger/conductor)
New Rhumba / Blues For Pablo / Springsville

SUNDAY 26 MAY 1956

Miles' 31st birthday.

MONDAY 27 MAY 1957

Recording session by Miles Davis with the Gil Evans Orchestra for Columbia in New York City.
MILES DAVIS (flugelhorn), BERNIE GLOW, ERNIE ROYAL, LOUIS MUCCI, TAFT JORDAN, JOHN CARISI (trumpet), FRANK REHAK, JIMMY CLEVELAND, JOE BENNETT (trombone), TOM MITCHELL (bass trombone), WILLIE RUFF, TONY MIRANDA, JIM BUFFINGTON (french horn), BILL BARBER (tuba), LEE KONITZ (alto sax), DANNY BANK (bass clarinet), ROMEO PENQUE, SID COOPER, EDWIN CAINE (clarinet/flute), PAUL CHAMBERS (bass), ART TAYLOR (drums), GIL EVANS (arranger/conductor)
I Don't Wanna Be Kissed / The Meaning Of The Blues / Lament

George Avakian (*seen at left with Miles*), jazz producer at Columbia, writes about *Miles Ahead* in the sleeve notes:

When Miles Davis signed with CBS, we found in each other a mutual interest in furthering the ideals of the nine-piece band. What direction this desire would take was uncertain, beyond the conviction that Gil Evans was the arranger we wanted. A series of discussions with Gil followed, out of which grew the basic conception (largely Miles') of this album; within the framework he wanted, Gil developed the details which produce the remarkable texture of a large jazz orchestra, a texture unique in tonal quality and breaking away from the roots which are to be found in the Davis group of the late forties.

SAT	1
SUN	2
MON	3
TUES	4
WED	5
THUR	6
FRI	7
SAT	8
SUN	9
MON	10
TUES	11
WED	12
THUR	13
FRI	14
SAT	15
SUN	16
MON	17
TUES	18
WED	19
THUR	20
FRI	21
SAT	22
SUN	23
MON	24
TUES	25
WED	26
THUR	27
FRI	28
SAT	29
SUN	30

MONDAY 17 JUNE 1957

The New Miles Davis Quintet (Miles Davis, trumpet; Sonny Rollins, tenor sax; Red Garland, piano; Paul Chambers, bass; Art Taylor, drums) open at Café Bohemia in New York City opposite the Al Cohn-Zoot Sims Quintet.

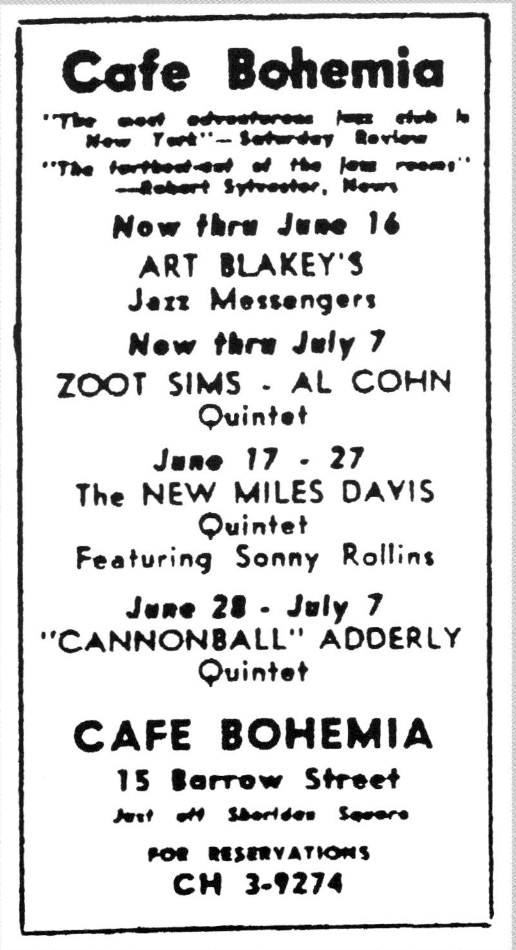

Cafe Bohemia
"The most adventurous jazz club in New York"—Saturday Review
"The hotbed-est of the jazz rooms" —Robert Sylvester, News

Now thru June 16
ART BLAKEY'S
Jazz Messengers

Now thru July 7
ZOOT SIMS - AL COHN
Quintet

June 17 - 27
The NEW MILES DAVIS
Quintet
Featuring Sonny Rollins

June 28 - July 7
"CANNONBALL" ADDERLY
Quintet

CAFE BOHEMIA
15 Barrow Street
Just off Sheridan Square

FOR RESERVATIONS
CH 3-9274

During the second week of the engagement *Down Beat* is present to review the show:

Al Cohn and Zoot Sims

Personnel: Cohn, tenor, clarinet, baritone; Sims, alto, clarinet and tenor; Teddy Kotick, bass; Bill Evans (subbing for Dave McKenna), piano; Nick Stabulas, drums.

Reviewed: Two sets in third week of six-week stand at Café Bohemia, New York.

Musical Evaluation: If anyone is looking for a free-swinging multicoloured group, stop right here.

In Cohn and Sims, you'll find two mainstream hornmen whose middle name is swing. Although most of the blowing right now is being done on two tenors, the duo is varying its group sound by pairing clarinets or by setting Zoot's virile alto against Al's fluid but biting baritone. On the sets caught, they teamed on clarinet for a number called *Two Funky People*. Although they seemed less comfortable wearing such straight instruments, they acquitted themselves nobly. Al's solo was as light and swinging as his touch on the tenor. Zoot's was rawer and as biting as his attack on tenor. They gave everyone a charge with the low flickering background they set up while Kotick soloed.

On *From A to Z*, Zoot blew alto and Al hefted baritone. Sims has become quite fluent on alto. The bite and drive he gets out of it is a source of excitement in itself. Cohn swings on baritone but not so fluently or consistently as on tenor.

On one original, the tenor blend was tight throughout the tricky theme. Zoot picked up the final figure and booted it nearly uptown during his choruses. Al's solo was smooth, but with rhythmic punch. During some fours passed around at the end, they showed a tight feeling for each other's ideas.

Audience Reaction: Attentive and favourable. The two-clarinet bit particularly intrigued the audience. Response was generous after solos.

Attitude of Performers: Al's placid manner and Zoot's bustling energy complement each other onstand. They appeared to be having a ball.

Commercial Potential: Where the group goes after mid-July was not yet determined, but it will be heard on records. Several firms already have bid for LPs by them.

Summary: What can you say after you say they're swinging?

T 1
N 2
ON 3
ES 4
ED 5
UR 6
I 7
T 8
N 9
ON 10
ES 11
ED 12
UR 13
I 14
T 15
N 16
ON 17
ES 18
ED 19
UR 20
I 21
T 22
N 23
ON 24
ES 25
ED 26
UR 27
I 28
T 29
N 30

Miles Davis Quintet

Personnel: Davis, trumpet; Sonny Rollins, tenor; Paul Chambers, bass; Red Garland, piano; Art Taylor, drums.

Reviewed: Café Bohemia, New York, two sets midway in second week of two-week stand.

Musical Evaluation: I first heard Davis play in person at the Newport Jazz festival two years ago. At that time, I was amazed that any human could achieve such a distillation of pure sound from an instrument so often thunderous. If anything, Miles has gone on making his tone purer and purer until it now is the gentlest of whispers when muted, and a subtle but somehow forceful and glowing sound on open horn.

He is ranging into exploration of dynamics as well as tone texture. On several of the originals, he built choruses expertly, one piece fitting neatly into the next, to a gleaming full shout, which, with Miles, is not loud but rather decorative. On other choruses, he would fall away to the subtlest of whispers, making of his solo line a vehicle as fleet and delicate as a glance.

Perhaps it is the forceful presence of Rollins in this group which is bringing out this burst of artistry in Miles. Surely, Rollins is of some effect on his leader. Sonny's choruses, too, are constructed with craftsmanship—now rough-edged and brimming with virility, now soft and nearly timid but always sure of footing and aimed at a goal constantly achieved before he takes his horn from his lips.

The third melodic voice in the group is Chambers, who always has sounded like a section on record. In person, his fullbodied tone brings him out of the rhythm section, and his melodic voice is felt constantly in ensembles and behind the horns.

Garland is flexible and strongly rhythmic in the group, and supple in solos. On *Diane*, for example, he varied the texture of his playing. From a longish line of dominantly right-hand phrases, he worked into a building series of powerful chords excitingly catapulting to a logical climax.

In addition to standing alone as a fine solo, it perfectly set off Miles, who followed with short bursts of melody blown in his liquid muted sound. Taylor's often bombastic drumming was edited to the dimensions of the pace set by Miles.

One final comment: *Bye Bye Blackbird*, long a sentimental favourite of mine, is as familiar a song as *Stardust*. But never have I heard it blown with such feeling and depth as by Miles, who, though muted, achieved more genuine emotional impact than many could with the fuller range of sound available on open horn.

Audience Reaction: A full house, rather unusual for midweek, remained remarkably quiet, and even more remarkably attentive to the group. The response was warm and sustained after each number, particularly after the solos.

Attitude of Performers: The group is neat in appearance, and on the sets caught was quite businesslike, apparently absorbed in its work. Miles was in a buoyant mood, strolling down into the audience after his solos to chat with friends.

The lone failing of the group is in not announcing titles of tunes and thereby giving the audience a peg on which to focus its concentration. It might help album sales, too.

Commercial Potential: This group, now very good, could well become great. It has the talent necessary. It is booked to return to this location in July and to record for Columbia this summer.

Summary: Miles is increasing in stature as an artist. But while savouring his playing, don't neglect the rest of the group. There is that much going on.

WEDNESDAY 19 JUNE 1957

Sonny Rollins and Paul Chambers record for Riverside in New York City. Sonny Clark and Roy Haynes are also on the session which becomes part of the Sonny Rollins Quartet album *The Sound of Sonny* on RLP 12-241.

THURSDAY 27 JUNE 1957

The New Miles Davis Quintet close at Café Bohemia in New York City.

MON	1
TUES	2
WED	3
THUR	4
FRI	5
SAT	6
SUN	7
MON	8
TUES	9
WED	10
THUR	11
FRI	12
SAT	13
SUN	14
MON	15
TUES	16
WED	17
THUR	18
FRI	19
SAT	20
SUN	21
MON	22
TUES	23
WED	24
THUR	25
FRI	26
SAT	27
SUN	28
MON	29
TUES	30
WED	31

CAFE BOHEMIA
15 Barrow Street
Just off Sheridan Square
FOR RESERVATIONS
CH 3-9274

MONDAY 8 JULY 1957

The Miles Davis Quintet open again at Café Bohemia in New York City, opposite the Randy Weston Trio.

SATURDAY 13 JULY 1957

The Miles Davis Quintet broadcast from Café Bohemia in New York City.
MILES DAVIS (trumpet), SONNY ROLLINS (tenor sax), RED GARLAND (piano), PAUL CHAMBERS (bass), ART TAYLOR (drums)
Four (Four Squared) / Bye Bye Blackbird / It Never Entered My Mind (SR out) / *Walkin' (Roy's Nappin' Now)*

SUNDAY 14 JULY 1957

Paul Chambers and Art Taylor record for Blue Note a the Rudy Van Gelder Studios in Hackensack, New Jersey. Hank Jones and Kenny Burrell are also on th album which is released as *Bass On Top* (BLP 1569).

THURSDAY 18 JULY 1957

John Coltrane opens with the Thelonious Monk Quartet at the Five Spot in New York City. This historic engagement will run until December, and Miles often goes to listen.

SATURDAY 20 JULY 1957

The Miles Davis Quintet broadcast on *Bandstand USA* from Café Bohemia in New York City.
Dear Old Stockholm / Bags' Groove / Nature Boy / S'posin

Below: John Coltrane with Thelonious Monk at the Five Spot. Drummer Shadow Wilson is visible behind Monk but bassist Wilbur Ware is out of shot.

ON **1**

JES **2**

ED **3**

HUR **4**

RI **5**

AT **6**

JN **7**

ON **8**

JES **9**

ED **10**

HUR **11**

RI **12**

AT **13**

JN **14**

ON **15**

JES **16**

ED **17**

HUR **18**

RI **19**

AT **20**

JN **21**

ON **22**

JES **23**

ED **24**

HUR **25**

RI **26**

AT **27**

JN **28**

ON **29**

JES **30**

ED **31**

SUNDAY 21 JULY 1957

The Miles Davis Quintet appear at the Great South Bay Jazz Festival in the afternoon. Also on the bill are Annie Ross and a band co-led by Marian and Jimmy McPartland.

In the evening they are at Café Bohemia where Randy Weston plays his final night.

MONDAY 22 JULY 1957

Miles opens in a week-long series of concerts in the open air in Central Park, New York. JAZZ UNDER THE STARS at 8.30 each evening of the week in the Wollman Memorial Theatre in Central Park, featuring Billie Holiday, George Shearing Quintet, Erroll Garner, Gerry Mulligan Quartet, Lester Young, Miles Davis, Jo Jones and Sonny Stitt, compered by Al 'Jazzbo' Collins and Jean Shepherd. Monday is the off-night at Café Bohemia.

TUESDAY 23 JULY 1957

After his appearance in JAZZ UNDER THE STARS in Central Park, Miles continues his engagement at Café Bohemia where his band are joined by the Cannonball Adderley Quintet. Miles talks to Cannonball about joining the band, but Cannonball has commitments and says he can't do it until October.

SATURDAY 27 JULY 1957

The Miles Davis Quintet broadcast on *Bandstand USA* from Café Bohemia in New York City.
Bye Bye Blackbird / Tune Up / A Foggy Day (trio only)

SUNDAY 28 JULY 1957

Miles closes his stint in the open air in Central Park, New York. JAZZ UNDER THE STARS continues for another week with a new cast, except for Billie Holiday who is held over.

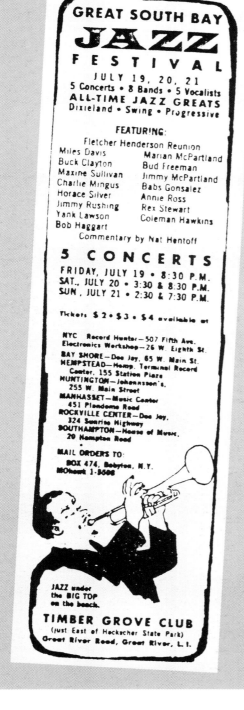

THUR	**1**
FRI	**2**
SAT	**3**
SUN	**4**
MON	**5**
TUES	**6**
WED	**7**
THUR	**8**
FRI	**9**
SAT	**10**
SUN	**11**
MON	**12**
TUES	**13**
WED	**14**
THUR	**15**
FRI	**16**
SAT	**17**
SUN	**18**
MON	**19**
TUES	**20**
WED	**21**
THUR	**22**
FRI	**23**
SAT	**24**
SUN	**25**
MON	**26**
TUES	**27**
WED	**28**
THUR	**29**
FRI	**30**
SAT	**31**

SUNDAY 11 AUGUST 1957

The Miles Davis Quintet close at Café Bohemia in New York City.

FRIDAY 23 AUGUST 1957

Red Garland and Paul Chambers record with John Coltrane and Art Taylor for Prestige at the Rudy Van Gelder Studios in Hackensack, New Jersey. The album is issued as *John Coltrane with the Red Garland Trio* on Prestige LP 7123.

The Miles Davis Quintet appears at the 2nd Annual New York Jazz Festival at Randall's Island.

Leonard Feather reviews the concert for *Down Beat*:

MILES CAME ON for a turbulent set in which Sonny Rollins and Paul Chambers stole the honors, the latter on his pizzicato solo only; the bowed solo was entirely lost, the result partly to a DC-7 overhead.

Playing fluegelhorn, Miles was as creatively fertile as ever, but his chops let him down—scarcely a phrase went by in which the mood wasn't spoiled by a fluffed note. Red Garland and Philly Joe Jones were effective on this set and accompanying several other acts, including Coleman Hawkins, who followed.

SATURDAY 31 AUGUST 1957

The Miles Davis Quintet opens at Café Bohemia in New York City opposite Bud Powell for a four-week engagement. Sonny Rollins, Art Taylor and Red Garland are in the quintet for the opening, but soon Sonny Rollins leaves to form his own band and Miles fires Art Taylor and Red Garland after disagreements. Bobby Jaspar replaces Rollins, Tommy Flanagan replaces Garland and Jimmy Cobb briefly displaces Art Taylor before Philly Joe Jones returns to the band. The finally settled quintet is captured in a radio broadcast from the club during September:
MILES DAVIS (trumpet), BOBBY JASPAR (tenor sax), TOMMY FLANAGAN (piano), PAUL CHAMBERS (bass), PHILLY JOE JONES (drums)
All Of Now / Four

SUNDAY 1 SEPTEMBER 1957

Paul Chambers records with the Sonny Clark Sextet for Blue Note at the Rudy Van Gelder Studios in Hackensack, New Jersey. Donald Byrd, John Coltrane, Curtis Fuller, Sonny Clark and Art Taylor are also on the session which is issued as *Sonny's Crib* on BLP 1576.

THURSDAY 5 SEPTEMBER 1957

Down Beat reports:

> Thelonious Monk sat in with Miles Davis' Quintet at the Café Bohemia (and broke up Miles by using his elbow several times during a solo). Horace Silver and Percy Heath sat in with Miles during a later set.

COOKIN' WITH THE MILES DAVIS QUINTET—Prestige 12″ LP 7094:

Airegin; Tune Up; When Lights Are Low; My Funny Valentine; Blues By Five

Personnel: Davis, trumpet; John Coltrane, tenor; Red Garland, piano; Paul Chambers, bass; Philly Joe Jones, drums.

Rating: *****

All the tremendous cohesion, the wild, driving swing, and the all-out excitement and controlled emotion that was present at the best moments of the Davis quintet has been captured on this record. Jones has said these sessions, made in 1956 and the last of Miles' Prestige recordings, are the best Davis has made. I am inclined to agree.

Miles was in exquisite form; Coltrane sounds better here than on any except the group's Columbia LP; Chambers is well recorded, and his solo on *Blues By Five* is particularly gratifying. Philly Joe and Garland work together in their intricate system of rhythmic feeding in a fashion that has been done seldom, if ever, before by any rhythm section.

There are many moments of pure music and emotional joy on this album. Note the traces of Davis in Coltrane's solo on *Airegin*; note Miles and Philly Joe at the end of Davis' first solo on *Tune Up*; note Jones and Garland behind Coltrane on the same tune; note how Jones doubles up against the pulse on *Lights Are Low*.

Garland contributes a golden solo on *Lights* and on *Five*. In the same tune, note how the rhythm section continues the melodic outline behind the solos.

As to Miles, his peculiar blend of pure melody and acidulous accents never has sounded better. His "squees" and "whees" come at the moment you least expect them. On his own composition, *Tune Up*, he gets a remarkable show tune type of sound in his statement of the melody and then prefaces his improvisation by a series of two-note phrases with the accent on the second one. This is extremely effective. *Valentine* is a slow one, done thoughtfully and almost sedately at times, with Jones on brushes behind Davis.

SUNDAY 15 SEPTEMBER 1957

Paul Chambers and Philly Joe Jones record with the John Coltrane Sextet for Blue Note at the Rudy Van Gelder Studios in Hackensack, New Jersey. Lee Morgan, John Coltrane, Curtis Fuller and Kenny Drew are also on the session which is issued as *Blue Train* on BLP 1577.

THURSDAY 19 SEPTEMBER 1957

Down Beat reviews Miles' latest album release:

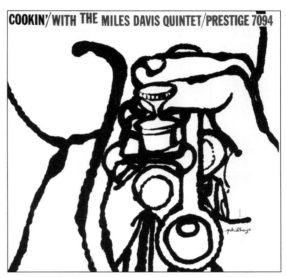

However, it is *When Lights Are Low*, Benny Carter's great tune which is mis-labeled *Just Squeeze Me* on my copy, that is the classic number. This is the second version of it Miles has recorded, and it is interesting to note that the tempo is almost exactly the same this time. This is one of the best arrangements this group had; an inventive melding of simplicity and thorough exploration of the harmonic and rhythmic possibilities.

Miles' wispy statement of the melody is followed by Coltrane's ruminative solo, Garland follows with his best work of the date, a long solo the second half of which is locked chords, and there is a short bit of Davis presaging the unison out chorus. This is one of the best LPs of the year and makes one wonder why the group rated so few votes in the Jazz Critics poll. (R.J.G.)

SUNDAY 22 SEPTEMBER 1957

Philly Joe Jones records with the Sonny Rollins Quartet for Blue Note at the Rudy Van Gelder Studios in Hackensack, New Jersey. Sonny Rollins, Wynton Kelly, and Doug Watkins are also on the session which is issued as *Newk's Time* on BLP 4001.

FRIDAY 27 SEPTEMBER 1957

The Miles Davis Quintet close at Café Bohemia in New York City.

TUES	**1**	FRI	**1**
WED	**2**	SAT	**2**
THUR	**3**	SUN	**3**
FRI	**4**	MON	**4**
SAT	**5**	TUES	**5**
SUN	**6**	WED	**6**
MON	**7**	THUR	**7**
TUES	**8**	FRI	**8**
WED	**9**	SAT	**9**
THUR	**10**	SUN	**10**
FRI	**11**	MON	**11**
SAT	**12**	TUES	**12**
SUN	**13**	WED	**13**
MON	**14**	THUR	**14**
TUES	**15**	FRI	**15**
WED	**16**	SAT	**16**
THUR	**17**	SUN	**17**
FRI	**18**	MON	**18**
SAT	**19**	TUES	**19**
SUN	**20**	WED	**20**
MON	**21**	THUR	**21**
TUES	**22**	FRI	**22**
WED	**23**	SAT	**23**
THUR	**24**	SUN	**24**
FRI	**25**	MON	**25**
SAT	**26**	TUES	**26**
SUN	**27**	WED	**27**
MON	**28**	THUR	**28**
TUES	**29**	FRI	**29**
WED	**30**	SAT	**30**
THUR	**31**		

FRIDAY 11 OCTOBER 1957

The Miles Davis Quintet, with Cannonball Adderley replacing Bobby Jaspar, open at Café Bohemia for a short engagement opposite the Frank Wess Quartet.

Cannonball Adderley recalls:

NOBODY WAS REALLY MAKING IT EXCEPT FOR MILES, CHICO AND BRUBECK. I HAD GOTTEN AN OFFER FROM DIZZY TO GO WITH HIS SMALL BAND. I WAS OPPOSITE MILES AT THE BOHEMIA, TOLD HIM I WAS GOING TO JOIN DIZZY, AND MILES ASKED ME WHY DIDN'T I JOIN HIM. I TOLD HIM HE'D NEVER ASKED ME… AND WHEN I FINALLY DECIDED TO CUT LOOSE IN OCTOBER 1957, I JOINED MILES. I FIGURED I COULD LEARN MORE THAN WITH DIZZY. NOT THAT DIZZY ISN'T A GOOD TEACHER, BUT HE PLAYED MORE COMMERCIALLY THAN MILES. THANK GOODNESS I MADE THE MOVE I DID.

MONDAY 14 OCTOBER 1957

Roy Eldridge and his Quartet replace Frank Wess at Café Bohemia.

WEDNESDAY 16 OCTOBER 1957

The Miles Davis Quintet close at Café Bohemia.

THURSDAY 17 OCTOBER 1957

The Miles Davis Quintet open at Birdland opposite the Stan Getz Quartet.

SATURDAY 19 OCTOBER 1957

The Miles Davis Quintet appear in concert at the Convention Hall in Philadelphia. Also on the bill are Dizzy Gillespie's Big Band, Chris Connor, Horace Silver, Jimmy Smith and Sonny Stitt.

WEDNESDAY 30 OCTOBER 1957

The Miles Davis Quintet and the Stan Getz Quartet close at Birdland.

SATURDAY 2 NOVEMBER 1957

The Miles Davis Quintet appear in a Jazz For Moderns concert at Carnegie Hall in New York City. Also on the bill are George Shearing's Sextet, Gerry Mulligan's Quintet, Chico Hamilton's Quintet, the Australian Jazz Quinte and Helen Merrill.

TUESDAY 12 NOVEMBER 1957

The Miles Davis Quintet appear in a Jazz For Moderns concert at Kiel Opera House in St Louis. Also on the bill are George Shearing's Sextet, Gerry Mulligan's Quintet, Chico Hamilton's Quintet, the Australian Jazz Quinte and Helen Merrill.

FRIDAY 15 NOVEMBER 1957

The Miles Davis Quintet appear in a Jazz For Moderns concert at the Orchestral Hall in Chicago. Also on the bill are George Shearing's Sextet, Gerry Mulligan's Quintet, Chico Hamilton's Quintet, the Australian Jazz Quintet and Helen Merrill.

At the conclusion of the Jazz For Moderns tour, Miles temporarily disbands and flies to Paris for a concert at the Olympia Theatre to be followed by a three-week residency at the Club St. Germain. He is met at the airport by Juliette Greco and film director Louis Malle, a keen Miles Davis fan, who asks Miles to write the musical score for his new film. Miles agrees.

SATURDAY 30 NOVEMBER 1957
Miles Davis and the Barney Wilen Quartet appear in concert at Olympia in Paris. The concert is taped. MILES DAVIS (trumpet), BARNEY WILEN (tenor sax), RENÉ URTREGER (piano), PIERRE MICHELOT (bass), KENNY CLARKE (drums)
Bags' Groove / Tune Up / Four / Rollins' Tune / Walkin' / Round About Midnight

Mike Zwerin, the trombonist who played with Miles' nonet at the Royal Roost, is living in Paris and recalls the Olympia concert:

THE OLYMPIA THEATRE WAS SOLD OUT THAT NIGHT, BUT BY CURTAIN TIME MILES' WHEREABOUTS WERE STILL A MYSTERY. FINALLY, THE CURTAIN WENT UP, REVEALING BARNEY WILEN, RENE URTREGER, PIERRE MICHELOT, AND KENNY CLARKE ALL SET UP. THEY STARTED PLAYING *WALKIN'* AND SOUNDED FINE. BUT NO MILES DAVIS. BARNEY TOOK A TENOR SOLO, AND AS HE WAS FINISHING, BACKING AWAY FROM THE MICROPHONE, MILES APPEARED FROM THE WINGS, AND ARRIVED AT THE MIKE WITHOUT BREAKING HIS STRIDE, JUST IN TIME TO START PLAYING – STRONG. IT WAS AN ENTRANCE WORTHY OF NIJINSKY. IF HIS CHOREOGRAPHY WAS GOOD, HIS PLAYING WAS PERFECT THAT NIGHT. HE HAD RECENTLY MADE HIS 'COMEBACK' AND WAS REALLY PUTTING THE POTS ON. HE WAS SERIOUS, AND HE WAS TRYING HARD INSTEAD OF JUST CATTING... FOR THE FIRST WEEK OF HIS STAY AT THE CLUB, AS WE CALLED THE ST. GERMAIN, I WAS DOWN THERE ALMOST EVERY NIGHT.

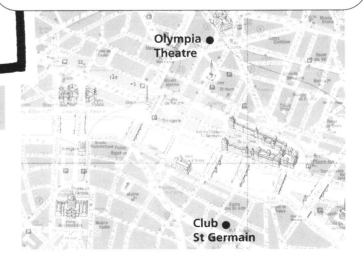

SATURDAY 23 NOVEMBER 1957
The Miles Davis Quintet appear in a Jazz For Moderns concert at the National Guard Armory in Washington. Also on the bill are George Shearing's Sextet, Gerry Mulligan's Quintet, Chico Hamilton's Quintet, the Australian Jazz Quintet and Helen Merrill.

SUN	**1**
MON	**2**
TUES	**3**
WED	**4**
THUR	**5**
FRI	**6**
SAT	**7**
SUN	**8**
MON	**9**
TUES	**10**
WED	**11**
THUR	**12**
FRI	**13**
SAT	**14**
SUN	**15**
MON	**16**
TUES	**17**
WED	**18**
THUR	**19**
FRI	**20**
SAT	**21**
SUN	**22**
MON	**23**
TUES	**24**
WED	**25**
THUR	**26**
FRI	**27**
SAT	**28**
SUN	**29**
MON	**30**
TUES	**31**

Above: A publicity shot for 'Ascenseur pour l'échafaud' with the star of the film, Jeanne Moreau.
Right: Miles discusses the score with the director Louis Malle (right).

WEDNESDAY 4 DECEMBER 1957

Miles Davis records the soundtrack for the Louis Malle film *Ascenseur pour l'échafaud*.
Miles Davis (trumpet), Barney Wilen (tenor sax), René Urtreger (piano), Pierre Michelot (bass), Kenny Clarke (drums)
Générique (BW out) / *L'assassinat de Carala* (BW out) / *Sur l'autoroute* (RU out) / *Julien dans l'ascenseur* (BW out) / *Florence dans les Champs-Elysées* / *Dîner au motel* (BW, RU out) / *Evasion de Julien* (BW, RU out) / *Visite du vigile* (MD, RU, BW out) / *Au bar du Petit Bac* / *Chez le photographe du motel* (BW out)

In a darkened room, Miles calls the key, sets the tempo, and the musicians improvise to the projected sequence of film. The music creates a very special atmosphere and Miles' first attempt at a film music score is a great success. The music is later issued on a Columbia album called *Jazz Track*.

THAT WAS FABULOUS. HE SAID, 'WAIT A MINUTE, RIGHT HERE! STOP! RIGHT HERE.' AND HE'D SAY, 'WE PLAY THIS, AND THIS RIGHT HERE' – 'CAUSE THIS SEEMED TO GO WITH THE SCENE AND IT WAS REALLY WELL THOUGHT OUT. AND WE DID THE MUSIC TO THE FILM RIGHT THEN AND THERE… IT TURNED OUT BEAUTIFUL. MILES REALLY PUT IT TOGETHER WONDERFULLY. AND, I MEAN, IT ALL HAPPENED ON THE SPUR OF THE MOMENT, YOU KNOW. AFTER ABOUT THREE HOURS, IT WAS OVER…

Drummer Kenny Clarke later recalls Miles' method of film music scoring:

UN **1**

ON **2**

UES **3**

VED **4**

HUR **5**

RI **6**

AT **7**

UN **8**

ON **9**

UES **10**

VED **11**

HUR **12**

RI **13**

AT **14**

UN **15**

ON **16**

UES **17**

VED **18**

HUR **19**

RI **20**

AT **21**

UN **22**

ON **23**

UES **24**

VED **25**

HUR **26**

RI **27**

AT **28**

UN **29**

ON **30**

UES **31**

Above: Miles and Juliette Greco in the Olympia dressing room.

The three-week residency at the Club St Germain is broken only by a short trip to Amsterdam.

SUNDAY 8 DECEMBER 1957

The Miles Davis / Barney Wilen Quintet broadcast from Amsterdam during a Sunday concert.

FRIDAY 20 DECEMBER 1957

Miles Davis' European tour ends.

Back in the States, Miles reforms the group, but decides to add another voice. John Coltrane returns on tenor to join the alto saxophone of Julian 'Cannonball' Adderley and Miles re-engages the original rhythm section of Red Garland, Paul Chambers and Philly Joe Jones. The Miles Davis Sextet opens at the Sutherland Lounge in Chicago around Christmas.

John Coltrane remembers his return to the group:

> I FOUND MILES IN THE MIDST OF ANOTHER STAGE OF HIS MUSICAL DEVELOPMENT. THERE WAS ONE TIME IN HIS PAST THAT HE DEVOTED TO MULTI-CHORDED STRUCTURES. HE WAS INTERESTED IN CHORDS FOR THEIR OWN SAKE. BUT NOW IT SEEMED THAT HE WAS MOVING IN THE OPPOSITE DIRECTION TO THE USE OF FEWER AND FEWER CHORD CHANGES IN SONGS. HE USED TUNES WITH FREE-FLOWING LINES AND CHORDAL DIRECTIONS. THIS APPROACH ALLOWED THE SOLOIST THE CHOICE OF PLAYING CHORDALLY OR MELODICALLY. IN FACT, DUE TO THE DIRECT AND FREE-FLOWING LINES IN HIS MUSIC, I FOUND IT EASY TO APPLY THE HARMONIC IDEAS THAT I HAD.

JANUARY **1958**

WED	**1**
THUR	**2**
FRI	**3**
SAT	**4**
SUN	**5**
MON	**6**
TUES	**7**
WED	**8**
THUR	**9**
FRI	**10**
SAT	**11**
SUN	**12**
MON	**13**
TUES	**14**
WED	**15**
THUR	**16**
FRI	**17**
SAT	**18**
SUN	**19**
MON	**20**
TUES	**21**
WED	**22**
THUR	**23**
FRI	**24**
SAT	**25**
SUN	**26**
MON	**27**
TUES	**28**
WED	**29**
THUR	**30**
FRI	**31**

THURSDAY 2 JANUARY 1958

The Miles Davis Sextet with John Coltrane, Cannonball Adderley, Red Garland, Paul Chambers and Philly Joe Jones, open at Birdland opposite the Johnny Richards Orchestra.

FRIDAY 3 JANUARY 1958

John Coltrane records two albums with Gene Ammons for Prestige at Rudy Van Gelder's Studio in Hackensack, New Jersey, *Groove Blues* and *The Big Sound*. Paul Quinichette, Pepper Adams, Jerome Richardson, Mal Waldron, George Joyner and Art Taylor are also on the session.

FRIDAY 10 JANUARY 1958

John Coltrane, Red Garland and Paul Chambers record for Prestige at Rudy Van Gelder's Studio in Hackensack, New Jersey. The tracks are for three albums under Coltrane's name, *Lush Life*, *The Believer* and *The Last Trane*. Donald Byrd and Louis Hayes are also on the session.

TUESDAY 21 JANUARY 1958

The Miles Davis Sextet open at The Continental in Brooklyn for a one-week engagement.

SUNDAY 26 JANUARY 1958

The Miles Davis Sextet close at the Continental in Brooklyn.

FRIDAY 31 JANUARY 1958

Paul Chambers and Philly Joe Jones record with Wynton Kelly and Kenny Burrell for Riverside at the Metropolitan Sound Studios in New York City. The album is released as *Wynton Kelly* (RLP 12-254).

WEDNESDAY 15 JANUARY 1958

The Miles Davis Sextet close at Birdland.

AT **1**
JN **2**
MON **3**
UES **4**
WED **5**
THUR **6**
RI **7**
AT **8**
JN **9**
MON **10**
UES **11**
WED **12**
THUR **13**
RI **14**
AT **15**
JN **16**
MON **17**
UES **18**
WED **19**
THUR **20**
RI **21**
AT **22**
UN **23**
MON **24**
UES **25**
WED **26**
THUR **27**
RI **28**

TUESDAY 4 FEBRUARY 1958

Recording session by the Miles Davis Sextet for Columbia at the 30th Street Studios in New York City.

MILES DAVIS (trumpet), JOHN COLTRANE (tenor sax), JULIAN 'CANNONBALL' ADDERLEY (alto sax), RED GARLAND (piano), PAUL CHAMBERS (bass), PHILLY JOE JONES (drums)

Two Bass Hit / Billy Boy (MD, JC, JCA out) */ Straight No Chaser / Milestones*

FRIDAY 7 FEBRUARY 1958

John Coltrane, Red Garland and Paul Chambers record *Soultrane* for Prestige at Rudy Van Gelder's Studio in Hackensack, New Jersey. Art Taylor is also on the session.

Top right and below: Miles at the Milestones session with pianist Red Garland and bassist Paul Chambers.

AT **1**
JN **2**
ON **3**
JES **4**
ED **5**
HUR **6**
.I **7**
AT **8**
JN **9**
ON **10**
JES **11**
ED **12**
HUR **13**
.I **14**
AT **15**
JN **16**
ON **17**
JES **18**
ED **19**
HUR **20**
.I **21**
AT **22**
JN **23**
ON **24**
JES **25**
ED **26**
HUR **27**
.I **28**

TUESDAY 11 FEBRUARY 1958
The Miles Davis Sextet with Cannonball Adderley open at the Copa in Pittsburgh for a one-week engagement.

SUNDAY 16 FEBRUARY 1958
The Miles Davis Sextet close at the Copa in Pittsburgh.

Opposite page: Miles listens to a playback during the Milestones session at Columbia's 30th Street Studios.

Miles Davis Sextet Comes to Copa

Miles Davis and his sextet of all-star jazz performers will be the attraction this week at Lenny Litman's Copa. Everyone in the group has been repeated winners of both the Downbeat and Metronome polls.

Miles has Julian "Cannonball" Adderley on alto sax, John Coltraine on tenor sax, Red Garland on piano, Philly Jo Jones on drums and Paul Chambers on bass. The Davis contingent will play 40-minute sets each hour of the evening.

NOW - ALL THIS WEEK - THE TITANS OF AMERICAN JAZZ
MILES DAVIS SEXTET
☆ MILES DAVIS · TRUMPET
☆ CANNONBALL ADDERLEY · ALTO SAX
☆ PAUL CHAMBERS · BASS ☆ RED GARLAND · PIANO
☆ JOHN COLTRAINE · TENOR SAX
☆ PHILLY JO JONES · DRUMS
PGH'S LEADING DOWNTOWN NITE CLUB
LENNY LITMAN'S COPA
818 LIBERTY AVE · CO.1-4200
FORTY MINUTE SETS EVERY HOUR
NEXT WEEK THE PLAYMATES "JO ANN"

SAT	**1**
SUN	**2**
MON	**3**
TUES	**4**
WED	**5**
THUR	**6**
FRI	**7**
SAT	**8**
SUN	**9**
MON	**10**
TUES	**11**
WED	**12**
THUR	**13**
FRI	**14**
SAT	**15**
SUN	**16**
MON	**17**
TUES	**18**
WED	**19**
THUR	**20**
FRI	**21**
SAT	**22**
SUN	**23**
MON	**24**
TUES	**25**
WED	**26**
THUR	**27**
FRI	**28**
SAT	**29**
SUN	**30**
MON	**31**

TUESDAY 4 MARCH 1958

Recording session by the Miles Davis Sextet for Columbia at the 30th Street Studios in New York City. MILES DAVIS (trumpet), JOHN COLTRANE (tenor sax), JULIAN 'CANNONBALL' ADDERLEY (alto sax), RED GARLAND (piano), PAUL CHAMBERS (bass), PHILLY JOE JONES (drums)

Dr Jekyll (Dr Jackle) (2 takes) / *Sid's Ahead (Walkin')* (RG out) / *Little Melonae* (6 takes, RG out)

Red Garland walks out of the session after an altercation with Miles. Miles plays piano on *Sid's Ahead,* and *Little Melonae,* which is never released, has no piano. Later, Bill Evans is brought in as Red's replacement.

This session completes the album later released as *Milestones* on Columbia CL1193.

Below: Miles poses in the famous green shirt for the Milestones album cover.

AT **1**

JN **2**

ON **3**

UES **4**

WED **5**

HUR **6**

RI **7**

AT **8**

JN **9**

ON **10**

UES **11**

WED **12**

HUR **13**

RI **14**

AT **15**

JN **16**

ON **17**

UES **18**

WED **19**

HUR **20**

RI **21**

AT **22**

JN **23**

ON **24**

UES **25**

WED **26**

HUR **27**

RI **28**

AT **29**

JN **30**

ON **31**

THURSDAY 6 MARCH 1958

Down Beat publishes an article in which Miles tells in his own words how his career started.

I spent my first week in New York and my first month's allowance looking for Charlie Parker.

If you can hear a note, you can play it.

You learn where to put notes so they'll sound right. You just don't do it because it's a funny chord. I used to change things because I wanted to hear them—substitute progressions and things. Now I have better taste.

People ask me if I respond to the audience. I wouldn't like to sit up there and play without anybody liking it. If it's a large audience, I'm very pleased because they are there anyway. If it's a small audience, sometimes it doesn't matter.

self-portrait: miles davis

You want me to tell you where I was born—that old story? It was in good old Alton, Ill. In 1926. And I had to call my mother a week before my last birthday and ask her how old I would be.

I started playing trumpet in grade school. Once a week we would hold notes. Wednesdays at 2.30. Everybody would fight to play best. Lucky for me, I learned to play the chromatic scale right away. A friend of my father's brought me a book one night and showed me how to do it so I wouldn't have to sit there and hold that note all the time.

My mother wanted to give me a violin for my birthday, but my father gave me a trumpet—because he loved my mother so much!

There was a very good instructor in town. He was having some dental work done by my father. He was the one that made my father get me the trumpet. He used to tell us all about jam sessions on the Showboat, about trumpet players like Bobby Hackett and Hal Baker. "Play without any vibrato," he used to tell us. "You're gonna get old anyway and start shaking," he used to say, "no vibrato!" That's how I tried to play. Fast and light—and no vibrato.

By the time I was 16, I was playing in a band—the Blue Devils—in East St. Louis. Sonny Stitt came to town with a band and heard us play one night. He told me, "You look like a man named Charlie Parker and you play like him, too. C'mon with us."

The fellows in his band had their hair slicked down, they wore tuxedos, and they offered me 60 whole dollars a week to play with them. I went home and asked my mother if I could go with them. She said no, I had to finish my last year of high school. I didn't talk to her for two weeks. And I didn't go with the band, either.

I knew about Charlie Parker in St. Louis, I even played with him there, while I was still in high school. We always used to try to play like Diz and Charlie Parker. When we heard that they were coming to town, my friend and I were the first people in the hall, me with a trumpet under

(Continued on Page 46)

a brilliant trumpeter tells in his own words how his career started

There's a certain feeling you get from playing that you can't get from composing. And when you play, it's like composition anyway. You make the outline.

If you play good for eight bars, it's enough. For yourself. And I don't tell anybody.

MARCH 1958

SAT	1
SUN	2
MON	3
TUES	4
WED	5
THUR	6
FRI	7
SAT	8
SUN	9
MON	10
TUES	11
WED	12
THUR	13
FRI	14
SAT	15
SUN	16
MON	17
TUES	18
WED	19
THUR	20
FRI	21
SAT	22
SUN	23
MON	24
TUES	25
WED	26
THUR	27
FRI	28
SAT	29
SUN	30
MON	31

FRIDAY 7 MARCH 1958
John Coltrane and Paul Chambers record *Kenny Burrell & John Coltrane* for New Jazz at Rudy Van Gelder's Studio in Hackensack, New Jersey. Tommy Flanagan and Jimmy Cobb are also on the session.

SUNDAY 9 MARCH 1958
Miles Davis records with Julian Adderley and the All Stars for Blue Note in New York City.
MILES DAVIS (trumpet), JULIAN 'CANNONBALL' ADDERLEY (alto sax), HANK JONES (piano), SAM JONES (bass), ART BLAKEY (drums)
Autumn Leaves / Somethin' Else / One For Daddy-O / Love For Sale / Dancing In The Dark (MD out) */ Alison's Uncle*
Miles appears by special arrangement with Columbia, probably to facilitate the release of Cannonball to appear with Miles on Columbia. The album is released as *Somethin' Else* (Blue Note BLP 81595)

THURSDAY 13 MARCH 1958
John Coltrane records *Mainstream 1958* with the Wilbur Harden Quintet for Savoy at Rudy Van Gelder's Studio in Hackensack, New Jersey. Tommy Flanagan, Doug Watkins and Louis Hayes are also on the session.

WEDNESDAY 26 MARCH 1958
John Coltrane, Red Garland and Paul Chambers record *Settin' The Pace* for Prestige at Rudy Van Gelder's Studio in Hackensack, New Jersey. Art Taylor is also on the session.

Miles and Frances Taylor begin living together in his apartment on 10th Avenue. Miles trades in his Mercedes-Benz for a white Ferrari.

TUES 1
WED 2
THUR 3
FRI 4
SAT 5
SUN 6
MON 7
TUES 8
WED 9
THUR 10
FRI 11
SAT 12
SUN 13
MON 14
TUES 15
WED 16
THUR 17
FRI 18
SAT 19
SUN 20
MON 21
TUES 22
WED 23
THUR 24
FRI 25
SAT 26
SUN 27
MON 28
TUES 29
WED 30

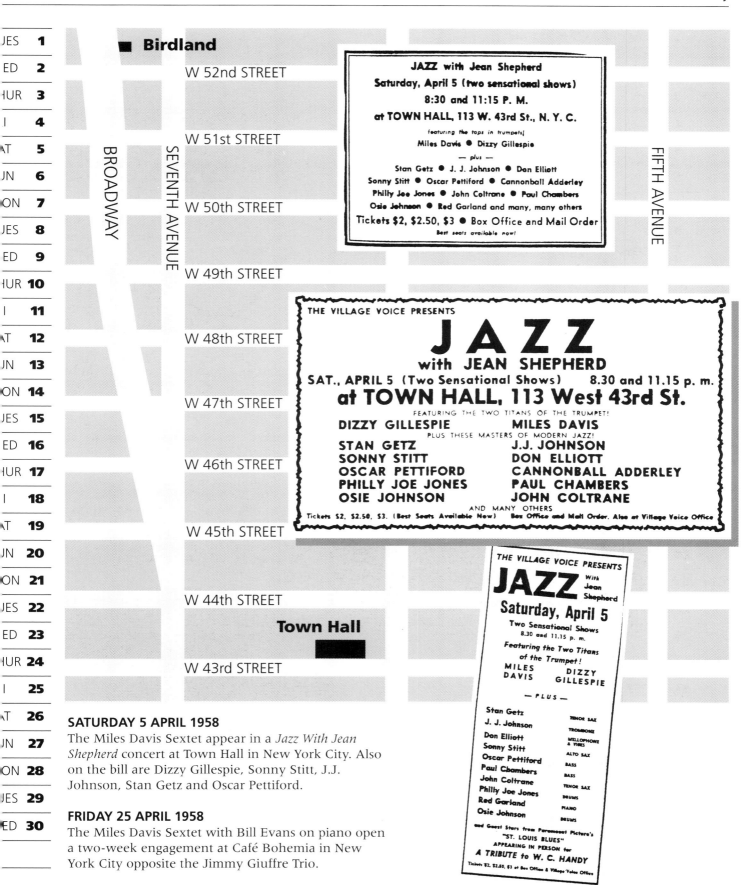

■ Birdland

BROADWAY · SEVENTH AVENUE · FIFTH AVENUE

W 52nd STREET
W 51st STREET
W 50th STREET
W 49th STREET
W 48th STREET
W 47th STREET
W 46th STREET
W 45th STREET
W 44th STREET
Town Hall
W 43rd STREET

JAZZ with Jean Shepherd
Saturday, April 5 (two sensational shows)
8:30 and 11:15 P. M.
at TOWN HALL, 113 W. 43rd St., N. Y. C.
featuring the tops in trumpets!
Miles Davis ● Dizzy Gillespie
— plus —
Stan Getz ● J. J. Johnson ● Don Elliott
Sonny Stitt ● Oscar Pettiford ● Cannonball Adderley
Philly Joe Jones ● John Coltrane ● Paul Chambers
Osie Johnson ● Red Garland and many, many others
Tickets $2, $2.50, $3 ● Box Office and Mail Order
Best seats available now!

THE VILLAGE VOICE PRESENTS
J A Z Z
with JEAN SHEPHERD
SAT., APRIL 5 (Two Sensational Shows) 8.30 and 11.15 p. m.
at TOWN HALL, 113 West 43rd St.
FEATURING THE TWO TITANS OF THE TRUMPET!
DIZZY GILLESPIE   MILES DAVIS
PLUS THESE MASTERS OF MODERN JAZZ!
STAN GETZ   J.J. JOHNSON
SONNY STITT   DON ELLIOTT
OSCAR PETTIFORD   CANNONBALL ADDERLEY
PHILLY JOE JONES   PAUL CHAMBERS
OSIE JOHNSON   JOHN COLTRANE
AND MANY OTHERS
Tickets $2, $2.50, $3. (Best Seats Available Now) Box Office and Mail Order. Also at Village Voice Office

THE VILLAGE VOICE PRESENTS
JAZZ With Jean Shepherd
Saturday, April 5
Two Sensational Shows
8.30 and 11.15 p. m.
Featuring the Two Titans
of the Trumpet!
MILES   DIZZY
DAVIS   GILLESPIE
— PLUS —
Stan Getz   TENOR SAX
J. J. Johnson   TROMBONE
Don Elliott   MELLOPHONE & VIBES
Sonny Stitt   ALTO SAX
Oscar Pettiford   BASS
Paul Chambers   BASS
John Coltrane   TENOR SAX
Philly Joe Jones   DRUMS
Red Garland   PIANO
Osie Johnson   DRUMS
and Guest Stars from Paramount Picture's
"ST. LOUIS BLUES"
APPEARING IN PERSON for
A TRIBUTE to W. C. HANDY
Tickets $2, $2.50, $3 at Box Office & Village Voice Office

SATURDAY 5 APRIL 1958
The Miles Davis Sextet appear in a *Jazz With Jean Shepherd* concert at Town Hall in New York City. Also on the bill are Dizzy Gillespie, Sonny Stitt, J.J. Johnson, Stan Getz and Oscar Pettiford.

FRIDAY 25 APRIL 1958
The Miles Davis Sextet with Bill Evans on piano open a two-week engagement at Café Bohemia in New York City opposite the Jimmy Giuffre Trio.

MAY 1958

THUR	1
FRI	2
SAT	3
SUN	4
MON	5
TUES	6
WED	7
THUR	8
FRI	9
SAT	10
SUN	11
MON	12
TUES	13
WED	14
THUR	15
FRI	16
SAT	17
SUN	18
MON	19
TUES	20
WED	21
THUR	22
FRI	23
SAT	24
SUN	25
MON	26
TUES	27
WED	28
THUR	29
FRI	30
SAT	31

SATURDAY 3 MAY 1958

The Miles Davis Sextet broadcast on Mutual's *Bandstand USA* from the Café Bohemia in New York City.
MILES DAVIS (trumpet), JOHN COLTRANE (tenor sax), JULIAN 'CANNONBALL' ADDERLEY (alto sax), BILL EVANS (piano), PAUL CHAMBERS (bass), PHILLY JOE JONES (drums)
Woody'n You / In Your Own Sweet Way / Night In Tunisia (incomplete)

MONDAY 12 MAY 1958

The Phineas Newborn Quartet replace Jimmy Giuffre's Trio opposite Miles at the Café Bohemia.

TUESDAY 13 MAY 1958

John Coltrane records with the Wilbur Harden Sextet for Savoy at Rudy Van Gelder's Studio in Hackensack, New Jersey. Also on the session are Wilbur Harden, Curtis Fuller, Howard Williams, Alvin Jackson and Art Taylor.

THURSDAY 15 MAY 1958

Down Beat reviews Miles' latest album release:

RELAXIN' WITH THE MILES DAVIS QUINTET— Prestige 7129:

If I Were A Bell; You're My Everything; I Could Write A Book; Oleo; It Could Happen To You; Woody'n You
Personnel: Davis, trumpet; John Coltrane, tenor; Red Garland, piano; Paul Chambers, bass; Philly Joe Jones, drums.
Rating: ★★★★

After all that walkin' and cookin', it's time for Miles and men to relax. That's what they do here. This is an informal, one-take-a-tune session, complete with asides from Miles to Prestige's Bob Weinstock and a false start on *Everything*.

Miles plays muted horn on all but *Woody'n* here. He plays with his customary delicate, intricate impact. Chambers is superb. Garland plays effectively in support and solos authoritatively. Jones, less oppressive here than in past conquests, contributes inspirationally, too. The material is of interest, with the standards particularly well handled. It's pleasant to hear a co-ordinated jazz group approach such tunes.

There is a hesitancy and lack of melodic content in Coltrane's playing at times here that hampers his effectiveness for me and lowers the rating of the LP. This is particularly true on the first two tracks, on which his solos seem to me to be rather aimless and somewhat strident. However, he is quite fluent on *Oleo* and *Book*. His efforts, throughout the LP, lack a consistent quality.

In general, however, this is an attractive set. And when all the members of the quintet are inspired, as on *Book* and *Oleo*, it is a valuable demonstration of conceptual prowess.

Ira Gitler's notes are frank and informative. (D.G.)

SATURDAY 17 MAY 1958

The Miles Davis Sextet broadcast on Mutual's *Bandstand USA* from the Café Bohemia in New York City. Cannonball is absent for the broadcast.
MILES DAVIS (trumpet), JOHN COLTRANE (tenor sax), BILL EVANS (piano), PAUL CHAMBERS (bass), PHILLY JOE JONES (drums), LEONARD FEATHER, DAN MORGENSTERN (announcements)
ann / *Four / Bye Bye Blackbird / Walkin' / Two Bass Hit* (incomplete) / ann

SUNDAY 18 MAY 1958

The Miles Davis Sextet close at Café Bohemia in New York City.
Philly Joe Jones quits to start his own band. His replacement is Jimmy Cobb.

FRIDAY 23 MAY 1958

John Coltrane, Red Garland and Paul Chambers record *Black Pearls* for Prestige at Rudy Van Gelder's Studio in Hackensack, New Jersey. Donald Byrd and Art Taylor are also on the session.

MONDAY 26 MAY 1958

Recording session by the Miles Davis Sextet for Columbia at the 30th Street Studios in New York City.
MILES DAVIS (trumpet), JOHN COLTRANE (tenor sax), JULIAN 'CANNONBALL' ADDERLEY (alto sax), BILL EVANS (piano), PAUL CHAMBERS (bass), JIMMY COBB (drums)
Green Dolphin Street / Fran Dance (2 takes) / *Stella By Starlight* (JCA out, 7 takes) / *Love For Sale*
The recordings are issued as *Jazz Track* on Columbia CL 1268.

Miles' 32nd birthday.

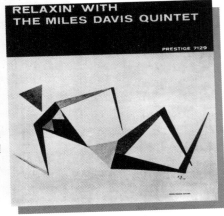

RELAXIN' WITH THE MILES DAVIS QUINTET

PRESTIGE 7129

TUESDAY 10 JUNE 1958

The Miles Davis Sextet open at the Spotlite Lounge in Washington, D.C. for a one-week engagement.

SUNDAY 15 JUNE 1958

The Miles Davis Sextet close at the Spotlite Lounge in Washington, D.C.

TUESDAY 24 JUNE 1958

John Coltrane records with the Wilbur Harden & Curtis Fuller Sextet for Savoy at Rudy Van Gelder's Studio in Hackensack, New Jersey. Also on the session are Wilbur Harden, Curtis Fuller, Tommy Flanagan, Alvin Jackson and Art Taylor.

The Miles Davis Sextet open at Smalls' Paradise in New York City for a one-week engagement.

WEDNESDAY 25 JUNE 1958

Miles, Coltrane, Evans and Chambers take part in a recording session by Michel Legrand and his Orchestra for Columbia in New York City.

MILES DAVIS (trumpet), JOHN COLTRANE (tenor sax), PHIL WOODS (alto sax), JEROME RICHARDSON (bass clarinet), HERBIE MANN (flute), BETTY GLAMANN (harp), EDDIE COSTA (vibes), BARRY GALBRAITH (guitar), BILL EVANS (piano), PAUL CHAMBERS (bass), KENNY DENNIS (drums), MICHEL LEGRAND (arranger/conductor)

Wild Man Blues / Round Midnight / Jitterbug Waltz / Django (JC, PW, JR out)

Miles doesn't play on the remainder of the album which is released as *Legrand Jazz* on Columbia CL 1250.

SUNDAY 29 JUNE 1958

The Miles Davis Sextet close at Smalls' Paradise in New York City.

TUES	**1**
WED	**2**
THUR	**3**
FRI	**4**
SAT	**5**
SUN	**6**
MON	**7**
TUES	**8**
WED	**9**
THUR	**10**
FRI	**11**
SAT	**12**
SUN	**13**
MON	**14**
TUES	**15**
WED	**16**
THUR	**17**
FRI	**18**
SAT	**19**
SUN	**20**
MON	**21**
TUES	**22**
WED	**23**
THUR	**24**
FRI	**25**
SAT	**26**
SUN	**27**
MON	**28**
TUES	**29**
WED	**30**
THUR	**31**

TUESDAY 1 JULY 1958

Cannonball Adderley and Bill Evans record for Riverside in New York City. Blue Mitchell, Sam Jones and Philly Joe Jones are also on the session which is released as *Portrait of Cannonball* on Riverside RLP12-269.

Miles drives up to Newport, Rhode Island, to take part in the 4th Annual Newport Jazz Festival. This is the first time Miles has returned to the scene of his 1955 triumph. The festival is being filmed by Bert Stern for his movie *Jazz on a Summer's Day*, but he somehow misses Miles Davis, Lester Young, Duke Ellington, Benny Goodman, Dave Brubeck and Willie 'The Lion' Smith.

Right: Miles chats with Symphony Sid Torin backstage at Newport. Behind them, it looks like record producer Bob Thiele (with cigarette) talking to Leonard Feather.

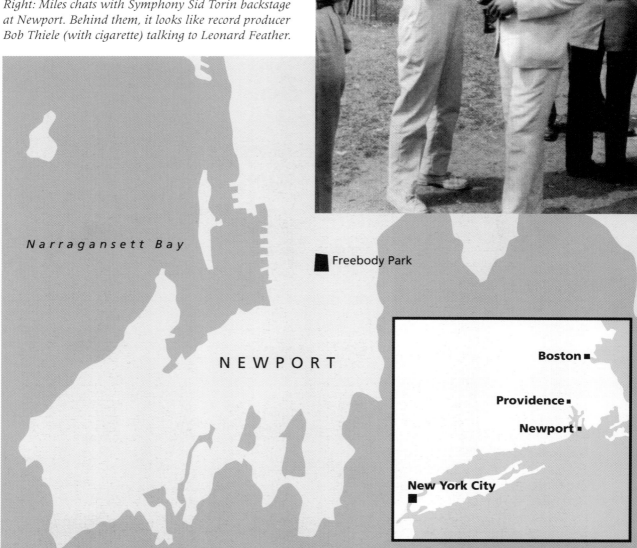

Narragansett Bay

■ Freebody Park

NEWPORT

Boston ■

Providence ■

Newport ■

New York City ■

ES **1**
ED **2**
UR **3**
4
T **5**
N **6**
ON **7**
ES **8**
ED **9**
UR **10**
11
T **12**
N **13**
ON **14**
ES **15**
ED **16**
UR **17**
18
T **19**
N **20**
ON **21**
ES **22**
ED **23**
UR **24**
25
T **26**
N **27**
ON **28**
ES **29**
ED **30**
UR **31**

THURSDAY 3 JULY 1958

Miles Davis Sextet appear at the Newport Jazz Festival in Newport, Rhode Island. The performance is recorded by Columbia.

MILES DAVIS (trumpet), JOHN COLTRANE (tenor sax), JULIAN 'CANNONBALL' ADDERLEY (alto sax), BILL EVANS (piano), PAUL CHAMBERS (bass), JIMMY COBB (drums), WILLIS CONOVER (announcer)
ann / *Ah-Leu-Cha* / *Straight No Chaser* / *Fran Dance* / *Two Bass Hit* / *Bye Bye Blackbird* / *The Theme*
These recordings are eventually released in the 60's as one half of an album entitled *Miles & Monk at Newport* on Columbia CL 2178.

Below: The sextet on stage at Newport.
L to r, Bill Evans, piano; Paul Chambers, bass;
Cannonball Adderley, alto sax; Miles, trumpet;
Jimmy Cobb, drums; John Coltrane, tenor sax.

Down Beat review the performance:

Next to arrive was the Miles Davis sextet, with Davis, trumpet; John Coltrane, tenor; Julian Adderley, alto; Bill Evans, piano; Paul Chambers, bass, and Jimmy Cobb, drums.

On an Ellington night, the Davis group's repertoire included six tunes, none associated with Duke. Included were Monk's *Straight No Chaser, Put Your Little Foot, Two Bass Hit,* and *Bye Bye Blackbird.* Asked backstage why his group did not perform Ellington tunes, Miles logically declared that performing familiar material effectively would be the best sort of tribute.

Unfortunately, the group did not perform effectively. Although Miles continues to play with delicacy and infinite grace, his group's solidarity is hampered by the angry young tenor of Coltrane. Backing himself into rhythmic corners on flurries of notes, Coltrane sounded like the the personification of motion-without-progress in jazz. What is equally important, Coltrane's playing apparently has influenced Adderley. The latter's playing indicated less concern for melodic structure than he has illustrated in the past.

Although Chambers continues to be one of jazz's most agile bassists, he was drowned often by Cobb's oppressive support. Evans, too, had little opportunity to speak as authoritatively as he has indicated he can speak.

With the exception of Miles' vital contribution, then, the group proved more confusing to listeners than educational.

TUES **1**

WED **2**

THUR **3**

FRI **4**

SAT **5**

SUN **6**

MON **7**

TUES **8**

WED **9**

THUR **10**

FRI **11**

SAT **12**

SUN **13**

MON **14**

TUES **15**

WED **16**

THUR **17**

FRI **18**

SAT **19**

SUN **20**

MON **21**

TUES **22**

WED **23**

THUR **24**

FRI **25**

SAT **26**

SUN **27**

MON **28**

TUES **29**

WED **30**

THUR **31**

TUES	**1**
WED	**2**
THUR	**3**
FRI	**4**
SAT	**5**
SUN	**6**
MON	**7**
TUES	**8**
WED	**9**
THUR	**10**
FRI	**11**
SAT	**12**
SUN	**13**
MON	**14**
TUES	**15**
WED	**16**
THUR	**17**
FRI	**18**
SAT	**19**
SUN	**20**
MON	**21**
TUES	**22**
WED	**23**
THUR	**24**
FRI	**25**
SAT	**26**
SUN	**27**
MON	**28**
TUES	**29**
WED	**30**
THUR	**31**

Left: Miles solos at Newport.

FRIDAY 11 JULY 1958

John Coltrane, Red Garland, Paul Chambers and Jimmy Cobb record *Standard Coltrane* with Wilbur Harden for Prestige at Rudy Van Gelder's Studio in Hackensack, New Jersey. They also record four tracks that are later used on the Coltrane albums *Stardust* and *Bahia*.

TUESDAY 22 JULY 1958

Recording session by Miles Davis with the Gil Evans Orchestra for Columbia in New York City.
MILES DAVIS (trumpet/flugelhorn), JOHN COLES, BERNIE GLOW, ERNIE ROYAL, LOUIS MUCCI (trumpet), FRANK REHAK, JIMMY CLEVELAND, JOE BENNETT (trombone), RICHARD HIXON (bass trombone), WILLIE RUFF, JULIUS WATKINS, GUNTHER SCHULLER (french horn), BILL BARBER (tuba), JULIAN 'CANNONBALL' ADDERLEY (alto sax), DANNY BANK (bass clarinet), PHIL BODNER, ROMEO PENQUE (flute), PAUL CHAMBERS (bass), PHILLY JOE JONES (drums), GIL EVANS (arranger/conductor)
My Man's Gone Now / Gone, Gone, Gone / Gone

The Miles Davis Sextet open at the Village Vanguard in New York City for a two-week engagement opposite singer Ethel Ennis.

TUESDAY 29 JULY 1958

Recording session by Miles Davis with the Gil Evans Orchestra for Columbia in New York City.
MILES DAVIS (trumpet/flugelhorn), JOHN COLES, BERN GLOW, ERNIE ROYAL, LOUIS MUCCI (trumpet), FRANK REHAK, JIMMY CLEVELAND, JOE BENNETT (trombone), RICHARD HIXON (bass trombone), WILLIE RUFF, JULIUS WATKINS, GUNTHER SCHULLER (french horn), BILL BARBER (tuba), JULIAN 'CANNONBALL' ADDERLEY (alto sax), DANNY BANK (bass clarinet), PHIL BODNER, ROMEO PENQUE (flute), PAUL CHAMBERS (bass), JIMMY COBB (drums), GIL EVANS (arranger/conductor)
Here Come De Honey Man / Bess You Is My Woman Now / It Ain't Necessarily So / Fisherman, Strawberry And Devil Crab

	1
T	**2**
N	**3**
ON	**4**
ES	**5**
ED	**6**
UR	**7**
	8
T	**9**
N	**10**
ON	**11**
ES	**12**
ED	**13**
UR	**14**
I	**15**
T	**16**
JN	**17**
ON	**18**
ES	**19**
ED	**20**
HUR	**21**
I	**22**
AT	**23**
JN	**24**
ON	**25**
ES	**26**
ED	**27**
HUR	**28**
I	**29**
AT	**30**
JN	**31**

SUNDAY 3 AUGUST 1958

The Miles Davis Sextet close at the Village Vanguard in New York City.

MONDAY 4 AUGUST 1958

Recording session by Miles Davis with the Gil Evans Orchestra for Columbia in New York City.
MILES DAVIS (trumpet/flugelhorn), JOHN COLES, BERNIE GLOW, ERNIE ROYAL, LOUIS MUCCI (trumpet), FRANK REHAK, JIMMY CLEVELAND, JOE BENNETT (trombone), RICHARD HIXON (bass trombone), WILLIE RUFF, JULIUS WATKINS, GUNTHER SCHULLER (french horn), BILL BARBER (tuba), JULIAN 'CANNONBALL' ADDERLEY (alto sax), DANNY BANK (bass clarinet), JEROME RICHARDSON, ROMEO PENQUE (flute), PAUL CHAMBERS (bass), JIMMY COBB (drums), GIL EVANS (arranger/conductor)
Prayer (Oh Doctor Jesus) / Bess Oh Where's My Bess / Buzzard Song

FRI	**1**
SAT	**2**
SUN	**3**
MON	**4**
TUES	**5**
WED	**6**
THUR	**7**
FRI	**8**
SAT	**9**
SUN	**10**
MON	**11**
TUES	**12**
WED	**13**
THUR	**14**
FRI	**15**
SAT	**16**
SUN	**17**
MON	**18**
TUES	**19**
WED	**20**
THUR	**21**
FRI	**22**
SAT	**23**
SUN	**24**
MON	**25**
TUES	**26**
WED	**27**
THUR	**28**
FRI	**29**
SAT	**30**
SUN	**31**

Comedy Club

Coming Aug. 12

JAZZ

JAZZ LTD.—THE BIGGEST NAMES IN JAZZ

OPENS   **MILES DAVIS**
TOMORROW   ALL STARS

Next Attraction
BUDDY RICH   **SPOTLITE**
Starts Tues., Aug. 12 | 1300 RHODE ISLAND AVE. N.E.

Tomorrow p. m. that cool school known as the Spotlite brings back Miles Davis and his All Stars for the devoted cheering sections. Mr. Davis will be around the sprawling premises thru next Sunday.

MILES DAVIS
and his
QUINTETTE
Jazz Session
Sat & Sun. 5 to 8

Coming Aug. 19
DINAH WASHINGTON

Comedy Club
1414 PENNA. AVE.
BALTIMORE

Above: Miles coaches drummer Jimmy Cobb at a recording session for the 'Porgy and Bess' album.
Opposite page: At the same session, Miles plays while Gil Evans conducts the orchestra (top) and in the bottom pictur Miles smiles as he listens to a playback.

TUESDAY 5 AUGUST 1958
The Miles Davis Sextet open at the Spotlite Lounge ir Washington D.C. for a one-week engagement.

SATURDAY 9 AUGUST 1958
The Miles Davis Sextet broadcast on Mutual's *Bandstand USA* from the Spotlite Lounge.
MILES DAVIS (trumpet), JOHN COLTRANE (tenor sax), JULIAN 'CANNONBALL' ADDERLEY (alto sax), BILL EVANS (piano), PAUL CHAMBERS (bass), JIMMY COBB (drums)
Walkin' / All Of You / 'Round About Midnight (incomplete

SUNDAY 10 AUGUST 1958
The Miles Davis Sextet close at the Spotlite Lounge ir Washington D.C.

TUESDAY 12 AUGUST 1958
The Miles Davis Sextet open at the Comedy Club in Baltimore for a one-week engagement.

SUNDAY 17 AUGUST 1958
The Miles Davis Sextet close at the Comedy Club in Baltimore.

	1
T	2
N	3
ON	4
ES	5
ED	6
HUR	7
I	8
T	9
N	10
ON	11
ES	12
ED	13
UR	14
N	15
T	16
N	17
ON	18
ES	19
ED	20
HUR	21
I	22
T	23
N	24
ON	25
ES	26
ED	27
HUR	28
RI	29
AT	30
JN	31

MONDAY 18 AUGUST 1958

Recording session by Miles Davis with the Gil Evans
Orchestra for Columbia in New York City.
MILES DAVIS (trumpet/flugelhorn), JOHN COLES, BERNIE
GLOW, ERNIE ROYAL, LOUIS MUCCI (trumpet), FRANK
REHAK, JIMMY CLEVELAND, JOE BENNETT (trombone),
RICHARD HIXON (bass trombone), WILLIE RUFF, JULIUS
WATKINS, GUNTHER SCHULLER (french horn), BILL
BARBER (tuba), JULIAN 'CANNONBALL' ADDERLEY (alto
sax), DANNY BANK (bass clarinet), JEROME RICHARDSON,
ROMEO PENQUE (flute), PAUL CHAMBERS (bass), JIMMY
COBB (drums), GIL EVANS (arranger/conductor)
*Summertime / There's A Boat That's Leaving Soon For New
York / I Loves You Porgy*

Meanwhile, John Coltrane is in the Savoy studios
recording an album for Wilbur Harden, *Jazz Way Out.*
Curtis Fuller, Tommy Flanagan, Alvin Jackson and
Art Taylor are also on the session.

WEDNESDAY 20 AUGUST 1958

Cannonball Adderley, with Bill Evans and Jimmy
Cobb, record with strings for EmArcy in New York
City.

FRI	**1**
SAT	**2**
SUN	**3**
MON	**4**
TUES	**5**
WED	**6**
THUR	**7**
FRI	**8**
SAT	**9**
SUN	**10**
MON	**11**
TUES	**12**
WED	**13**
THUR	**14**
FRI	**15**
SAT	**16**
SUN	**17**
MON	**18**
TUES	**19**
WED	**20**
THUR	**21**
FRI	**22**
SAT	**23**
SUN	**24**
MON	**25**
TUES	**26**
WED	**27**
THUR	**28**
FRI	**29**
SAT	**30**
SUN	**31**

THURSDAY 21 AUGUST 1958
Cannonball Adderley, Bill Evans and Jimmy Cobb complete the strings session for EmArcy in New York City. The album is released as *Jump For Joy* on EmArcy SR80017.

The results of the *Down Beat* 1958 International Jazz Critics Poll are published and Miles wins the trumpet category, with the previous year's winner, Dizzy Gillespie, finishing second.

SATURDAY 23 AUGUST 1958
The Miles Davis Sextet appear at the New York Jazz Festival at Randall's Island.

MONDAY 25 AUGUST 1958
John Coltrane records *Tanganyika Strut* with Wilbur Harden for Savoy in New York City. Curtis Fuller, Howard Williams, Alvin Jackson and Art Taylor are also on the session.

COMBO
Modern Jazz Quartet	**102**
Jimmy Giuffre 3	30
Gerry Mulligan Quartet	28
Oscar Peterson Trio	21
Miles Davis Quintet	20
Tony Scott Quintet	20
Thelonious Monk Quartet	13
Chico Hamilton Quintet	10
Buddy Tate Septet	10
Dave Brubeck Quartet	8
Art Blakey's Jazz Messengers	8
Bobby Hackett Sextet	5
Louis Armstrong All-Stars	3
Horace Silver Quintet	3
Ben Webster Quartet	2

TRUMPET
Miles Davis	**101**
Dizzy Gillespie	64
Louis Armstrong	36
Clark Terry	13
Billy Butterfield	13
Chet Baker	10
Joe Newman	10
Jonah Jones	10
Roy Eldridge	7
Buck Clayton	5
Bobby Hackett	5
Art Farmer	4
Ruby Braff	3
Donald Byrd	3
Maynard Ferguson	3
Doc Cheatham	1
Emmett Berry	1

ON	**1**	WED	**1**
ES	**2**	THUR	**2**
ED	**3**	FRI	**3**
UR	**4**	SAT	**4**
	5	SUN	**5**
	6	MON	**6**
N	**7**	TUES	**7**
ON	**8**	WED	**8**
ES	**9**	THUR	**9**
ED	**10**	FRI	**10**
UR	**11**	SAT	**11**
	12	SUN	**12**
T	**13**	MON	**13**
N	**14**	TUES	**14**
ON	**15**	WED	**15**
ES	**16**	THUR	**16**
ED	**17**	FRI	**17**
UR	**18**	SAT	**18**
	19	SUN	**19**
T	**20**	MON	**20**
N	**21**	TUES	**21**
ON	**22**	WED	**22**
ES	**23**	THUR	**23**
ED	**24**	FRI	**24**
UR	**25**	SAT	**25**
	26	SUN	**26**
T	**27**	MON	**27**
N	**28**	TUES	**28**
ON	**29**	WED	**29**
ES	**30**	THUR	**30**
		FRI	**31**

Above: Miles and Billie Holiday at the Plaza Hotel for the Columbia party on 9 September.

TUESDAY 9 SEPTEMBER 1958

Miles Davis Sextet appear in the Persian Room of the Plaza Hotel in New York at a party thrown by Columbia Records. Also appearing are Duke Ellington and his Orchestra, Billie Holiday and Jimmy Rushing.

MILES DAVIS (trumpet), JOHN COLTRANE (tenor sax), JULIAN 'CANNONBALL' ADDERLEY (alto sax), BILL EVANS (piano), PAUL CHAMBERS (bass), JIMMY COBB (drums)

Straight No Chaser / My Funny Valentine (JC, JCA out) / *If I Were A Bell* (JCA out) / *Oleo*

FRIDAY 12 SEPTEMBER 1958

John Coltrane records *New York N.Y.* with George Russell's Orchestra for Decca in New York City. Bill Evans is also on the session.

THURSDAY 25 SEPTEMBER 1958

John Coltrane plays in an informal jam session in Joe Brazil's basement in Detroit.

MONDAY 13 OCTOBER 1958

John Coltrane records with the Cecil Taylor Quintet for United Artists in New York City. Kenny Dorham, Cecil Taylor, Chuck Israels and Louis Hayes are also on the session.

FRIDAY 17 OCTOBER 1958

The Miles Davis Sextet open at the Apollo Theatre in Harlem for a one-week engagement. Also on the bill are Sarah Vaughan, The Wailers, Johnny Richards Band and Symphony Sid.

THURSDAY 23 OCTOBER 1958

The Miles Davis Sextet close at the Apollo Theatre in Harlem.

TUESDAY 28 OCTOBER 1958

Cannonball Adderley records for Riverside in New York City. Milt Jackson, Wynton Kelly, Percy Heath and Art Blakey are also on the session which is released as *Things Are Getting Better* on Riverside RLP12-286.

WEDNESDAY 29 OCTOBER 1958

The Miles Davis Sextet open at the Spotlite Lounge in Washington, D.C.

SAT	1
SUN	2
MON	3
TUES	4
WED	5
THUR	6
FRI	7
SAT	8
SUN	9
MON	10
TUES	11
WED	12
THUR	13
FRI	14
SAT	15
SUN	16
MON	17
TUES	18
WED	19
THUR	20
FRI	21
SAT	22
SUN	23
MON	24
TUES	25
WED	26
THUR	27
FRI	28
SAT	29
SUN	30

SATURDAY 1 NOVEMBER 1958

The Miles Davis Sextet broadcast on Mutual's *Bandstand USA* from the Spotlite Lounge in Washington, D.C.
MILES DAVIS (trumpet), JOHN COLTRANE (tenor sax), JULIAN 'CANNONBALL' ADDERLEY (alto sax), BILL EVANS (piano), PAUL CHAMBERS (bass), JIMMY COBB (drums)
ann / *Sid's Ahead* / ann / *Bye Bye Blackbird* / ann / *Straight, No Chaser* / ann

SUNDAY 2 NOVEMBER 1958

The Miles Davis Sextet close at the Spotlite Lounge in Washington D.C. after a one-week engagement.

TUESDAY 4 NOVEMBER 1958

The Miles Davis Sextet open at the Village Vanguard in New York City for a two-week engagement.

TUESDAY 11 NOVEMBER 1958

Singer Ernestine Anderson joins the Miles Davis Sextet on the bill at the Village Vanguard.

SUNDAY 16 NOVEMBER 1958

The Miles Davis Sextet close at the Village Vanguard in New York City.
Bill Evans leaves the band and Red Garland temporarily rejoins. Both Coltrane and Cannonball are keen to start their own bands. In order to keep the group together Miles gets his agent to take bookings for Trane's group and Cannonball's group while both are still playing with Miles.

FRIDAY 28 NOVEMBER 1958

The Miles Davis Sextet appear in concert at Town Hall in New York City. There are two shows, at 8pm and 11pm. Also on the bill are Thelonious Monk's Band, the Gerry Mulligan Quartet and the Jimmy Giuffre Trio.

MON **1**
TUES **2**
WED **3**
THUR **4**
5
T 6
N 7
MON **8**
TUES **9**
WED **10**
THUR **11**
12
T 13
N 14
MON **15**
TUES **16**
WED **17**
THUR **18**
19
T 20
MON **21**
MON **22**
TUES **23**
WED **24**
THUR **25**
26
T 27
MON **28**
MON **29**
TUES **30**
WED **31**

FRIDAY 12 DECEMBER 1958

The Miles Davis Sextet open at the Howard Theatre in Washington D.C. for a one-week engagement.

THURSDAY 18 DECEMBER 1958

The Miles Davis Sextet close at the Howard Theatre in Washington D.C.

THURSDAY 25 DECEMBER 1958

Miles is the runaway winner of the trumpet award in the annual *Down Beat* Readers' Poll. He is also named Personality of the Year.

TRUMPET

1.	Miles Davis	2352
2.	Dizzy Gillespie	696
3.	Maynard Ferguson	309
4.	Chet Baker	276
5.	Art Farmer	216
6.	Jonah Jones	180
7.	Louis Armstrong	144
7.	Shorty Rogers	144
9.	Roy Eldridge	123
10.	Donald Byrd	114
11.	Harry James	102
12.	Ruby Braff	81
13.	Kenny Dorham	72
14.	Harry Edison	69
15.	Don Fagerquist	66
16.	Conte Candoli	60
17.	Clark Terry	54
17.	Lee Morgan	54
17.	Joe Newman	54
20.	Bobby Hackett	45
21.	Charlie Shavers	42
22.	Thad Jones	36

FRIDAY 26 DECEMBER 1958

John Coltrane, Red Garland and Paul Chambers record as the John Coltrane Quartet for Prestige at Rudy Van Gelder's Studio in Hackensack, New Jersey. Also on the session are Art Taylor and Freddie Hubbard. The recordings are issued as *The Believer* on LP 7292.

SATURDAY 27 DECEMBER 1958

The Miles Davis Sextet appear in concert at Town Hall in New York City. Jimmy Cobb is sick and Philly Joe Jones deps for him. There are two shows, at 8.30pm and 11.30pm. Also on the bill are the J. J. Johnson Quintet, the Sonny Rollins Trio, Art Blakey & the Jazz Messengers and Anita O'Day.

THUR	**1**	SUN	**1**
FRI	**2**	MON	**2**
SAT	**3**	TUES	**3**
SUN	**4**	WED	**4**
MON	**5**	THUR	**5**
TUES	**6**	FRI	**6**
WED	**7**	SAT	**7**
THUR	**8**	SUN	**8**
FRI	**9**	MON	**9**
SAT	**10**	TUES	**10**
SUN	**11**	WED	**11**
MON	**12**	THUR	**12**
TUES	**13**	FRI	**13**
WED	**14**	SAT	**14**
THUR	**15**	SUN	**15**
FRI	**16**	MON	**16**
SAT	**17**	TUES	**17**
SUN	**18**	WED	**18**
MON	**19**	THUR	**19**
TUES	**20**	FRI	**20**
WED	**21**	SAT	**21**
THUR	**22**	SUN	**22**
FRI	**23**	MON	**23**
SAT	**24**	TUES	**24**
SUN	**25**	WED	**25**
MON	**26**	THUR	**26**
TUES	**27**	FRI	**27**
WED	**28**	SAT	**28**
THUR	**29**		
FRI	**30**		
SAT	**31**		

THURSDAY 1 JANUARY 1959

The Miles Davis Sextet, with Wynton Kelly on piano, open at Birdland in New York for a two-week engagement opposite the Maynard Ferguson Orchestra. During the engagement, Miles is presented with *Down Beat* plaques for top trumpet of 1958 in both the readers' and Critics' Poll.

SATURDAY 3 JANUARY 1959

The Miles Davis Sextet broadcast on Mutual's *Bandstand USA* from Birdland.
MILES DAVIS (trumpet), JOHN COLTRANE (tenor sax), JULIAN 'CANNONBALL' ADDERLEY (alto sax), WYNTON KELLY (piano), PAUL CHAMBERS (bass), JIMMY COBB (drums), LEONARD FEATHER (announcer)
ann / *Bags' Groove* / *All Of You* (incomplete)

WEDNESDAY 14 JANUARY 1959

The Miles Davis Sextet close at Birdland in New York City.

THURSDAY 15 JANUARY 1959

John Coltrane and Paul Chambers record *Bags and Trane* with Milt Jackson for Atlantic at the Atlantic Recording Studios in New York City. Hank Jones and Connie Kay are also on the session.

WEDNESDAY 21 JANUARY 1959

The Miles Davis Sextet open at the Sutherland Lounge in Chicago for a two-week engagement.

MONDAY 2 FEBRUARY 1959

The Miles Davis Sextet close at the Sutherland Lounge in Chicago.
Paul Chambers, Cannonball Adderley, Wynton Kelly and Jimmy Cobb record for VeeJay in Chicago. Freddie Hubbard is on trumpet.

TUESDAY 3 FEBRUARY 1959

The Sextet, minus their leader Miles Davis, record as *Cannonball Adderley Quintet in Chicago* for Mercury at Universal Studios in Chicago. Paul Chambers, Cannonball, Kelly and Philly Joe Jones (replacing Cobb) complete the Vee Jay album begun the previous day (VJLP 1014

SATURDAY 14 FEBRUARY 1959

The Miles Davis Sextet appear in concert at th Civic Opera House in Chicago. Thelonious Monk, Gerry Mulligan and Sarah Vaughan are also on the bill.

TUESDAY 17 FEBRUARY 1959

The Miles Davis Sextet open at the Blackhawk in San Francisco for a one-week engagement.

SUNDAY 22 FEBRUARY 1959

The Miles Davis Sextet close at the Blackhawk in San Francisco.

N 1
ON 2
ES 3
ED 4
UR 5
6
T 7
N 8
ON 9
ES 10
ED 11
UR 12
13
T 14
N 15
ON 16
ES 17
ED 18
UR 19
20
T 21
N 22
ON 23
ES 24
ED 25
UR 26
27
T 28
N 29
ON 30
ES 31

MONDAY 2 MARCH 1959
Recording session by the Miles Davis Sextet for Columbia at the 30th Street Studios in New York City. This is the first session for Miles' new album, *Kind of Blue*.
MILES DAVIS (trumpet), JOHN COLTRANE (tenor sax), JULIAN 'CANNONBALL' ADDERLEY (alto sax), WYNTON KELLY (piano), PAUL CHAMBERS (bass), JIMMY COBB (drums)
Freddie Freeloader (5 takes)
BILL EVANS (piano) replaces Wynton Kelly:
So What (3 takes) / *Blue In Green* (JCA out, 6 takes)

TUESDAY 10 MARCH 1959
Wynton Kelly, Paul Chambers and Jimmy Cobb record as a trio to complete the Riverside album *Kelly Blue* begun on 19 February (RLP 12-298).

FRIDAY 13 MARCH 1959
The Miles Davis Sextet open at the Apollo Theatre in Harlem for a one-week engagement. Also on the bill are Ruth Brown, Thelonious Monk and the Johnny Richards Band.
After the show, the sextet drive to Brooklyn for a midnight concert at Loew's Valencia Theatre.

THURSDAY 19 MARCH 1959
The Miles Davis Sextet close at the Apollo Theatre in Harlem.

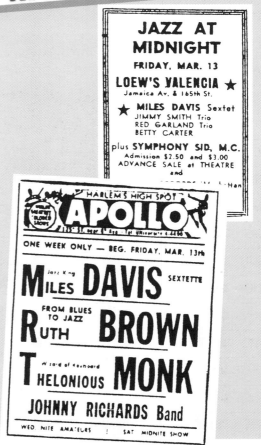

WED	**1**
THUR	**2**
FRI	**3**
SAT	**4**
SUN	**5**
MON	**6**
TUES	**7**
WED	**8**
THUR	**9**
FRI	**10**
SAT	**11**
SUN	**12**
MON	**13**
TUES	**14**
WED	**15**
THUR	**16**
FRI	**17**
SAT	**18**
SUN	**19**
MON	**20**
TUES	**21**
WED	**22**
THUR	**23**
FRI	**24**
SAT	**25**
SUN	**26**
MON	**27**
TUES	**28**
WED	**29**
THUR	**30**

WEDNESDAY 1 APRIL 1959

John Coltrane and Paul Chambers record with Cedar Walton and Lex Humphries for Atlantic in New York City. This is Coltrane's first session of his new contract with Atlantic Records.

THURSDAY 2 APRIL 1959

Miles, Gil Evans and the Quintet appear on the Robert Herridge Theatre Show, a CBS television programme on the arts, at CBS Studio 61 in New York City. The band is reduced to a quintet because Cannonball Adderley is ill, and unable to appear.

Miles Davis Quintet: MILES DAVIS (trumpet), JOHN COLTRANE (tenor sax), WYNTON KELLY (piano), PAUL CHAMBERS (bass), JIMMY COBB (drums)
So What

Miles Davis with Gil Evans and his Orchestra: MILES DAVIS (trumpet/flugelhorn), ERNIE ROYAL, CLYDE REASINGER LOUIS MUCCI, JOHNNY COLES, EMMETT BERRY (trumpet), FRANK REHAK, JIMMY CLEVELAND, BILL ELTON, ROD LEVITT (trombone), JULIUS WATKINS, BOB NORTHERN (french horn), BILL BARBER (tuba), DANNY BANK (bass clarinet), ROMEO PENQUE, EDDIE CAINE (woodwinds), JOHN COLTRANE (alto sax), PAUL CHAMBERS (bass), JIMMY COBB (drums), GIL EVANS (arranger/conductor)
The Duke / Blues For Pablo / New Rhumba

The programme is recorded and eventually transmitted on 21 July 1960.

ED **1**	FRI **1**	MON **1**
HUR **2**	SAT **2**	TUES **2**
RI **3**	SUN **3**	WED **3**
AT **4**	MON **4**	THUR **4**
UN **5**	TUES **5**	FRI **5**
ON **6**	WED **6**	SAT **6**
JES **7**	THUR **7**	SUN **7**
ED **8**	FRI **8**	MON **8**
HUR **9**	SAT **9**	TUES **9**
RI **10**	SUN **10**	WED **10**
AT **11**	MON **11**	THUR **11**
UN **12**	TUES **12**	FRI **12**
ON **13**	WED **13**	SAT **13**
JES **14**	THUR **14**	SUN **14**
ED **15**	FRI **15**	MON **15**
HUR **16**	SAT **16**	TUES **16**
RI **17**	SUN **17**	WED **17**
AT **18**	MON **18**	THUR **18**
UN **19**	TUES **19**	FRI **19**
ON **20**	WED **20**	SAT **20**
JES **21**	THUR **21**	SUN **21**
ED **22**	FRI **22**	MON **22**
HUR **23**	SAT **23**	TUES **23**
RI **24**	SUN **24**	WED **24**
AT **25**	MON **25**	THUR **25**
UN **26**	TUES **26**	FRI **26**
ON **27**	WED **27**	SAT **27**
JES **28**	THUR **28**	SUN **28**
ED **29**	FRI **29**	MON **29**
HUR **30**	SAT **30**	TUES **30**
	SUN **31**	

MONDAY 6 APRIL 1959

Recording session by the Miles Davis Sextet for Columbia at the 30th Street Studio in New York City.
MILES DAVIS (trumpet), JOHN COLTRANE (tenor sax), JULIAN 'CANNONBALL' ADDERLEY (alto sax), BILL EVANS (piano), PAUL CHAMBERS (bass), JIMMY COBB (drums)
Flamenco Sketches (6 takes) / *All Blues* (2 takes)
This session completes the recording of the album *Kind of Blue* (Columbia CL1355).

SUNDAY 12 APRIL 1959

Cannonball Adderley, Wynton Kelly, Paul Chambers and Jimmy Cobb record for Riverside in New York City. The album is released as *Cannonball Takes Charge* on Riverside RLP12-303.

THURSDAY 16 APRIL 1959

The Miles Davis Sextet open at Birdland in New York City for a two-week engagement opposite Gil Evans' 14-piece Orchestra.

WEDNESDAY 29 APRIL 1959

The Miles Davis Sextet and the Gil Evans Orchestra close at Birdland in New York City.

MONDAY 4 MAY 1959

John Coltrane records *Giant Steps* for Atlantic in New York City. Tommy Flanagan, Paul Chambers and Art Taylor are also on the session.

TUESDAY 5 MAY 1959

John Coltrane completes the recording of *Giant Steps* for Atlantic in New York City.

WEDNESDAY 6 MAY 1959

The Miles Davis Sextet open at the Sutherland Lounge in Chicago for a two-week engagement.

TUESDAY 12 MAY 1959

Cannonball Adderley and Wynton Kelly complete recording for the album *Cannonball Takes Charge* for Riverside in New York City. Percy Heath and Albert Heath are also on this session.

MONDAY 18 MAY 1959

The Miles Davis Sextet close at the Sutherland Lounge in Chicago.

TUESDAY 26 MAY 1959

Miles' 33rd birthday.

FRIDAY 29 MAY 1959

The Miles Davis Sextet open at the Blackhawk in San Francisco for a two-week engagement

THURSDAY 11 JUNE 1959

The Miles Davis Sextet close at the Blackhawk in San Francisco.

WED	**1**
THUR	**2**
FRI	**3**
SAT	**4**
SUN	**5**
MON	**6**
TUES	**7**
WED	**8**
THUR	**9**
FRI	**10**
SAT	**11**
SUN	**12**
MON	**13**
TUES	**14**
WED	**15**
THUR	**16**
FRI	**17**
SAT	**18**
SUN	**19**
MON	**20**
TUES	**21**
WED	**22**
THUR	**23**
FRI	**24**
SAT	**25**
SUN	**26**
MON	**27**
TUES	**28**
WED	**29**
THUR	**30**
FRI	**31**

WEDNESDAY 1 JULY 1959

The Miles Davis Sextet open at Jazz Seville in Los Angeles.
Down Beat reviews the opening night:

Caught in the Act: Miles Davis Sextet at Jazz Seville, Hollywood

Personnel: Miles Davis, trumpet; Julian 'Cannonball' Adderley, alto; John Coltrane, tenor; Wynton Kelly, piano; Paul Chambers, bass; Jimmy Cobb, drums

In his first appearance on the west coast in over two years, Miles Davis presented not a group as such but a very good rhythm section backing three star soloists. Not only were all six musicians not onstand together during any set on opening night, but there was no ensemble playing to speak of and, when the group was reviewed, Cannonball laid out completely during two consecutive sets.

The character of the sextet's engagement—for a reputed $2,500 a week—threw into razor-sharp focus the question of night club entertainment vs. untrammeled expression by jazz artists of varying maturity. While there can be no questioning the validity of the instrumentalists' right to express themselves in the jazz art, the debatable point remains of social responsibility to an audience paying through the nose to hear and see them.

Miles would informally open a number, blowing down into the mike, oblivious of the audience. Coltrane would follow, strolling out of backstage shadows, to blow long and searchingly on the changes of, say, *All of You*, or the blues. Pianist Kelly, from his spot on floor level invisible to most of the audience, would solo for, perhaps, four easy and funky choruses. Then Miles would appear onstand again to take the tune out.

As to the individual solo work, Cannonball was forthright and original in expression; Miles raw and searing with open horn, insinuating and subtle with mute tight on the mike. Coltrane communicated a sense of inhibition (sometimes even frustration) with his calculated understatement and contrived dissonance. On the whole, the tenor man's contributions suggested superficially stimulating, lonely and rather pathetic self-seeking. Is this truly the dilemma of the contemporary American jazz artist? One hesitates to believe so.

For all the showcasing of the frequently brilliant soloists, one yearned to hear ensemble performance by these three horns of established merit. But apparently nobody had eyes—or the musicians were not prepared to offer such fare.

Some highlights of the solo work included: Cannonball's compulsive strength and vigorous attack on a medium blues; Coltrane's multi-noted minor exposition leading to an extended solo characterized by quick and frequent long flurries of notes which seemed vainly to seek the anchoring of a definitive feel for the solo mood; Chambers' infrequent arco solo excursions, brilliantly and facilely executed, and Miles' close-muted incisiveness.

Predictably, the audience—which packed the Seville opening night—expressed appreciation with much palm-beating. (Possibly the jam-session atmosphere engendered by the attitude of the musicians onstand go through to the customers...) In any event, this lon overdue appearance by Miles and companions in L Angeles set the locals straight on the current New Yo mode of jazz presentation.

During the run at Jazz Seville Coltrane gives notice and Jimmy Heath flies out from New York to join the band on tenor sax. Following the Seville gig, Heath and Cobb elect to drive to the next job in Chicago in Cannonball Adderley's Fleetwood Cadillac. Jimmy Cobb does the driving while Cannonball meditates!

FRIDAY 17 JULY 1959

Billie Holiday dies in New York City.

WEDNESDAY 22 JULY 1959

The Miles Davis Sextet, with Jimmy Heath, Cannonball Adderley, Wynton Kelly, Paul Chambers and Jimmy Cobb, appear at the Canadian Jazz Festival in Toronto.

Above: Jimmy Heath at Idlewild Airport in New York, on hi way to join the Miles Davis Sextet in Los Angeles.

ED 1
UR 2
I 3
AT 4
IN 5
ON 6
IES 7
ED 8
IUR 9
I 10
I 11
AT 11
IN 12
ON 13
IES 14
ED 15
IUR 16
I 17
AT 18
IN 19
ON 20
IES 21
ED 22
IUR 23
I 24
AT 25
IN 26
ON 27
IES 28
ED 29
IUR 30
I 31

THURSDAY 23 JULY 1959

Down Beat magazine reviews the *Porgy and Bess* album:

Miles Davis/Gil Evans
PORGY AND BESS—Columbia CL1274
The Buzzard Song; Bess, You Is My Woman Now; Gone, Gone, Gone; Summertime; Bess, Oh Where's My Bess; Prayer (Oh Doctor Jesus); Fisherman, Strawberry and Devil Crabs; My Man's Gone Now; It Ain't Necessarily So; Here Come de Honey Man; I Loves You, Porgy; There's A Boat That's Leaving Soon For New York.
Rating: *****

The inherent pensiveness of Gil Evans' writing and the introversion of Miles Davis' playing produces something akin to a gas flame turned as low as it can be without going out. Its heat is quiet, but very intense.

What is it possible to say now about Gil Evans? This man has genius. He is one of the few living composers whose magic passes all the technical tests for stature without dying in the process. He has taken what he wanted and needed from the classical tradition, and yet remained a jazz writer, safely evading the lure of contemporary classical music, which has written itself up a blind alley. In his control and reserve (notice *Summertime*) he can put you in mind of Sibelius, who may have been the last classical composer to express himself naturally and without calculation of effects and because he felt it that way. Yet Evans is unique, and his development has been quite personal. His debts are to himself: there are things in this album, soaked up by the personalities—or rather, the joint personality—of Evans and Davis. You forget the underlying structures and, since the music used is not in the standard AABA pop song form to begin with, the album becomes a remarkable jazz experience, both for the musicians and the listener, who will be forcibly reminded of the great seriousness and the serious greatness in jazz, the universality in it that Andre Hodeir is always talking about.

Some of the best of Miles is to be heard in this album—along with some of the sloppiest. There are cracked and fuzzed notes and others that just shouldn't have been let go. (*Strawberry* may make all but the most uncritical Davis fans squirm.) Why these things were let pass is anybody's guess. Maybe Miles didn't care. Maybe they were let pass in accordance with the dubious faith that even mistakes are part of the whole and therefore to be admired in jazz. Maybe it is because the executives-in-charge think that Miles' stature is such that these considerations are small in comparison—which, as a matter of fact, is true.

In any case, the Davis-Evans relationship has again produced superb music. In the jazz albums of *Porgy*, this one is in a class by itself. Which figures: it named its own terms.

FRIDAY 24 JULY 1959

The Miles Davis Sextet, with Jimmy Heath, Cannonball Adderley, Wynton Kelly, Paul Chambers and Jimmy Cobb, open at the Regal Theatre in Chicago for a one-week engagement. Dakota Staton shares top billing.

THURSDAY 30 JULY 1959

The Miles Davis Sextet close at the Regal Theatre in Chicago.

FRIDAY 31 JULY 1959

The Miles Davis Sextet are due to appear at the French Lick Jazz Festival, but two of the sextet fail to arrive on time and the appearance is rescheduled for Sunday evening.

SAT	**1**
SUN	**2**
MON	**3**
TUES	**4**
WED	**5**
THUR	**6**
FRI	**7**
SAT	**8**
SUN	**9**
MON	**10**
TUES	**11**
WED	**12**
THUR	**13**
FRI	**14**
SAT	**15**
SUN	**16**
MON	**17**
TUES	**18**
WED	**19**
THUR	**20**
FRI	**21**
SAT	**22**
SUN	**23**
MON	**24**
TUES	**25**
WED	**26**
THUR	**27**
FRI	**28**
SAT	**29**
SUN	**30**
MON	**31**

SUNDAY 2 AUGUST 1959
The Miles Davis Sextet, with Jimmy Heath, Cannonball
Adderley, Wynton Kelly, Paul Chambers and Jimmy
Cobb, appear at the French Lick Jazz Festival.

AT 1
SUN 2
MON 3
TUES 4
WED 5
THUR 6
FRI 7
AT 8
SUN 9
MON 10
TUES 11
WED 12
THUR 13
FRI 14
AT 15
SUN 16
MON 17
TUES 18
WED 19
THUR 20
FRI 21
AT 22
SUN 23
MON 24
TUES 25
WED 26
THUR 27
FRI 28
AT 29
SUN 30
MON 31

Above: Miles relaxes with Dizzy Gillespie backstage at the French Lick Jazz Festival.
Opposite page: The Miles Davis Sextet on stage at the French Lick Festival. L to r: Jimmy Heath, Cannonball Adderley, Paul Chambers and Miles.

SAT	1
SUN	2
MON	3
TUES	4
WED	5
THUR	6
FRI	7
SAT	8
SUN	9
MON	10
TUES	11
WED	12
THUR	13
FRI	14
SAT	15
SUN	16
MON	17
TUES	18
WED	19
THUR	20
FRI	21
SAT	22
SUN	23
MON	24
TUES	25
WED	26
THUR	27
FRI	28
SAT	29
SUN	30
MON	31

Prior to the Playboy Jazz Festival in Chicago, Jimmy Heath goes to see his family in Philadelphia. His parole officer tells him he has to stay within a 60-mile radius of Philadelphia as a condition of his parole. Despite Miles' attempts to pull strings Heath has no choice but to leave the band.

FRIDAY 7 AUGUST 1959

The Miles Davis group, now reduced to a quintet following the loss of Jimmy Heath, appear at the Playboy Jazz Festival at the Chicago Stadium in Chicago. Also on the bill are Count Basie and his Orchestra, Dakota Staton, Dave Brubeck Quartet, Dizzy Gillespie, Kai Winding and Mort Sahl. Gene Lees, editor of *Down Beat*, reports:

Even Miles seemed in good mood. He came close to acknowledging that the audience existed; once he even smiled. No amount of incredulity from the profession will deny the truth: Miles smiled … and played beautifully.

SUNDAY 9 AUGUST 1959

The Miles Davis Quintet appear in concert at the Berkshire Music Barn in Lenox, Massachusetts.

WEDNESDAY 12 AUGUST 1959

Wynton Kelly and Paul Chambers record for VeeJay in New York City. Lee Morgan, Wayne Shorter and Philly Joe Jones are also on the album which is released as *Kelly Great!* on VJ 3004.

THURSDAY 13 AUGUST 1959

The Miles Davis Sextet, probably with Coltrane back on tenor, open at Birdland opposite the Chico Hamilton Quintet for a two-week engagement. Opening night is standing-room only.

SUNDAY 23 AUGUST 1959

The Miles Davis Quintet appear at the Randall's Island Jazz Festival in New York City. Also on the Sunday night bill are the Ahmad Jamal Trio, the Modern Jazz Quartet, Dakota Staton and Stan Kenton and his Orchestra.

TUESDAY 25 AUGUST 1959

Between sets at Birdland, Miles escorts a white girl acquaintance out of the club and puts her into a cab. It's a hot, muggy night, and Miles stays on the sidewalk to get some air. A white policeman tells him to move along. 'What for?' says Miles, 'I'm working downstairs.' The policeman tells him to move along anyway, or he'll be arrested. When Miles objects, he is brutally beaten by the policeman and a detective who happens upon the incident. Miles is arrested and marched to the 54th Street Precinct where he is booked for disorderly conduct and assault. Frances arrives and makes sure Miles gets hospital treatment. The gash in his head needs ten stitches before Miles is returned to the station and kept overnight.

WEDNESDAY 26 AUGUST 1959

In the morning, with headlines in all the New York papers, manager Harold Lovett arrives and posts bail. The hearing is set for Friday 18 September.

Nat Adderley deputises for Miles and the quintet is held over for another week at Birdland. Cannonball Adderley and John Coltrane assume leadership of the group.

The shameful story makes headlines around the world. Above right: Miles, in handcuffs and bleeding, arrives at the 54th Street Precinct.

PROBE INTO BIRDLAND BEATING-UP

From REN GREVATT and BURT KORALL

NEW YORK, Wednesday.—New York Police Commissioner Stephen P. Kennedy is to probe the alleged beating-up of jazz trumpeter Miles Davis by two Broadway cops outside the famed Birdland jazz club.

A battered and bleeding Davis was hauled away in a squad car. Only police reinforcements stopped an angry mob of onlookers from joining in a fracas that jammed the sidewalks and blocked traffic.

The crowd later gathered outside the 54th Street Precinct, where Davis was held. As reported in last week's **MELODY MAKER**, he was booked for assault and disorderly conduct. Kept in jail overnight, he was released on a $500 bond.

HEADLINES

On Tuesday, the disorderly conduct charge was postponed until September 18. The assault summons will be held in special sessions court at a date to be announced.

The incident brought screaming headlines in the New York newspapers.

Thirty-three-year-old Davis told reporters that he had just finished making a 27-minute recording for the Armed Services to aid a Bond sales drive for free America.

When he went outside Birdland for a few minutes, a policeman approached and

Back Page, Col. 2

Melody Make[r]

September 12, 1959 — FOR THE BEST IN JAZZ — Every Friday 6d.

see Page 20

← THIS IS WHAT THEY DID TO MILES DAVIS

THE battered, bleeding figure on the left is trumpeter Miles Davis, one of the great names of modern jazz and the idol of a million disc collectors and fans. This dramatic picture, flown to the MELODY MAKER from New York, shows Davis, still bleeding from head wounds, being marched into the city's West 54th Street Police Station House by Patrolman Gerald Kilduff.

BEATEN

A few minutes earlier he had been taking a breather between sessions at the world-famous jazz haunt, Birdland, when he was told to move on by Kilduff.

Miles alleges that the next

TUES	1	THUR	1
WED	2	FRI	2
THUR	3	SAT	3
FRI	4	SUN	4
SAT	5	MON	5
SUN	6	TUES	6
MON	7	WED	7
TUES	8	THUR	8
WED	9	FRI	9
THUR	10	SAT	10
FRI	11	SUN	11
SAT	12	MON	12
SUN	13	TUES	13
MON	14	WED	14
TUES	15	THUR	15
WED	16	FRI	16
THUR	17	SAT	17
FRI	18	SUN	18
SAT	19	MON	19
SUN	20	TUES	20
MON	21	WED	21
TUES	22	THUR	22
WED	23	FRI	23
THUR	24	SAT	24
FRI	25	SUN	25
SAT	26	MON	26
SUN	27	TUES	27
MON	28	WED	28
TUES	29	THUR	29
WED	30	FRI	30
		SAT	31

The advertised appearance of the Miles Davis Quintet at the Cotton Club in Atlantic City (*right*) is one of the casualties of the Birdland beating.

WEDNESDAY 16 SEPTEMBER 1959

The Miles Davis Sextet, with Nat Adderley depping for Miles, close at Birdland. Cannonball Adderley leaves the band.

THURSDAY 1 OCTOBER 1959

Down Beat magazine reviews a Prestige reissue and the *Kind of Blue* album:

Miles Davis

MILES DAVIS AND THE MODERN JAZZ GIANTS—Prestige 7150
The Man I Love (Take 2)*; Swing Spring; 'Round about Midnight; Bemsha Swing; The Man I Love* (Take 1). Personnel: Tracks 1,2,4,5: Davis, trumpet; Milt Jackson, vibes; Thelonious Monk, piano; Percy Heath, bass; Kenny Clarke, drums. Track 3: Davis, trumpet; John Coltrane, tenor; Red Garland, piano; Paul Chambers, bass; Philly Joe Jones, drums.
Rating: ****½

There are few jazzmen whose creative resources are so great that <u>any</u> recorded example of their work is of interest. This reissue of 1954 and 1956 Davis sessions includes at least three such men: Milt Jackson, Thelonious Monk, and Davis himself.

The earlier date (all titles but *Midnight*), which also produced *Bags' Groove*, reveals a somewhat uncomfortable Miles, blowing with and against a free-wheeling, but only half-sympathetic group. Davis' approach to jazz, which leans heavily upon the sensitivity of his pianist, is left tattered by the jarring individualism of pianist Monk, whose playing is not designed to flatter or inspire Miles. In spite of all this, enough memorable moments came from the session to make this a very worthwhile LP.

Swing Spring, in particular, demonstrates that Davis was ready to lead the way out of the cliche-ridden I-can-blow-stronger-than-you arena into which many jazzmen had stampeded by the mid 50s.

Midnight, performed by the most esthetically satisfying of all Davis groups, is a musical essay on the virtues of lyricism and horizontal structure, combined with harmonic insight, a classic performance that should be in any thoughtful collector's library.

Miles Davis

KIND OF BLUE—Columbia CL 1355:
So What?; Freddie Freeloader; Blue in Green; Flamenco Sketches; All Blues.
Personnel: Davis, trumpet; Julian Adderley, alto; John Coltrane, tenor; Bill Evans, piano (all tracks except Freeloader); Wynton Kelly, piano (Track 2); Paul Chambers, bass; James Cobb, drums.
Rating: *****

This is a remarkable album. Using very simple but effective devices, Miles has constructed an album of extreme beauty and sensitivity. This is not to say that this LP is a simple one—far from it. What is remarkable is that the men have done so much with the stark, skeletal material.

All the compositions bear the mark of the Impressionists and touches of Bela Bartok. For example, *So What?* is built on two scales, which sound somewhat like the Hungarian minor, giving the performance a Middle Eastern flavor; *Flamenco* and *All Blues* reflect a strong Ravel influence.

Flamenco and *Freeloader* are both blues, but each is of a different mood and conception: *Sketches* is in 6/8, which achieves a rolling, highly charged effect, while *Freeloader* is more in the conventional blues vein. The presence of Kelly on *Freeloader* may account partly for the difference between the two.

Miles' playing throughout the album is poignant, sensitive, and at times, almost morose; his linear concept never falters. Coltrane has some interesting solos; his angry solo on *Freeloader* is in marked contrast to his lyrical romanticism on *All Blues*. Cannonball seems to be under wraps on all the tracks except *Freeloader* when his irrepressible joie de vivre bubbles forth. Chambers, Evans, and Cobb provide a solid, sympathetic backdrop for the horns.

This is the soul of Miles Davis, and it's a beautiful soul.

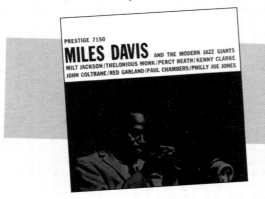

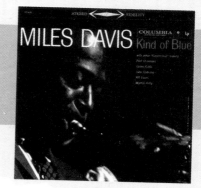

UR	1
	2
T	3
N	4
ON	5
ES	6
ED	7
UR	8
	9
T	10
N	11
ON	12
ES	13
ED	14
UR	15
N	16
T	17
JN	18
ON	19
ES	20
ED	21
HUR	22
I	23
T	24
JN	25
ON	26
ES	27
ED	28
HUR	29
RI	30
T	31

SUNDAY 4 OCTOBER 1959

The Miles Davis Quintet appear at the *Jazz For Civil Rights* concert at the Hunter College Auditorium on Park Avenue at 69th Street in New York City. Also on the bill are Thelonious Monk, Dakota Staton and Tony Scott.

JAZZ FOR CIVIL RIGHTS

SUN., OCT. 4th at 8:30 P.M.   BENEFIT: N.A.A.C.P.

HUNTER COLLEGE AUDITORIUM 69th ST. & PARK AVE.

MILES DAVIS Sextet

DAKOTA STATON

NEWPORT YOUTH BAND ● TYREE GLENN Orch. ● ART BLAKEY ● HORACE SILVE Quintet ● BILLY TAYLOR ● DON ELLIOTT ● CRYSTAL JOY ● OZZIE BAILEY ● RANDY WESTON Trio ● MAXINE SULLIVAN ● TIMMIE ROGERS ● THE TRENIERS ● BABS GONZALES ● KENNY BURRELL Trio ● BUDDY RICH ● REX STEWART ● BILL HENDERSON ● TONY SCOTT ● JEROME RICHARDSON

Prices: $2 20, 3 30, 4.40 TICKETS NOW ON SALE: N. A. A. C. P. 20 W. 40 St., N.Y.C. Colony Record Center 1671 Broadway The Record Shack 274 W. 125th St.

SUNDAY 11 OCTOBER 1959

Miles Davis appears in a concert at the Academy of Music in Philadelphia. Also on the bill are Ray Charles, Horace Silver, Sonny Stitt and Philly Joe Jones.

FRIDAY 16 OCTOBER 1959

The Miles Davis Quintet open at the Howard Theatre in Washington for a one-week engagement. Also on the show are Dakota Staton, Red Garland's Trio, singer Leon Thomas and comedian Redd Foxx.

THURSDAY 22 OCTOBER 1959

The Miles Davis Quintet close at the Howard Theatre in Washington.

FRIDAY 23 OCTOBER 1959

The Miles Davis Quintet open at the Paramount Theatre in Brooklyn for a one-week engagement. Also on the bill are the Count Basie Orchestra with Joe Williams, Dakota Staton, George Shearing's Quintet, Lambert, Hendricks & Ross with MCs Don Adams and Symphony Sid.

SATURDAY 24 OCTOBER 1959

The charges against Miles re the Birdland incident are dismissed when a panel of three judges rule that the arrest was illegal.

THURSDAY 29 OCTOBER 1959

The Miles Davis Quintet close at the Paramount Theatre in Brooklyn.

Miles Davis featured in Jazz for Civil Rights

NEW YORK — Trumpeter Miles Davis whose episode with police outside Birdland led to brutality allegations will headline the "Jazz for Civil Rights" concert at the Hunter College auditorium, 69th St. and Park Ave., on Oct. 4.

Proceeds from the star-studded affair will go to the NAACP Freedom Fund. The concert is being sponsored by Miss Elsie Carrington, a member of the Association's Committee of 50 pledged to raise $250,000 for the civil rights organization.

Allan Morrison, magazine associate editor, is concert chairman. Mr. Morrison said Thursday sponsors anticipate a net profit of $5,000 from the jazz show.

HE STATED that some of the artists volunteered their services for the benefit affair. Others, he said, agreed quickly when approached to participate.

JAZZ AT THE HOWARD

NOW THRU THURS., OCT. 22 — MIDNITE SHOWS FRI. & SAT., OCT. 16-17. ALL MIDNITE SEATS UNRESERVED $2.00 — MATS. $1.00 — EVES. & ALL DAY SUN. $1.50.

"LATE LATE SHOW" . . . "TIME TO SWING"

★ **DAKOTA STATON**

"KIND OF BLUE" "PORGY AND BESS"

★ **MILES DAVIS** SEXTETTE

"GARLAND OF RED" . . . "BLUESVILLE"

★ **RED GARLAND** AND TRIO

NEW SINGING DISCOVERY

★ **LEON THOMAS**

LAFF OF THE PARTY

★ **REDD FOXX**

1 WEEK ONLY!

OCT. 23 thru OCT. 29

ON STAGE IN PERSON CONTINUOUS PERFORMANCES

COUNT BASIE and his orchestra featuring **JOE WILLIAMS**

DAKOTA STATON

MILES DAVIS and his sextet

GEORGE SHEARING and his sextet

LAMBERT, HENDRICKS & ROSS

DON ADAMS

"SYMPHONY SID"

plus on screen **"THE YOUNG LAND"**

BROOKLYN **Paramount** Flatbush and DeKalb

NOVEMBER 1959

SUN	1
MON	2
TUES	3
WED	4
THUR	5
FRI	6
SAT	7
SUN	8
MON	9
TUES	10
WED	11
THUR	12
FRI	13
SAT	14
SUN	15
MON	16
TUES	17
WED	18
THUR	19
FRI	20
SAT	21
SUN	22
MON	23
TUES	24
WED	25
THUR	26
FRI	27
SAT	28
SUN	29
MON	30

THURSDAY 5 NOVEMBER 1959
The Miles Davis Quintet open a three-week engagement at Birdland in New York City opposite the Johnny Smith Trio.

TUESDAY 10 NOVEMBER 1959
The first recording session for the new Miles Davis/Gil Evans collaboration, *Sketches of Spain*, is scheduled. Miles is taken ill during the session which is then used for rehearsal.

SUNDAY 15 NOVEMBER 1959
Rehearsal for *Sketches of Spain*.

THURSDAY 19 NOVEMBER 1959
Harry Edison's Quintet replace the Johnny Smith Trio as the Miles Davis Quintet begin their third week at Birdland.

FRIDAY 20 NOVEMBER 1959
Recording session for *Sketches of Spain* by Miles Davis with the Gil Evans Orchestra for Columbia in New York City.
MILES DAVIS (trumpet/flugelhorn), BERNIE GLOW, TAFT JORDAN, ERNIE ROYAL, LOUIS MUCCI (trumpet), FRANK REHAK, RICHARD HIXON (trombone), DANNY BANK (bass clarinet/alto flute), ALBERT BLOCK (piccolo flute), EDDIE CAINE (flute), HAROLD FELDMAN (oboe/bass clarinet), LOREN GLICKMAN (bassoon), JOHN BARROWS, JIMMY BUFFINGTON, EARL CHAPIN (french horn), JAMES MCALLISTER (tuba), JANET PUTMAN (harp), PAUL CHAMBERS (bass), JIMMY COBB, ELVIN JONES (drums), GIL EVANS (arranger/conductor)
Concierto de Aranjuez

TUESDAY 24 NOVEMBER 1959
John Coltrane, Wynton Kelly, Paul Chambers and Jimmy Cobb record for Atlantic in New York City. The tracks are later used on the album *Coltrane Jazz*.

WEDNESDAY 25 NOVEMBER 1959
The Miles Davis Quintet close at Birdland in New York City and are replaced the next night by Cannonball Adderley's new Quintet.

FRIDAY 27 NOVEMBER 1959
The Miles Davis Quintet appear at a Jazz Festival & Dance at the St. Nicholas Arena in New York City. Also appearing are Tito Puente and his Orchestra.

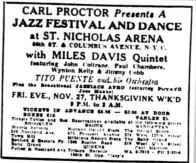

ES **1**
ED **2**
UR **3**
4
T **5**
N **6**
ON **7**
ES **8**
ED **9**
UR **10**
11
T **12**
N **13**
ON **14**
ES **15**
ED **16**
UR **17**
18
T **19**
N **20**
ON **21**
ES **22**
ED **23**
UR **24**
25
T **26**
N **27**
ON **28**
ES **29**
ED **30**
UR **31**

WEDNESDAY 2 DECEMBER 1959

John Coltrane, Wynton Kelly, Paul Chambers and Jimmy Cobb record more tracks for the album *Coltrane Jazz* for Atlantic in New York City.

WEDNESDAY 23 DECEMBER 1959

John Coltrane and his family move to a house in St. Albans, Queens.

THURSDAY 24 DECEMBER 1959

Miles is again the runaway winner of the trumpet award in the annual *Down Beat* Readers' Poll. He is also named Personality of the Year and the Miles Davis Sextet are third in the combo poll.

FRIDAY 25 DECEMBER 1959

The Miles Davis Quintet open at the Regal Theatre in Chicago for a one-week engagement. Also on the bill are Art Blakey's Jazz Messengers and Betty Carter.

THURSDAY 31 DECEMBER 1959

The Miles Davis Quintet close at the Regal Theatre in Chicago.

FRI	1
SAT	2
SUN	3
MON	4
TUES	5
WED	6
THUR	7
FRI	8
SAT	9
SUN	10
MON	11
TUES	12
WED	13
THUR	14
FRI	15
SAT	16
SUN	17
MON	18
TUES	19
WED	20
THUR	21
FRI	22
SAT	23
SUN	24
MON	25
TUES	26
WED	27
THUR	28
FRI	29
SAT	30
SUN	31

THURSDAY 7 JANUARY 1960

Miles is featured in a four-page article by Barbara J. Gardner in *Down Beat*:

> Ask any jazz fan who Miles Davis is. Most will say, "He's a fink, but he sure can play." Ask any club owner where he has worked. Most will say, "He's a headache, but the customers flock to hear him." Ask any musician. He will probably say, "He's an evil little bastard, but he certainly can play." In other words, two points seem glaringly in evidence — Miles is a difficult person to deal with, and Miles can play his instrument.

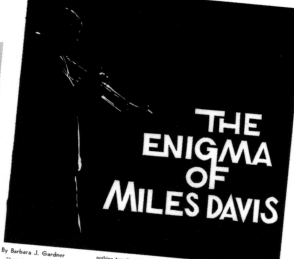

THE ENIGMA OF MILES DAVIS

By Barbara J. Gardner

There is no room for the middle stance. You choose up sides, and you play on your team. He is either the greatest living musician or he is just a cool bopper. He is handsome and a wonderful individual or he is ugly and a drag. His trumpet prowess is getting greater every day or his scope is becoming more and more limited.

Any current jazz discussion can be enlivened simply by dropping in the magic name—Miles Davis.

Yet these arguments can be mystifying in the frequency with which the opponents switch positions. A musician in a conversation with fellow workers is likely to blast Davis. The same musician discussing Miles with his dinner host and hostess may change tunes in the middle of the chorus and sing nothing but the highest praise for the trumpeter.

Unaware of the chain of events they were beginning, Dr. and Mrs. Miles Davis, on May 25, 1926, named their first son Miles Dewey. Miles, his parents and an older sister, Dorothy, moved from Alton, Ill. to East St. Louis, Ill. in 1927. There, Miles' brother Vernon was born. The first 12 years included all the usual brother-sister squabbles. Yet, though there were normal childhood frictions, Miles was gregarious, amiable, and had many friends.

Musically, his career began uneventfully on his 13th birthday when his father gave him a trumpet. Only his immediate attraction and dedication to the horn gave an indication of the mastery of the instrument he would later achieve. Even his family admits that in the beginning, the growing pains were considerable and Miles was no instant threat to any trumpet player.

"We still have a record packed away someplace that we cut with some rhythm and blues outfit," his sister recalled. "He was pretty awful. They don't even mention his name."

But the woodshed was nearby, and Miles used it.

By the time Billy Eckstine brought his big band through East St. Louis in the early 1940s, the growing pains were over. Dizzy Gillespie and Eckstine convinced both Miles and his father that the quiet, reserved youngster should continue to study music. While the band was in town, Miles had the exciting experience of sitting in. He was so awe-stricken by Charlie Parker and Gillespie that he could hardly play.

Miles pulled up stakes in 1945 and

20 • DOWN BEAT

rived at because he has endured a series of cold, degrading, and demoralizing experiences.

An instance: arriving in Chicago during the summer of 1959, Davis rolled his imported Ferrari into a motel on Lake Michigan's shore only to be to, there was a mix-up in the reservations. Sorry. Jazz great or not, there was no room available.

His refusal to accept publicly a poll award from a national men's magazine was prompted by his dissatisfaction with the discriminatory policies of the publication. Davis talked, as well as corresponded, with the publisher, explaining why he could not, in good faith, accept any commendation from the publication. In spite of the best efforts of the publisher, he has been unable to sway Davis' attitude.

This adherence to principle runs through his relationships. Once he has made up his mind, and cast his lot, he is more than reluctant to change his position. This is especially true regarding sidemen working with him. Both his present pianist and his drummer went through periods during which

22 • DOWN BEAT

Miles had to adjust to and acquaint himself with their styles of playing.

"Miles thinks there is only one drummer in the entire world," a musician said at the beginning of 1959, "and that one is Philly Joe Jones." Miles seemed to give credence to this idea long after Jones had been replaced by Jimmy Cobb. Several times, he recorded only when he was able to secure Jones as his drummer. Gradually, this attitude began to fade, and Cobb at last was free to function without the ghostly sizzle of his predecessor behind him. Several months ago, questioned about Miles' affinity to Philly Joe, the same musician expressed amazement. "Well, Miles has that clean-cut Jimmy Cobb sound in his ear now," he said.

The exact pattern was followed when pianist Wynton Kelly replaced Red Garland. For months Miles was attuned to the blockish Garland swing, and he couldn't hear it in the melodic, stylish Kelly. But, sticking by their personal styles, and drawing from Miles' subtle hints in technique and execution, Kelly and Cobb came to be highly regarded by their employer.

Davis' ability to pick top musicians as sidemen is unerring, and the influence he wields over their musical expression is almost phenomenal. Sometimes by subtle suggestion, at times by brutal frankness, Miles whips a musical unit into a cohesive, tight-knit, power-generating single voice.

Not only does he usually walk away with top trumpet honors in trade polls, but like a powerful politician, he carries the ticket, and individual members of his group wind up well inside the first 10 of their categories.

This has been referred to as the "Miles magic." What are some of the elements that form the man and the magician in this trumpeter?

There is an undercurrent of loyalty and dedication to conviction that runs well hidden beneath a temperamental guise. Examples of his generosity and loyalty are described throughout the industry.

Earlier this year in Chicago, a man wielding a knife appeared backstage and began threatening the trumpeter. A prominent New York musician —

unexpectedly out of work, down on his luck, and hung up in Chicago — was nearby. Seeing the man with the knife move in on Miles, the New Yorker knocked him cold with an uppercut.

Miles walked calmly away without saying so much as "thank you." Some bystanders were annoyed. Wasn't this more than adequate proof of Miles' insolence and ingratitude? Few if any of them knew the reason the New Yorker was present. Miles, hearing the man was in financial trouble, had invited him to play the date with his group. He had no need of the man, but offering a handout would perhaps have hurt the New Yorker's pride. The fee Miles paid him was big enough to get him out of town and on to the next gig.

A contributing factor to Miles' attraction is his glow of freedom and individuality. This exhibition strikes a chord within many persons who, on the surface, are critical of his attitude. He seldom allows anyone to bore him with small talk. A chatterbox is likely to find himself talking to empty space as Miles walks quietly away.

Although there are several individual writers and disc jockeys among his personal friends, as a profession, Miles has little use for persons in communications. He seldom gives interviews to writers and almost never appears for radio or television interviews. One reason he will not do them is that he is, in his speech habits, impetuously profane.

But perhaps more important than that is his extreme sensitivity about the loss of his normal speaking voice.

After a throat operation a few years ago, Miles was told by the doctors not to speak at all for several days. Someone provoked him, and Miles blurted out a retort. The damage was done. Now he speaks in a soft, rasping, gravelly voice. It is curiously attractive, when you become accustomed to it, and stranger of all, it somehow resembles the tightly restrained sound of his muted trumpet.

The striking, delicate-featured man who stands in almost shy uneasiness, mute against the microphone, is the antithesis of the confident, self-contained offstage Miles. There are those who believe this restless musician is the real Miles. Certainly his exquisite—at times even fragile—playing would not seem to be the expression of a braggart or a bully.

Standing somewhere between the unapproachable loner and the onstage lonely trumpeter is Miles Dewey Davis. At present, Miles is unwilling to share that person with the public. He expresses his conviction that each person has a right and a duty to live an independent existence.

If this attitude rubs many persons the wrong way, his popularity evidently rises with each disparagement.

It was not surprising that Miles in the past few months has won both the *Down Beat* International Jazz Critics poll and the magazine's Readers poll. What is surprising, however, is that despite all the criticism of his stage manner, the readers also voted him jazz personality of the year.

Apparently a club owner was right when, not too long ago, he threw up his hands in exasperation as Miles sauntered offstage after a solo. After reciting to Miles a list of his sins, he said, "The trouble with you is that everybody *likes* you, you little son of a bitch."

January 7, 1960 • 71

	1
T	2
N	3
ON	4
ES	5
ED	6
UR	7
	8
T	9
N	10
ON	11
ES	12
ED	13
UR	14
	15
T	16
N	17
ON	18
ES	19
ED	20
UR	21
	22
T	23
UN	24
ON	25
ES	26
ED	27
HUR	28
	29
AT	30
UN	31

FRIDAY 15 JANUARY 1960

The Miles Davis Quintet open at the Apollo Theatre in Harlem for a one-week engagement. Also starring on the bill are Dakota Staton and the James Moody Band.

THURSDAY 21 JANUARY 1960

The Miles Davis Quintet close at the Apollo Theatre in Harlem.

Below: Paul Chambers and Miles Davis at the Apollo.

MON	1
TUES	2
WED	3
THUR	4
FRI	5
SAT	6
SUN	7
MON	8
TUES	9
WED	10
THUR	11
FRI	12
SAT	13
SUN	14
MON	15
TUES	16
WED	17
THUR	18
FRI	19
SAT	20
SUN	21
MON	22
TUES	23
WED	24
THUR	25
FRI	26
SAT	27
SUN	28
MON	29

WEDNESDAY 10 FEBRUARY 1960

The Miles Davis Quintet are due to open at the Sutherland Hotel Lounge in Chicago for a two-week engagement opposite Ornette Coleman. A snow storm forces their plane to land at Indianapolis and they have to bus to Chicago. Paul Chambers is stranded in New York.

SUNDAY 21 FEBRUARY 1960

The Miles Davis Quintet close at the Sutherland Hotel Lounge in Chicago.
John Coltrane gives notice and by 1 March is back in New York to open at the Five Spot with Mal Waldron's Trio.

SATURDAY 27 FEBRUARY 1960

The Miles Davis Quintet plus Buddy Montgomery (vibes) appear in concert with the Modern Jazz Quartet at the Shrine Auditorium in Los Angeles. John Tynan reviews the concert in *Down Beat*:

MILES DAVIS QUINTETTE

TUESDAY NITE — JAZZ CONCERT

PARKING BY UNIFORMED ATTENDANTS

SUTHERLAND HOTEL & LOUNGE
47th and DREXEL BOULEVARD

Caught In The Act

JAZZ CONCERT
Shrine Auditorium, Los Angeles
Personnel: Miles Davis Sextet; Modern Jazz Quartet; Paul Horn Quintet; Jackie Cain & Roy Kral

…The climax came with the appearance of the Miles Davis Sextet. Reportedly Miles was miffed on arrival at the auditorium because the group had to wait to go on stage and possibly this accounted for his casual approach to his horn in the trio of tunes performed by himself, tenorist John Coltrane, vibist Buddy Montgomery, pianist Wynton Kelly, bassist Paul Chambers, and drummer Jimmy Cobb.

Davis seemed reluctant to work seriously for the audience, doodled around *All Of You* and, between the first chorus and the out blowing, stood in the background behind the group watching over his men like a fussy mother hen. His muted, closely miked *All Of You* was in solo remote and whimsical, indeed, with moments of moving lyric beauty.

Slashing at the canvas of his own creation, Coltrane erupted in a fantastic onrush of surrealism and disconnected musical thought best appreciated within the dark corridors of his personal psyche. The philosophical implications of his performance; with its overtones of neurotic compulsion and contempt for an audience, belong in another area of journalistic examination.

Miles, whose bearing resembles more and more that of Frank Sinatra, could have been most proud of soloists Kelly and Montgomery.

Kelly's final solo of the evening was a joy to hear, following as it did that of the anarchistic Coltrane. It revealed real concept of beauty and a structure logically built to climax after climax. Montgomery's vibes statements disclosed genuine development in his attempt to create a rising tide of jazz excitement. One had the feeling, though, that Buddy was but a disconnected entity in this front line of wandering egos.

MONDAY 29 FEBRUARY 1960

Wynton Kelly, Paul Chambers and Jimmy Cobb record with Art Pepper for Contemporary in Hollywood. Conte Candoli is also on the album which is released as *Gettin' Together* (M3573).

THURSDAY 3 MARCH 1960

The Miles Davis Quintet with Buddy Montgomery (vibes) appear in concert at San José.

FRIDAY 4 MARCH 1960

The Miles Davis Quintet with Buddy Montgomery (vibes) appear in concert at the San Francisco Civic Auditorium.

SATURDAY 5 MARCH 1960

The Miles Davis Quintet with Buddy Montgomery (vibes) appear in concert at the Oakland Auditorium Arena.

THURSDAY 10 MARCH 1960

Recording session by Miles Davis with the Gil Evans Orchestra for Columbia in New York City.
MILES DAVIS (trumpet/flugelhorn), BERNIE GLOW, ERNIE ROYAL, JOHN COLES (trumpet), FRANK REHAK, RICHARD HIXON (trombone), DANNY BANK (bass clarinet/alto flute), ALBERT BLOCK (piccolo flute), EDDIE CAINE, HAROLD FELDMAN (flute), ROMEO PENQUE (oboe), JACK KNITZER (bassoon), JOE SINGER, TONY MIRANDA, JIMMY BUFFINGTON (french horn), BILL BARBER (tuba), JANET PUTMAN (harp), PAUL CHAMBERS (bass), JIMMY COBB, ELVIN JONES (drums), ELDEN C. BAILEY (percussion), GIL EVANS (arranger/conductor)
The Pan Piper (2 takes) / *Song Of Our Country* (11 takes)

FRIDAY 11 MARCH 1960

Recording session by Miles Davis with the Gil Evans Orchestra for Columbia in New York City.
MILES DAVIS (trumpet/flugelhorn), BERNIE GLOW, ERNIE ROYAL, JOHN COLES, LOUIS MUCCI (trumpet), FRANK REHAK, RICHARD HIXON (trombone), DANNY BANK (bass clarinet/alto flute), ALBERT BLOCK (piccolo flute), EDDIE CAINE, HAROLD FELDMAN (flute), ROMEO PENQUE (oboe), JACK KNITZER (bassoon), JOE SINGER, TONY MIRANDA, JIMMY BUFFINGTON (french horn), BILL BARBER (tuba), JANET PUTMAN (harp), PAUL CHAMBERS (bass), JIMMY COBB, ELVIN JONES (drums), ELDEN C. BAILEY (percussion), GIL EVANS (arranger/conductor)
Solea / Will O' The Wisp / Saeta

MILES DAVIS (trumpet/flugelhorn), ERNIE ROYAL, CLYDE REASINGER, JOHN COLES, LOUIS MUCCI, EMMETT BERRY (trumpet), FRANK REHAK, JIMMY CLEVELAND, BILL ELTON, ROD LEVITT (trombone), DANNY BANK (bass clarinet), EDDIE CAINE, ROMEO PENQUE (woodwinds), JOHN COLTRANE (tenor sax), JULIUS WATKINS, BOB NORTHERN (french horn), BILL BARBER (tuba), PAUL CHAMBERS (bass), JIMMY COBB, ELVIN JONES (drums), GIL EVANS (arranger/conductor)
Song Of Our Country

TUES	**1**
WED	**2**
THUR	**3**
FRI	**4**
SAT	**5**
SUN	**6**
MON	**7**
TUES	**8**
WED	**9**
THUR	**10**
FRI	**11**
SAT	**12**
SUN	**13**
MON	**14**
TUES	**15**
WED	**16**
THUR	**17**
FRI	**18**
SAT	**19**
SUN	**20**
MON	**21**
TUES	**22**
WED	**23**
THUR	**24**
FRI	**25**
SAT	**26**
SUN	**27**
MON	**28**
TUES	**29**
WED	**30**
THUR	**31**

THURSDAY 17 MARCH 1960

Down Beat reviews Miles' latest album release:

WORKIN' WITH THE MILES DAVIS QUINTET—Prestige 7166:
It Never Entered My Mind; Four; In Your Own Sweet Way; The Theme (take 1); Trane's Blues; Ahmad's Blues; Half Nelson; The Theme (take 2).
Personnel: Davis, trumpet; John Coltrane, tenor; Red Garland, piano; Paul Chambers, bass; Philly Joe Jones, drums.
Rating: *****

Even if it is quite possible that this is the least earth-shattering of the three Miles' LPs from this series of sessions, it still rates ***** because it is the sort of thing that is going to be owned and played and dug and redug for all time.

Few bands in the history of jazz have had the quality of this group. And not the least indication of its total importance is the individual importance of all its members then and now. Would that somebody had had the sense and initiative to take King Oliver and his Creole Jazz band into the studio and leave them alone to cut their book, or that Eckstine's great band had been let go at length. We can be everlastingly grateful to Bob Weinstock of Prestige for these recordings.

By now, everyone is familiar with the pattern and sound of this group. It does not seem sensible to essay any particular analysis here. Just let it go down like this: Red Garland plays particularly well on *Ahmad's Blues* (it's a trio) and Coltrane on *Trane's Blues*. But that's just the way it hits me. Actually, the whole LP is a gas. I don't see how anyone can do without it. (R.J.G.)

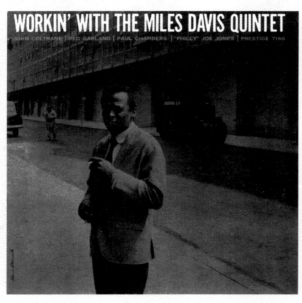

The quintet are contracted to a European tour for Norman Granz' JATP, but John Coltrane wants to leave and form his own band. Miles persuades him to go to Europe and to quit after the tour. Coltrane grumbles throughout the tour.

MONDAY 21 MARCH 1960

Miles Davis Quintet (Miles, trumpet; John Coltrane, tenor sax; Wynton Kelly, piano; Paul Chambers, bass; Jimmy Cobb, drums) appear at a JATP concert at the Olympia in Paris. Also on the bill are the Stan Getz Quartet and the Oscar Peterson Trio.
Part of the concert is recorded:
MILES DAVIS (trumpet), JOHN COLTRANE (tenor sax), WYNTON KELLY (piano), PAUL CHAMBERS (bass), JIMMY COBB (drums)
All Of You / So What / On Green Dolphin Street / Walkin' / Bye Bye Blackbird / Round About Midnight / Oleo / The Theme

Above: Jimmy Cobb and Miles in the Customs Hall at Stockholm airport on arrival in Sweden.

TUESDAY 22 MARCH 1960

Miles Davis Quintet appear at two JATP concerts at the Konserthuset in Stockholm, Sweden. Also on the bill are the Stan Getz Quartet and the Oscar Peterson Trio.
Part of the concerts are recorded:
MILES DAVIS (trumpet), JOHN COLTRANE (tenor sax), WYNTON KELLY (piano), PAUL CHAMBERS (bass), JIMMY COBB (drums)
First concert: *So What / Fran Dance / Walkin' / The Theme*
Second concert: *So What / On Green Dolphin Street / All Blues / The Theme*

JES **1**

VED **2**

HUR **3**

RI **4**

AT **5**

JN **6**

ON **7**

JES **8**

VED **9**

HUR **10**

RI **11**

AT **12**

JN **13**

ON **14**

JES **15**

VED **16**

HUR **17**

RI **18**

AT **19**

JN **20**

ION **21**

JES **22**

VED **23**

HUR **24**

RI **25**

AT **26**

JN **27**

ION **28**

JES **29**

VED **30**

HUR **31**

Above: A quick kiss from Frances before Miles, Jimmy Cobb and Paul Chambers (below) head for the Konserhuset stage for the 9 o'clock performance.

TUES	**1**
WED	**2**
THUR	**3**
FRI	**4**
SAT	**5**
SUN	**6**
MON	**7**
TUES	**8**
WED	**9**
THUR	**10**
FRI	**11**
SAT	**12**
SUN	**13**
MON	**14**
TUES	**15**
WED	**16**
THUR	**17**
FRI	**18**
SAT	**19**
SUN	**20**
MON	**21**
TUES	**22**
WED	**23**
THUR	**24**
FRI	**25**
SAT	**26**
SUN	**27**
MON	**28**
TUES	**29**
WED	**30**
THUR	**31**

Above: Miles receives a bouquet from Norman Granz in the Stockholm dressing room. Wynton Kelly seems amused. Opposite page: More pictures from Stockholm; Miles and Frances chat with Stan Getz backstage; a young Swedish fan makes friends with Miles; John Coltrane and Miles take a breather on the stage of the Konserthuset.

WEDNESDAY 23 MARCH 1960

Miles Davis Quintet appear at a JATP concert at the Njårdhallen in Oslo, Norway. Also on the bill are the Stan Getz Quartet and the Oscar Peterson Trio.

THURSDAY 24 MARCH 1960

Miles Davis Quintet appear at a JATP concert at the Tivoli Konsertsal in Copenhagen, Denmark. Also on the bill are the Stan Getz Quartet and the Oscar Peterson Trio.

Part of the concert is broadcast on Denmark Radio:
MILES DAVIS (trumpet), JOHN COLTRANE (tenor sax), WYNTON KELLY (piano), PAUL CHAMBERS (bass), JIMMY COBB (drums)

ann / *So What / Green Dolphin Street / All Blues / The Theme*

TUES	**1**
WED	**2**
THUR	**3**
FRI	**4**
SAT	**5**
SUN	**6**
MON	**7**
TUES	**8**
WED	**9**
THUR	**10**
FRI	**11**
SAT	**12**
SUN	**13**
MON	**14**
TUES	**15**
WED	**16**
THUR	**17**
FRI	**18**
SAT	**19**
SUN	**20**
MON	**21**
TUES	**22**
WED	**23**
THUR	**24**
FRI	**25**
SAT	**26**
SUN	**27**
MON	**28**
TUES	**29**
WED	**30**
THUR	**31**

FRIDAY 25 MARCH 1960

Miles Davis Quintet appear at a JATP concert at the Niedersachsenhalle in Hanover, West Germany. Also on the bill are the Stan Getz Quartet and the Oscar Peterson Trio.

SATURDAY 26 MARCH 1960

Miles Davis Quintet appear at a JATP concert at the Weser-Ems-Halle in Oldenburg, West Germany. Also on the bill are the Stan Getz Quartet and the Oscar Peterson Trio.

SUNDAY 27 MARCH 1960

Miles Davis Quintet appear at a JATP concert at the Sportpalast in Berlin, West Germany. Also on the bill are the Stan Getz Quartet and the Oscar Peterson Trio.

MONDAY 28 MARCH 1960

Miles Davis Quintet (appear at two JATP concerts (6pm and 9pm) at the Deutsches Museum in Munich, West Germany. Also on the bill are the Stan Getz Quartet and the Oscar Peterson Trio.

TUESDAY 29 MARCH 1960

Miles Davis Quintet appear at a JATP concert at the Musikhalle in Hamburg, West Germany. Also on the bill are the Stan Getz Quartet and the Oscar Peterson Trio.

WEDNESDAY 30 MARCH 1960

Miles Davis Quintet appear at a JATP concert at the Kongresshalle in Frankfurt-am-Main, West Germany Also on the bill are the Stan Getz Quartet and the Oscar Peterson Trio.

THURSDAY 31 MARCH 1960

Miles Davis Quintet appear at a JATP concert at the Teatro Dell Arte in Milan, Italy. Also on the bill are the Stan Getz Quartet and the Oscar Peterson Trio.

I 1
AT 2
JN 3
ON 4
JES 5
ED 6
HUR 7
RI 8
AT 9
JN 10
ON 11
JES 12
ED 13
HUR 14
RI 15
AT 16
JN 17
ION 18
JES 19
VED 20
HUR 21
RI 22
AT 23
JN 24
ION 25
JES 26
VED 27
HUR 28
RI 29
AT 30

SATURDAY 2 APRIL 1960

Miles Davis Quintet appear at a JATP concert at the Messehalle in Cologne, West Germany. Also on the bill are the Stan Getz Quartet and the Oscar Peterson Trio.

MONDAY 4 APRIL 1960

Miles Davis Quintet, without Miles who is absent from this concert, appear at a JATP concert at the Rheinhalle in Düsseldorf, West Germany. Also on the bill are the Stan Getz Quartet and the Oscar Peterson Trio.

TUESDAY 5 APRIL 1960

Miles Davis Quintet appear at a JATP concert at the Donauhalle in Ulm, West Germany. Also on the bill are the Stan Getz Quartet and the Oscar Peterson Trio.

WEDNESDAY 6 APRIL 1960

Miles Davis Quintet appear at a JATP concert at the Stadthalle in Vienna, Austria. Also on the bill are the Stan Getz Quartet and the Oscar Peterson Trio.

THURSDAY 7 APRIL 1960

Miles Davis Quintet appear at a JATP concert at the Messehalle in Nuremberg, West Germany. Also on the bill are the Stan Getz Quartet and the Oscar Peterson Trio.

FRIDAY 8 APRIL 1960

Miles Davis Quintet appear at a JATP concert at the Kongresshaus in Zürich, Switzerland. Also on the bill are the Stan Getz Quartet and the Oscar Peterson Trio. Part of the concert is privately taped:
MILES DAVIS (trumpet), JOHN COLTRANE (tenor sax), WYNTON KELLY (piano), PAUL CHAMBERS (bass), JIMMY COBB (drums)
If I Were A Bell / Fran-Dance / So What / All Blues / Theme

SATURDAY 9 APRIL 1960

Miles Davis Quintet appear at a JATP concert at the Kurhaus in Scheveningen, Holland starting at 8.15pm. Also on the bill are the Stan Getz Quartet and the Oscar Peterson Trio.
Part of the concert is broadcast on VARA Radio Station:
MILES DAVIS (trumpet), JOHN COLTRANE (tenor sax), WYNTON KELLY (piano), PAUL CHAMBERS (bass), JIMMY COBB (drums)
ann / *On Green Dolphin Street / So What / Round About Midnight / Walkin' / Theme*
At midnight the troupe all appear at a JATP concert at the Concertgebouw in Amsterdam, Holland.

SUNDAY 10 APRIL 1960

Miles Davis Quintet appear at two JATP concerts (5pm and 8.30pm) at the Liederhalle in Stuttgart, West Germany. Also on the bill are the Stan Getz Quartet and the Oscar Peterson Trio.

WEDNESDAY 27 APRIL 1960

Back in New York, Wynton Kelly and Paul Chambers record a trio album for VeeJay with Philly Joe Jones on drums. The album is released as *Kelly at Midnight*.

SUN	**1**	WED	**1**
MON	**2**	THUR	**2**
TUES	**3**	FRI	**3**
WED	**4**	SAT	**4**
THUR	**5**	SUN	**5**
FRI	**6**	MON	**6**
SAT	**7**	TUES	**7**
SUN	**8**	WED	**8**
MON	**9**	THUR	**9**
TUES	**10**	FRI	**10**
WED	**11**	SAT	**11**
THUR	**12**	SUN	**12**
FRI	**13**	MON	**13**
SAT	**14**	TUES	**14**
SUN	**15**	WED	**15**
MON	**16**	THUR	**16**
TUES	**17**	FRI	**17**
WED	**18**	SAT	**18**
THUR	**19**	SUN	**19**
FRI	**20**	MON	**20**
SAT	**21**	TUES	**21**
SUN	**22**	WED	**22**
MON	**23**	THUR	**23**
TUES	**24**	FRI	**24**
WED	**25**	SAT	**25**
THUR	**26**	SUN	**26**
FRI	**27**	MON	**27**
SAT	**28**	TUES	**28**
SUN	**29**	WED	**29**
MON	**30**	THUR	**30**
TUES	**31**		

When the quintet return to the States John Coltrane quits the band and opens at the Jazz Gallery in New York with his own quartet on Tuesday 3 May.

Miles searches for a replacement for Coltrane. Jimmy Heath is still bound by his parole restrictions, so Miles asks Wayne Shorter to join the band. Wayne is playing with Art Blakey's Jazz Messengers and unable to get away so Miles settles on Sonny Stitt. The quintet now comprises Miles Davis, trumpet; Sonny Stitt, alto & tenor; Wynton Kelly, piano; Paul Chambers, bass; Jimmy Cobb, drums.

THURSDAY 26 MAY 1960
Miles' 34th birthday.

FRIDAY 17 JUNE 1960
The Miles Davis Quintet including Sonny Stitt appear at Los Angeles' second annual Jazz Festival at the Hollywood Bowl. The festival is opened by the Stan Kenton Orchestra followed by the Hollywood Jazz Greats and the Steve Allen All Stars. The second half of the concert features the Miles Davis Quintet, Ernestine Anderson and the Gerry Mulligan 13-piece Orchestra.

Down Beat reports:

TUESDAY 21 JUNE 1960
The Miles Davis Quintet open at the Blackhaw in San Francisco for a one-week engagement. Opening night sees one of the biggest houses o the year at the club.

MONDAY 27 JUNE 1960
The Miles Davis Quintet close at the Blackhaw in San Francisco.

Green trumpet and all, Miles Davis opened the concert's second half to deliver himself of some of the greatest trumpet jazz ever heard. His brilliance and consistency was possibly due to the presence of Sonny Stitt, whose alto and tenor playing brooked the severest and most responsible competition. The other three members of the quintet were Wynton Kelly, piano; Paul Chambers, bass, and Jimmy Cobb, drums, all of whom, despite the poor pickup on Chambers' bass and overbalance on the drums, remained a surging power plant throughout the set.

Miles waxed rough-edged and laconic on *On Green Dolphin Street* while Stitt was the epitome of controlled, pulsing invention on tenor. They maintained the wondrously exalted level through *All Blue* and *'Round Midnight* with Stitt an ideal counterbalance to Miles, whether digging in deep on tenor or soaring on alto. Kelly and Chambers also soloed forcefully, the latter in a bowed excursion on *Dolphin*.

SATURDAY 9 JULY 1960

The Miles Davis Quintet open at the Sutherland Hotel Lounge in Chicago for a nine-day engagement.

SUNDAY 17 JULY 1960

The Miles Davis Quintet close at the Sutherland Hotel Lounge in Chicago.

THURSDAY 21 JULY 1960

The Sound of Miles Davis, filmed in April 1959, is shown on New York's WCBS-TV (non network) channel.

FRIDAY 22 JULY 1960

The Miles Davis Quintet open at the Apollo Theatre in Harlem for a one-week engagement. Also on the bill are the Thelonious Monk Trio, the James Moody Band, Betty Carter and Moms Mabley.

THURSDAY 28 JULY 1960

The Miles Davis Quintet are due to close at the Apollo Theatre but the show is held over for the weekend.

SUNDAY 31 JULY 1960

The Miles Davis Quintet close at the Apollo Theatre.

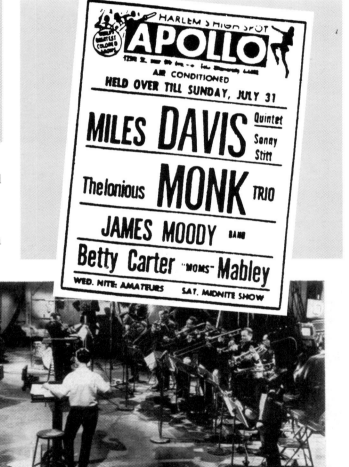

THE SOUND OF MILES

Miles Davis's first music teacher in East St. Louis, Ill., was adamant on one point: he told the future jazz great, "No vibrato! You're going to get old and start shaking, so play without any vibrato." Miles was 13, and in grade school.

Twenty years later, taping a half-hour television film for CBS films, Miles described his own playing as, "fast, light, and still no vibrato."

The film, *The Sound of Miles Davis,* is one of a series of 26 on subjects ranging from drama to ballet, produced by Robert Herridge. The only other jazz film in the series is a half-hour on pianist Ahmad Jamal.

Made over a year ago, the films are now ready for syndication to CBS outlets across the country as *The Robert Herridge Theater.* Six of the episodes, including the Davis film, are being shown during July and August on New York's WCBS-TV (non-network). The Davis film was shown Thursday, July 21. It was the trumpeter's first major

Penque, Danny Banks, and Ed Caine, woodwinds; John Coltrane, alto saxophone (in place of Adderley); John Barber, tuba; Paul Chambers, bass, and Jimmy Cobb, drums.

Davis, concentrating on the music in his brooding manner, is seen and heard performing *The Duke,* a tribute to Duke Ellington written by Dave Brubeck; *Blues for Pablo,* a ballad by Gil ... *New Rhumba.*

Teagarden visited Bangkok on their respective U. S. State Department tours, they were invited to the Royal Amphorn palace for jam sessions with the king.

The young Eastern ruler also composes in the American manner, although native Thai music is in a five-note scale. His song *Blue Night* was presented on Broadway in Mike Todd's *Peep Show* 10 years ago. Another of his tunes,

Miles Davis and Gil Evans, recording for TV film

MON	**1**
TUES	**2**
WED	**3**
THUR	**4**
FRI	**5**
SAT	**6**
SUN	**7**
MON	**8**
TUES	**9**
WED	**10**
THUR	**11**
FRI	**12**
SAT	**13**
SUN	**14**
MON	**15**
TUES	**16**
WED	**17**
THUR	**18**
FRI	**19**
SAT	**20**
SUN	**21**
MON	**22**
TUES	**23**
WED	**24**
THUR	**25**
FRI	**26**
SAT	**27**
SUN	**28**
MON	**29**
TUES	**30**
WED	**31**

TUESDAY 2 AUGUST 1960

The Miles Davis Quintet with Sonny Stitt open a two-week engagement at the Village Vanguard in New York City opposite the Walter Bishop Trio.

THURSDAY 4 AUGUST 1960

In the *Down Beat* Critics' Poll Miles ties with Dizzy Gillespie for first place in the trumpet section. In the combo section, Miles' band is second to the Modern Jazz Quartet.

Trumpet

Dizzy Gillespie	40
Miles Davis	40
Art Farmer	15

Louis Armstrong 13; Clark Terry 11; Roy Eldridge 9; Buck Clayton 4; Lee Morgan 4.

Combo

Modern Jazz Quartet	38
Miles Davis' group	13
Oscar Peterson Trio	11

Cannonball Adderley Quintet 9; Horace Silver Quintet 9; Charlie Mingus' group 8; Dizzy Gillespie Quintet 6; The Jazz Messengers 6; Dave Brubeck Quartet 5; Thelonious Monk Quartet 5; Buddy Tate Quartet 4.

SUNDAY 14 AUGUST 1960

The Miles Davis Quintet with Sonny Stitt close at the Village Vanguard in New York City.

MONDAY 15 AUGUST 1960

The Miles Davis Quintet with Sonny Stitt open at the Brandywine Music Box near Wilmington, south of Philadelphia for a one-week engagement opposite Lambert, Hendricks & Ross.

SATURDAY 20 AUGUST 1960

The Miles Davis Quintet with Sonny Stitt close at the Brandywine Music Box.

SUNDAY 21 AUGUST 1960

The Miles Davis Quintet featuring Sonny Stitt appear at the Randall's Island Jazz Festival in New York City. Also on the Sunday night bill are Dinah Washington, the Dave Brubeck Quartet, Lambert, Hendricks & Ross, the Les McCann Trio and Maynard Ferguson & his Orchestra.

... the show will feature the Miles Davis Quintet, with alto-tenor man Sonny Stitt, as a festival exclusive. The group has not and will not appear at any other jazz festival this summer. Davis is reported to be composing a special group of themes for the event.

Davis was originally scheduled to be featured with the Gil Evans Orchestra playing behind him. This was changed when the Davis-Evans combination was quoted at $10,000 for the Sunday night appearance.

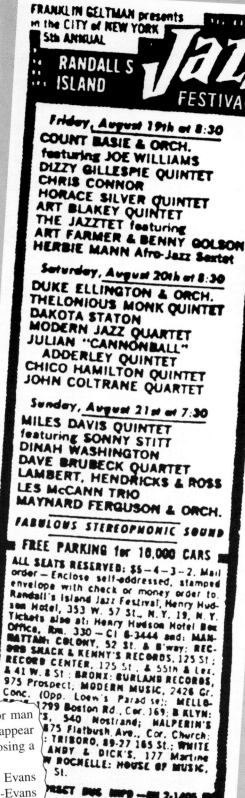

HUR **1**

RI **2**

AT **3**

UN **4**

ION **5**

JES **6**

VED **7**

HUR **8**

RI **9**

AT **10**

UN **11**

ION **12**

JES **13**

VED **14**

HUR **15**

RI **16**

AT **17**

UN **18**

ION **19**

UES **20**

VED **21**

HUR **22**

RI **23**

AT **24**

UN **25**

ION **26**

UES **27**

VED **28**

HUR **29**

RI **30**

MONDAY 19 SEPTEMBER 1960

Wynton Kelly, Paul Chambers and Jimmy Cobb record with Walter Benton for Jazzland in New York City. Freddie Hubbard is also on the session which is released as *Out of this World* (JLP 28).

Miles is now scheduled to make his first visit to Britain and, as part of the promotional build-up, Leonard Feather writes a long feature on Miles for London's *Melody Maker*:

Miles today is a wealthy man, owning some $50,000 worth of stock. He just bought an entire building in a good section of Manhattan, where he lives on the first two floors renting out the rest of the building as apartments. He drives a Ferrari that cost $12,500 and he likes to drive fast. He has a substantial five-figure annual income from Columbia Records. Miles' apparent aloofness on the stand has a devastating effect on women, who often find his good looks more irresistible than his most lyrical solo. Recently he was married to a lovely, petite girl named Frances Taylor, who teaches dancing. He has remained close to his daughter and two sons (seventeen, fourteen and ten) by an early marriage.

SATURDAY 24 SEPTEMBER 1960

The Miles Davis Quintet appear at the Gaumont Theatre, Hammersmith, London.

SUNDAY 25 SEPTEMBER 1960

The Miles Davis Quintet appear at the Guildhall, Portsmouth.

MONDAY 26 SEPTEMBER 1960

The Miles Davis Quintet appear at the De Montfort Hall, Leicester.

TUESDAY 27 SEPTEMBER 1960

The Miles Davis Quintet appear in two concerts at the Free Trade Hall, Manchester. Part of the concert is recorded:
MILES DAVIS (trumpet), SONNY STITT (tenor sax, alto sax), WYNTON KELLY (piano), PAUL CHAMBERS (bass), JIMMY COBB (drums)
First concert: *Four / All Of You / Walkin'* (inc)
Second concert: *Four* (inc) / *All Blues / Well You Needn't / Autumn Leaves / So What / Stardust* (MD out) / *The Theme*

WEDNESDAY 28 SEPTEMBER 1960

The Miles Davis Quintet appear at the Philharmonic Hall, Liverpool.

FRIDAY 30 SEPTEMBER 1960

The Miles Davis Quintet appear at the Colston Hall, Bristol.

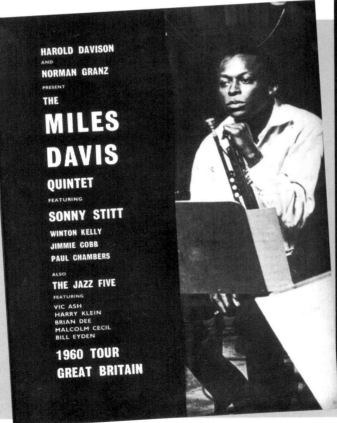

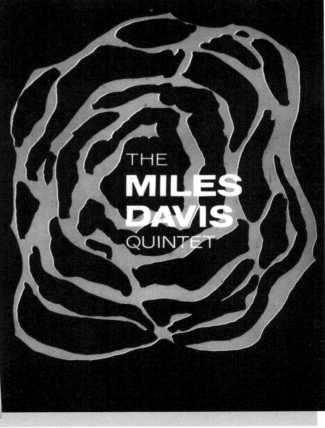

OCTOBER 1960

SAT	1
SUN	2
MON	3
TUES	4
WED	5
THUR	6
FRI	7
SAT	8
SUN	9
MON	10
TUES	11
WED	12
THUR	13
FRI	14
SAT	15
SUN	16
MON	17
TUES	18
WED	19
THUR	20
FRI	21
SAT	22
SUN	23
MON	24
TUES	25
WED	26
THUR	27
FRI	28
SAT	29
SUN	30
MON	31

SATURDAY 1 OCTOBER 1960
The Miles Davis Quintet appear at the Astoria Theatre, Finsbury Park, London.

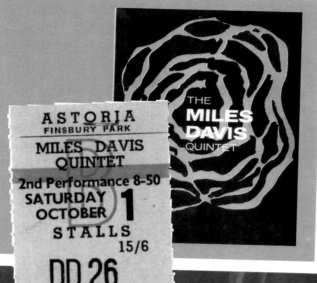

SUNDAY 2 OCTOBER 1960
The Miles Davis Quintet appear at the Gaumont Theatre, Lewisham, London.

WEDNESDAY 5 OCTOBER 1960
The Miles Davis Quintet appear at the Town Hall, Birmingham.

FRIDAY 7 OCTOBER 1960
The Miles Davis Quintet appear at the City Hall, Newcastle.

SATURDAY 8 OCTOBER 1960
The Miles Davis Quintet appear at the Gaumont Theatre, Hammersmith, London.

SUNDAY 9 OCTOBER 1960
The Miles Davis Quintet appear at the Gaumont State Theatre, Kilburn, London.

Below and opposite: Miles and Sonny Stitt in London.

SAT **1**
SUN **2**
MON **3**
TUES **4**
WED **5**
THUR **6**
FRI **7**
SAT **8**
SUN **9**
MON **10**
TUES **11**
WED **12**
THUR **13**
FRI **14**
SAT **15**
SUN **16**
MON **17**
TUES **18**
WED **19**
THUR **20**
FRI **21**
SAT **22**
SUN **23**
MON **24**
TUES **25**
WED **26**
THUR **27**
FRI **28**
SAT **29**
SUN **30**
MON **31**

SAT	**1**
SUN	**2**
MON	**3**
TUES	**4**
WED	**5**
THUR	**6**
FRI	**7**
SAT	**8**
SUN	**9**
MON	**10**
TUES	**11**
WED	**12**
THUR	**13**
FRI	**14**
SAT	**15**
SUN	**16**
MON	**17**
TUES	**18**
WED	**19**
THUR	**20**
FRI	**21**
SAT	**22**
SUN	**23**
MON	**24**
TUES	**25**
WED	**26**
THUR	**27**
FRI	**28**
SAT	**29**
SUN	**30**
MON	**31**

TUESDAY 11 OCTOBER 1960

The Miles Davis Quintet appear at the Olympia in Paris.

Part of the concert is recorded:

MILES DAVIS (trumpet), SONNY STITT (tenor sax), WYNTON KELLY (piano), PAUL CHAMBERS (bass), JIMMY COBB (drums)

So What

THURSDAY 13 OCTOBER 1960

The Miles Davis Quintet appear in two concerts at the Konserthuset in Stockholm.

Part of the concert is recorded:

MILES DAVIS (trumpet), SONNY STITT (tenor sax, alto sax), WYNTON KELLY (piano), PAUL CHAMBERS (bass), JIMMY COBB (drums)

First concert:

1st set: *Walkin' / Autumn Leaves / So What / Round About Midnight / The Theme*

2nd set: *June Night* (trio) / *Stardust* (MD out) / *On Green Dolphin Street / All Blues / The Theme*

Second concert:

1st set: *All Of You / Walkin' / Autumn Leaves / The Theme*

2nd set: *Softly As In A Morning Sunrise* (trio) / *Makin' Whoopee* (trio) / *If I Were A Bell / No Blues / The Theme*

AT 1
UN 2
ION 3
UES 4
VED 5
HUR 6
RI 7
AT 8
UN 9
ION 10
UES 11
VED 12
HUR 13
RI 14
AT 15
UN 16
ION 17
UES 18
VED 19
HUR 20
RI 21
AT 22
UN 23
ION 24
UES 25
VED 26
HUR 27
RI 28
AT 29
UN 30
ION 31

Opposite and below: Miles and the quintet in Stockholm.

KONSERTHUSET
Torsdag 13 okt. kl. 19 o. 21.15

Norman Granz
presents

MILES DAVIS
orchestra
SONNY STITT
WINTON KELLY   PAUL CHAMBERS
JIMMY COBBS

BILJETTER från i morgon hos Svala & Söderlund. Konserthusets
kassa, NK, PUB o. tidn. dep.-kont. ● Bechsteinflygel fr. Hoffmans
◆◆◆ *Arrangör:* KARUSELL KONSERTBYRÅ ◆◆

SAT	**1**
SUN	**2**
MON	**3**
TUES	**4**
WED	**5**
THUR	**6**
FRI	**7**
SAT	**8**
SUN	**9**
MON	**10**
TUES	**11**
WED	**12**
THUR	**13**
FRI	**14**
SAT	**15**
SUN	**16**
MON	**17**
TUES	**18**
WED	**19**
THUR	**20**
FRI	**21**
SAT	**22**
SUN	**23**
MON	**24**
TUES	**25**
WED	**26**
THUR	**27**
FRI	**28**
SAT	**29**
SUN	**30**
MON	**31**

FRIDAY 21 OCTOBER 1960

The Miles Davis Quintet open at the Regal Theatre in Chicago for a one-week engagement. Jimmy Heath replaces Sonny Stitt for the week. Also on the show are Lambert, Hendricks & Ross, the Modern Jazz Quartet and the Ike Isaacs Trio.

THURSDAY 27 OCTOBER 1960

The Miles Davis Quintet close at the Regal Theatre in Chicago.

FRIDAY 28 OCTOBER 1960

Jimmy Heath, Wynton Kelly and Jimmy Cobb record with Bunky Green for Exodus in Chicago. Donald Byrd and Larry Ridley are also on the session.

TUES	**1**	THUR	**1**
WED	**2**	FRI	**2**
THUR	**3**	SAT	**3**
FRI	**4**	SUN	**4**
SAT	**5**	MON	**5**
SUN	**6**	TUES	**6**
MON	**7**	WED	**7**
TUES	**8**	THUR	**8**
WED	**9**	FRI	**9**
THUR	**10**	SAT	**10**
FRI	**11**	SUN	**11**
SAT	**12**	MON	**12**
SUN	**13**	TUES	**13**
MON	**14**	WED	**14**
TUES	**15**	THUR	**15**
WED	**16**	FRI	**16**
THUR	**17**	SAT	**17**
FRI	**18**	SUN	**18**
SAT	**19**	MON	**19**
SUN	**20**	TUES	**20**
MON	**21**	WED	**21**
TUES	**22**	THUR	**22**
WED	**23**	FRI	**23**
THUR	**24**	SAT	**24**
FRI	**25**	SUN	**25**
SAT	**26**	MON	**26**
SUN	**27**	TUES	**27**
MON	**28**	WED	**28**
TUES	**29**	THUR	**29**
WED	**30**	FRI	**30**
		SAT	**31**

SUNDAY 13 NOVEMBER 1960

Wynton Kelly and Paul Chambers record with Hank Mobley for Blue Note at Rudy Van Gelder's studio in Hackensack, New Jersey. Freddie Hubbard and Art Blakey are also on the session which is released as *Roll Call* (BLP4058).

TUESDAY 15 NOVEMBER 1960

The Miles Davis Quintet including Sonny Stitt open a two-week engagement at the Village Vanguard in New York City opposite the Bill Evans Trio.

SUNDAY 27 NOVEMBER 1960

The Miles Davis Quintet close at the Village Vanguard in New York City.

FRIDAY 2 DECEMBER 1960

The Miles Davis Quintet open at the Howard Theatre in Washington for a one-week engagement. Also on the show are Sarah Vaughan, James Moody's Orchestra, dancer Bunny Briggs and comedian Clay Tyson.

THURSDAY 8 DECEMBER 1960

The Miles Davis Quintet close at the Howard Theatre in Washington. This is Sonny Stitt's final appearance with the quintet. Miles chooses Hank Mobley to replace him.

WEDNESDAY 21 DECEMBER 1960

Miles and Frances Taylor are married in New York City. This is the first time Miles has been officially married.

MONDAY 26 DECEMBER 1960

The Miles Davis Quintet with Hank Mobley on tenor sax open at The Cloister in Chicago for a two-week engagement. Gil Evans flies in from New York to hear the band.

SUN	**1**	WED	**1**
MON	**2**	THUR	**2**
TUES	**3**	FRI	**3**
WED	**4**	SAT	**4**
THUR	**5**	SUN	**5**
FRI	**6**	MON	**6**
SAT	**7**	TUES	**7**
SUN	**8**	WED	**8**
MON	**9**	THUR	**9**
TUES	**10**	FRI	**10**
WED	**11**	SAT	**11**
THUR	**12**	SUN	**12**
FRI	**13**	MON	**13**
SAT	**14**	TUES	**14**
SUN	**15**	WED	**15**
MON	**16**	THUR	**16**
TUES	**17**	FRI	**17**
WED	**18**	SAT	**18**
THUR	**19**	SUN	**19**
FRI	**20**	MON	**20**
SAT	**21**	TUES	**21**
SUN	**22**	WED	**22**
MON	**23**	THUR	**23**
TUES	**24**	FRI	**24**
WED	**25**	SAT	**25**
THUR	**26**	SUN	**26**
FRI	**27**	MON	**27**
SAT	**28**	TUES	**28**
SUN	**29**		
MON	**30**		
TUES	**31**		

SUNDAY 8 JANUARY 1961
The Miles Davis Quintet close at The Cloister in Chicago.

SUNDAY 15 JANUARY 1961
Hank Mobley and Paul Chambers record with Kenny Dorham for Blue Note at Rudy Van Gelder's studio in Englewood, New Jersey. Kenny Drew and Philly Joe Jones are also on the album which is issued as *Whistle Stop* (BLP4063).

THURSDAY 16 FEBRUARY 1961
Miles features on the front page of *Down Beat*. The two-page article by Marc Crawford looks at the friendship between Miles and Gil Evans.

TUESDAY 28 FEBRUARY 1961
The Miles Davis Quintet open at the Village Vanguard in New York City for a two-week engagement opposite the Lee Konitz-Jim Hall Group.

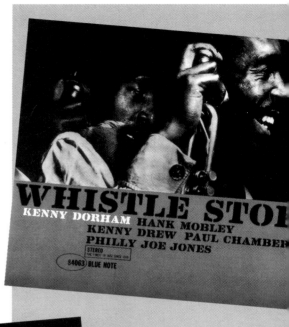

> 66
>
> I used to think you had to use a lot of notes and stuff to be writing. Now I've learned enough about writing *not* to write. I just let Gil write. I give him an outline of what I want and he finishes it. I can even call him on the phone and just tell him what I got in mind, and when I see the score, it is exactly what I wanted.
>
> 99

ED 1
UR 2
3
T 4
N 5
ON 6
ES 7
ED 8
UR 9
10
T 11
N 12
ON 13
ES 14
ED 15
UR 16
17
T 18
N 19
ON 20
ES 21
ED 22
UR 23
24
T 25
N 26
ON 27
ES 28
ED 29
UR 30
31

TUESDAY 7 MARCH 1961

Recording session by the Miles Davis Quintet for Columbia in New York City. Teo Macero is the producer.

MILES DAVIS (trumpet), HANK MOBLEY (tenor sax), WYNTON KELLY (piano), PAUL CHAMBERS (bass), JIMMY COBB (drums)

Drad-dog / Pfrancing

SUNDAY 12 MARCH 1961

The Miles Davis Quintet close at the Village Vanguard in New York City.

MONDAY 20 MARCH 1961

Recording session by the Miles Davis Quintet for Columbia at the 30th Street Studio in New York City.

MILES DAVIS (trumpet), HANK MOBLEY (tenor sax), WYNTON KELLY (piano), PAUL CHAMBERS (bass), JIMMY COBB (drums)

Old Folks

JOHN COLTRANE (tenor sax) is added for one number: *Someday My Prince Will Come*

TUESDAY 21 MARCH 1961

Recording session by the Miles Davis Quintet, with John Coltrane replacing Hank Mobley, for Columbia at the 30th Street Studio in New York City.

MILES DAVIS (trumpet), JOHN COLTRANE (tenor sax), WYNTON KELLY (piano), PAUL CHAMBERS (bass), JIMMY COBB (drums)

Teo / I Thought About You (JC out)

MILES DAVIS (trumpet), WYNTON KELLY (piano), PAUL CHAMBERS (bass), PHILLY JOE JONES (drums)

Blues No.2 (JC out)

Teo Macero, the producer, utilises spliced tape and over-dubbed solos by Miles and Trane to produce the album released as *Someday My Prince Will Come* (CL1656). A photograph of Frances is used on the cover.

Miles is unhappy with Hank Mobley's playing and is becoming bored with the band. He is also suffering a lot of pain from the arthritis in his joints caused by sickle-cell anaemia. To give himself time to think he decides to drive out to California for an upcoming engagement at the Blackhawk in San Francisco.

SUNDAY 26 MARCH 1961

Hank Mobley, Wynton Kelly and Paul Chambers record for Blue Note at Rudy Van Gelder's studio in Englewood Cliffs, New Jersey. Grant Green and Philly Joe Jones are also on the session which is released as *Workout* (BLP4080).

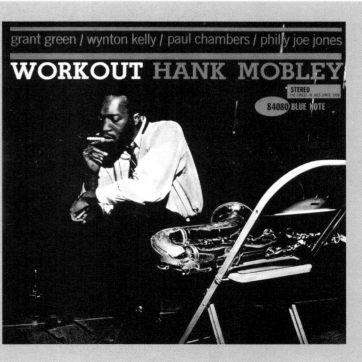

WED	**1**
THUR	**2**
FRI	**3**
SAT	**4**
SUN	**5**
MON	**6**
TUES	**7**
WED	**8**
THUR	**9**
FRI	**10**
SAT	**11**
SUN	**12**
MON	**13**
TUES	**14**
WED	**15**
THUR	**16**
FRI	**17**
SAT	**18**
SUN	**19**
MON	**20**
TUES	**21**
WED	**22**
THUR	**23**
FRI	**24**
SAT	**25**
SUN	**26**
MON	**27**
TUES	**28**
WED	**29**
THUR	**30**
FRI	**31**

Miles Davis is big business and both Columbia and Prestige take full page advertisements to promote their recordings.

ED 1
UR 2
3
T 4
N 5
ON 6
ES 7
ED 8
UR 9
10
T 11
N 12
ON 13
ES 14
ED 15
UR 16
17
T 18
N 19
ON 20
ES 21
ED 22
UR 23
24
T 25
N 26
ON 27
ES 28
ED 29
UR 30
31

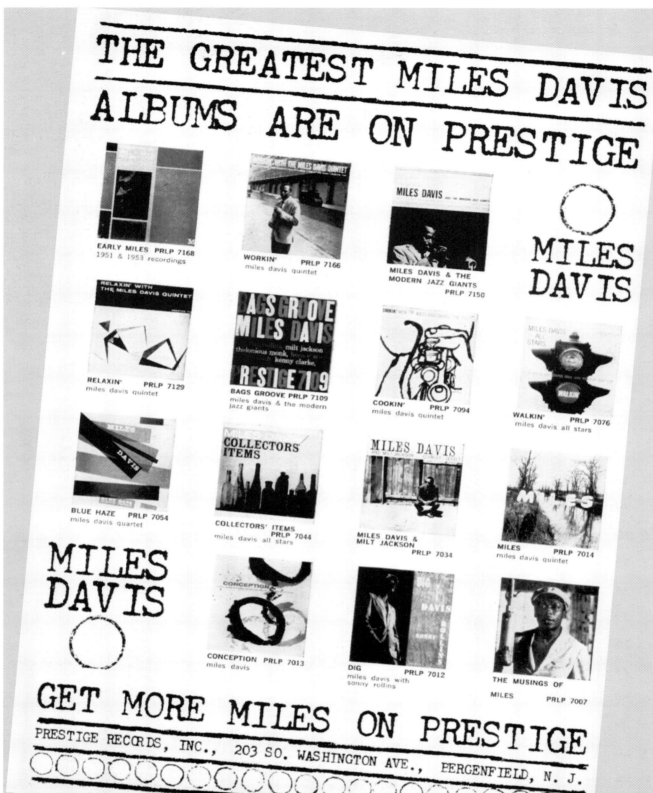

SAT	**1**
SUN	**2**
MON	**3**
TUES	**4**
WED	**5**
THUR	**6**
FRI	**7**
SAT	**8**
SUN	**9**
MON	**10**
TUES	**11**
WED	**12**
THUR	**13**
FRI	**14**
SAT	**15**
SUN	**16**
MON	**17**
TUES	**18**
WED	**19**
THUR	**20**
FRI	**21**
SAT	**22**
SUN	**23**
MON	**24**
TUES	**25**
WED	**26**
THUR	**27**
FRI	**28**
SAT	**29**
SUN	**30**

TUESDAY 4 APRIL 1961
The Miles Davis Quintet open at the Blackhawk in San Francisco for a four-week engagement.

FRIDAY 14 APRIL 1961
The Miles Davis Quintet is recorded live at the Blackhawk:
MILES DAVIS (trumpet), HANK MOBLEY (tenor sax), WYNTON KELLY (piano), PAUL CHAMBERS (bass), JIMMY COBB (drums)
Walkin' / Bye Bye Blackbird / All Of You (HM out) / *No Blues / Bye Bye / Love I've Found You* (WK out)

BLACKHAWK—Miles Davis and his Sextet in their second week: one of the great groups in contemporary jazz; nightly except Monday; jam 3:30 Sunday.

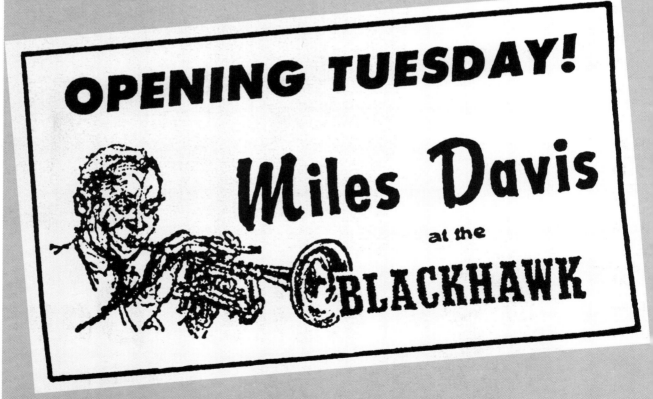

Now Appearing!
Song Stylist — Anita O'Day
AT THE
BLACKHAWK
Opening Tuesday, April 4th
Miles Davis Sextet

OPENING TUESDAY!
Miles Davis
at the
BLACKHAWK

T **1**

N **2**

ON **3**

ES **4**

ED **5**

UR **6**

7

T **8**

N **9**

ON **10**

ES **11**

ED **12**

UR **13**

14

T **15**

N **16**

ON **17**

ES **18**

ED **19**

UR **20**

21

T **22**

N **23**

ON **24**

ES **25**

ED **26**

UR **27**

28

T **29**

N **30**

SATURDAY 15 APRIL 1961

The Miles Davis Quintet is recorded live at the Blackhawk:
MILES DAVIS (trumpet), HANK MOBLEY (tenor sax), WYNTON KELLY (piano), PAUL CHAMBERS (bass), JIMMY COBB (drums)
Well You Needn't / Fran-Dance / So What / Oleo / If I Were A Bell (HM out) */ Neo*

FRIDAY 21 APRIL 1961

The Miles Davis Quintet is recorded live at the Blackhawk:
MILES DAVIS (trumpet), HANK MOBLEY (tenor sax), WYNTON KELLY (piano), PAUL CHAMBERS (bass), JIMMY COBB (drums)
On Green Dolphin Street

SATURDAY 22 APRIL 1961

The Miles Davis Quintet is recorded live at the Blackhawk:
MILES DAVIS (trumpet), HANK MOBLEY (tenor sax), WYNTON KELLY (piano), PAUL CHAMBERS (bass), JIMMY COBB (drums)
'Round Midnight

SUNDAY 30 APRIL 1961

The Miles Davis Quintet close at the Blackhawk in San Francisco.

MON	1
TUES	2
WED	3
THUR	4
FRI	5
SAT	6
SUN	7
MON	8
TUES	9
WED	10
THUR	11
FRI	12
SAT	13
SUN	14
MON	15
TUES	16
WED	17
THUR	18
FRI	19
SAT	20
SUN	21
MON	22
TUES	23
WED	24
THUR	25
FRI	26
SAT	27
SUN	28
MON	29
TUES	30

FRIDAY 19 MAY 1961

The Miles Davis Quintet and the Gil Evans Orchestra appear in concert at Carnegie Hall in New York City. The concert is a benefit for the African Research Foundation and is sold out. Part of the concert is recorded:

MILES DAVIS (trumpet), HANK MOBLEY (tenor sax), WYNTON KELLY (piano), PAUL CHAMBERS (bass), JIMMY COBB (drums)

So What / No Blues / Oleo / Someday My Prince Will Come / Teo / Walkin' / I Thought About You

MILES DAVIS, ERNIE ROYAL, JOHNNY COLES, BERNIE GLOW, LOUIS MUCCI (trumpet), JIMMY KNEPPER, RICHARD HIXON, FRANK REHAK (trombone), JULIUS WATKINS, PAUL INGRAHAM, BOB SWISSHELM (french horn), BILL BARBER (tuba), ROMEO PENQUE, JEROME RICHARDSON, EDDIE CAINE, BOB TRICARICO, DANNY BANK (reeds), JANET PUTMAN (harp), PAUL CHAMBERS (bass), JIMMY COBB (drums), BOBBY ROSENGARDEN (percussion), GIL EVANS (arranger, conductor)

Spring Is Here / Someday My Prince Will Come / The Meaning Of The Blues / Lament / I Had The Greatest Dream / New Rhumba / Saeta / Solea / Concierto de Aranjuez

The resulting album is released as *Miles Davis at Carnegie Hall — The Legendary Performance of May 19, 1961* (CL1812).

FRIDAY 26 MAY 1961

Miles' 35th birthday.

Miles Davis is named "Fashion Personality for the Month of May" by *Gentlemen's Quarterly*. The magazine printed a photo of Miles wearing a jacket of his own design.

Miles Davis promises innovations galore at his May 19 Carnegie Hall concert, among them a flamenco guitarist in the hall's bar during intermission.

ON 1
ES 2
ED 3
UR 4
5
T 6
N 7
ON 8
ES 9
ED 10
UR 11
12
T 13
N 14
ON 15
ES 16
ED 17
UR 18
19
T 20
N 21
ON 22
JES 23
ED 24
HUR 25
26
T 27
JN 28
ON 29
JES 30

The concert is a great success, despite an interruption by Max Roach who leads a demonstration against the African Research Foundation with placards reading AFRICA FOR THE AFRICANS! FREEDOM NOW! Roach is removed by security men and Miles returns to the stage, seething with anger, to play with even greater fire and intensity.

The critics are unanimous in their praise for the performance.

Few jazz performances have touched the heights of that evening. It was jazz at its finest.

MILES DAVIS JOINS EVANS IN CONCERT

Trumpeter and His Quartet Heard in Jazz Program

Some of the most provocative jazz recordings made during the last four years have been the product of arrangements for a large orchestra written and conducted by Gil Evans and featuring the solo trumpet of Miles Davis. Last night at Carnegie Hall Mr. Davis made his first public appearance with Mr. Evans' orchestra in a program that also included Mr. Davis' quintet.

The evening was a triumph for Mr. Davis. He played brilliantly, particularly in the sections with his quintet. And although he has often been charged with treating his audiences disdainfully he not only smiled on a couple of occasions but acknowledged applause with a quick glance over the footlights and a slight nod of his head.

Ever since his arrival in New York in the mid-Forties, Mr. Davis has had an ardent group of supporters, although for many years his technical limitations kept him from challenging the virtuoso accomplishments of as facile a contemporary as Dizzy Gillespie.

Last night, however, Mr. Davis seemed intent on proving his all-round capabilities on the trumpet. He played with tremendous fire and spirit, soaring off into high note runs with confidence and precision, building lines bristling with searing emotion and yet retaining all the warmest singing elements of his gentler side. He was in the spotlight almost throughout the evening, yet he never faltered, never seemed to tire and poured out a stunning series of magnificent trumpet solos.

Most of his more forceful playing occurred with his quintet, a situation that left his pianist, Wynton Kelly, and his tenor saxophonist, Hank Mobley in unenviable positions, because they always had to follow him with solos of their own. Mr. Kelly, a highly resourceful and compelling pianist, rose to these occasions extremely well, but Mr. Mobley seemed quite unenterprising in such company.

The selections played by Mr. Davis with Mr. Evans' orchestra, which included "The Meaning of the Blues," "New Rhumba" and "Concierto de Aranjuez," were marked by rich, somber tonal mixtures that served as a suitable contrast to Mr. Davis' fiery performances with his quintet.

The concert, a benefit for the African Research Foundation, was interrupted briefly as Mr. Davis' quintet was playing the first selection following the intermission when a man in a white jacket walked out to the middle of the stage, sat down directly behind the footlights and held aloft a sign reading "Africa for the Africans".

When it became apparent that the man intended to stay there, Mr. Davis halted the music and walked off the stage. After a momentary pause, three men came out and carried the sign-carrier off. Mr. Davis returned to tumultuous applause, dismissed the selection that had been interrupted and bit tartly into another number with no evidence that he was in the least bit flustered.

JOHN S. WILSON.

Although Miles seems to be at the peak of his career, both artistically and financially, he is still restless and unfulfilled. His personal musical odyssey will see him become an influential figure in the fusing of jazz with rock and electronic music. Miles is to remain a vital innovator during the next three decades.

MILES DEWEY DAVIS III
1926–1991